Development of the Labor Movement in Milwaukee

Development of the
Labor Movement
in Milwaukee

THOMAS W. GAVETT

70047

HD6519
.M5
G28

THE UNIVERSITY OF WISCONSIN PRESS

Madison and Milwaukee, 1965

Published by
THE UNIVERSITY OF WISCONSIN PRESS
Madison and Milwaukee
P.O. Box 1379, Madison, Wisconsin 53701

Copyright © 1965
by the Regents of the University of Wisconsin

Printed in the United States of America by
Wisconsin Cuneo Press, Inc., Milwaukee, Wisconsin

Library of Congress Catalog Number 65-13501

 3

Preface

THIS book traces the development of the Milwaukee labor movement from its origins to the end of its alliance with Socialism during World War II. The only sections covering developments since that time are Chapter XVI, on the purge of the Communists, and a very brief sketch in Chapter XVII on developments from the war to the merger of the local labor movement in 1959.

Since the real significance of the Milwaukee labor movement lies in its flirtations with ideology, World War II is a more suitable cutoff point than the date of the merger.

I should like to express my appreciation for the two-year scholarship established by the Milwaukee labor movement in honor of J. F. Friedrick, then general secretary of the Federated Trades Council. The scholarship, administered by the University of Wisconsin, made possible the completion of the original draft of this book. The State Historical Society of Wisconsin has long collected documents relevant to the history of labor, and the staff of the Society was most helpful in making those records available. The library of West Virginia University helped in procuring a few of the more recent documents, and the Institute of Industrial Relations of that university financed the typing and retyping of the manuscript. Mrs. Kathryn DuBois, the typist, competently deciphered my handwriting.

Dean Edwin Young, the late Edwin E. Witte, J. F. Friedrick, and Milton Derber read various drafts of the manuscript. They and the editors of the University of Wisconsin Press made many helpful, if at times painful, criticisms. The late Selig Perlman was my major professor during the time I was a graduate student at the University of Wisconsin, and the intellectual stimulation he provided hardly needs additional testimonials. I should also mention the contribution of my wife,

[v

Pat, who guarded me from unnecessary interruptions while I was working on the revision and was a helpful proofreader.

As always, any errors of fact or interpretation are the responsibility of the author.

T.W.G.

Morgantown, West Virginia
February, 1963

Contents

Development of the Labor Movement in Milwaukee

CHAPTER I

The Genesis of Unionism

THE alliance of labor and Socialism is the outstanding fact in the history of unionism in Milwaukee. Though Socialism achieved notable success in other cities, nowhere was its relationship with labor as strong and enduring as in Milwaukee. Ideologically liberal but conservative in action, the labor movement provided the base for a revisionist Socialism that held political power in the city for over thirty years.

Dynamic and contentious leaders held the stage. Paul Grottkau of the Central Labor Union, Robert Schilling of the Knights of Labor, Frank Weber of the Federated Trades Council, and Victor L. Berger of the Socialist Party were the major performers in the early years. Though the story they helped write was part of the mainstream of American history, their efforts produced a unique experiment in ideology. A look at the early trade unions will perhaps explain why Milwaukee became fertile ground for such an experiment.

Unionism entered Milwaukee history at a comparatively late date. No Workingmen's Party, as there was in Philadelphia and New York in 1828, nor any trace of the National Trades Union of the mid-1830's was to be found in early Milwaukee. In 1840 the village, with a population of less than 2,000, lay on the industrial fringe of America and had few wage earners.

The continuing westward migration, however, brought significant changes in the following years. Milwaukee's position at the junction of Lake Michigan and the Milwaukee River made it a gateway to the sparsely inhabited hinterland. The city became a major trading center for the area and later, an important part of the manufacturing complex on the southern shore of the lake. During the 1840's the population increased tenfold, and by 1900 Milwaukee had become a city of over 285,000 people.

Foreign-born immigrants contributed a large number to that increase. In 1850, 64 per cent of the population was foreign-born; more than half of these were Germans. In the years that followed the percentage of the population born abroad decreased, but at the turn of the century it still included almost one-third of the population, of which two-thirds were German.

The surge of population brought a working class. As late as 1860 there were fewer than 3,500 wage earners in Milwaukee County, but their number approached 50,000 by the turn of the century. This growth in the labor force paralleled the growth in the number of firms, from about 550 in 1860 to almost 3,500 in 1900. The capital investment of 3 million dollars in 1860 increased to 110 million by the end of the century.[1]

The few legislative attempts to improve the condition of labor prior to the 1880's were generally ineffective. A mechanics' lien law, regulation of apprenticeships, limitations on garnishment of wages, restriction of child labor, and limitations on employers' traditional defenses against liability claims were on the statute books. These laws provided meager protection and were inadequately enforced. The era of protective labor legislation had not really begun to arrive.[2]

As time went on, there were also a few attempts by employers to improve conditions for their workers. These were early experiments in employer paternalism. In 1881 T. A. Chapman instructed his agents to select sites in the First Ward near his store. He intended to build blocks of low-rent tenement houses for his employees. E. P. Allis organized the Allis Mutual Aid Society for his employees in April, 1883. The Society provided disability benefits of $5.25 a week and a death benefit of $50. Employees were charged 50 cents to join and 25 cents monthly dues, Allis contributing an equal amount.[3]

None of these early attempts to improve the condition of labor are, however, the vital part of the story of a labor movement. Not until unions appeared on the scene would attitudes change significantly. Prior to that event, the Milwaukee *Daily Sentinel* was able to editorialize in 1845:

The mechanics of our city are evincing a spirit that will redown to their everlasting credit. At several meetings recently held by them, at different places, they have matured plans for the organization of a Literary and Scientific Society, and an Association, or "Trades Union." The former, as its name indicates, is intended for the mental cultivation and literary qualification of its members; and the latter to exercise a prudent supervision of the Mechanical and producing interests of the city generally.

It is gratifying to observe these movements on the part of our operatives and it speaks much for their intelligence, enterprise and patriotism. Let them press boldly on the consummation of their object, so devoutly desired, and there is no . . . doubt but that the most abundant success will crown their efforts. Labor must and will have its rights asserted and secured, and reap a fair and liberal reward, if all classes of operatives so will it.[4]

This attitude of the community would soon change when the workers adopted a more aggressive attitude.

Early Unions

The 1840's and 1850's were years of relative inactivity for unions in America. The aggressive union movement of the 1830's had all but perished in the long depression beginning in 1837. Nevertheless, on the local level unionism survived, however sporadically. In Milwaukee the first evidence of unionism appeared in August, 1847. At that time forty masons and bricklayers struck for an increase in their daily wage from $1.50 to $1.75. In April 1848 the journeymen coopers held a protest meeting against a reduction in the rate for flour barrels, apparently unsuccessful.[5]

In July, 1848, a strike of journeymen shoemakers at a shop owned by Benjamin Bosworth displayed the problems and tactics of the very early labor organizations and the attitude of management. Bosworth had brought a number of journeymen shoemakers from Boston and paid their expenses with the understanding that they would work for him until their passage had been repaid. He had promised to pay them 20 per cent more than they had received in Boston, but to retain the increase to pay for their transportation debts. According to Bosworth, as quoted in the Milwaukee *Sentinel* of August 1, 1848, he had actually paid them 50 per cent more than they had been receiving in Boston. "They were perfectly satisfied," he claimed, "till some meddlesome pile drivers, that knew no more about making Ladies fine work than an ass (as they themselves expressed it about the one that drew up their list of wages) . . . first enticed them to join their society, then brought their list of prices to me to sign."

Bosworth refused to sign the list, claiming that some operations in the production of shoes had been omitted and some were priced too high. However, he finally did sign the list on the promise that the union would submit a new list at its next meeting. But when the next meeting was held, the union refused to submit a new list since other manufacturers had refused to sign. Therefore, Bosworth claimed the right to manufacture any kind of shoe he wished and to set his own prices. Evidently Bosworth continued to use the former list of prices as a guide, but a strike was precipitated when he refused to pay nineteen cents more to put the bottoms on "Goat bootees" which the "Captain of the Lodge" claimed were "Gaiter bootees" since they laced up. The strikers voted to continue the protest until Bosworth agreed to abide by a price list that had recently been developed. Bosworth refused, terming it a "bungling list, that they all admit is wrong." The strikers put a letter in the newspaper claiming that Bosworth ran a scab shop. According to Bosworth, the strikers also gave five dollars to two men owing him money so they could leave town, "thinking thereby to punish me . . . ." Bosworth charged that the strikers had been humbugged and intimidated by foreigners and that their blustering was the result of alcohol. He ignored the strikers, and evidently their demands failed.

The first successful strike in Milwaukee was called in September, 1848, by a Ship Carpenters and Caulkers Association at the shipbuilding company of George Barber. The skilled workers demanded improvements in hours and wages, and a restriction on the number of unskilled workers—"barndoor joiners" as the strikers dubbed them—employed. With a number of contracts to fill, the employers conceded the demands after one month. The strikers won a reduction in hours from twelve to ten, an increase in wages for all skilled workers, and a restriction in the number of apprentices.

In the fall of 1848 a Cabinetmakers and Joiners Union with sixty-one members made an agreement with employers for an increase in wages and a restriction of the number of apprentices. When the agreement was broken, the union members, for the first time in Milwaukee, decided to start a cooperative store and warehouse with $1,200. The union members purchased supplies from the cooperative and displayed their finished work in the cooperative salesroom. However, internal dissension soon arose, and the enterprise was closed.[6]

The first time a labor dispute in the area was brought into the courts was in August, 1851. The schooner *Bristol* of Montreal had come to Milwaukee from Burlington, Vermont. On August 27, 1851, the schooner left Milwaukee for Chicago, but when it was off Racine, the crew refused to obey orders unless their wages were increased to the rates paid on Lake Michigan. The captain refused their demand and, with the mate and the cook, brought the vessel back to the Milwaukee port and appealed to the law for assistance. The sailors were brought to court but discharged by Justice Walworth on the grounds that he did not have jurisdiction.

On August 30 of the same year there was another strike of sailors—some unemployed and others employed on the brigs *Mechanic* and the *David Smart*—for higher wages. Since some of the employed sailors refused to strike, a fight started. Because of threats of further violence,

three or four of the leaders were arrested and brought before Justice
Walworth, who sent them to jail to await examination.[7]

The problem of female labor as a "competitive menace" came to
Milwaukee in the spring of 1852. At that time, Madame Mathilde
Franziska Anneke founded the first woman-suffrage paper of the
state, *Die Frauen Zeitung*. Madame Anneke had been offered the use
of Moritz Schoeffler's printshop where the first German daily of the
state, the *Wisconsin Banner*, was published. However, the printers
at Schoeffler's establishment refused to set the type, perhaps because
of their opposition to a woman-suffrage paper, but more likely because of Madame Anneke's advocacy of female compositors. The
printers organized a Typographical Union and set forth a number of
demands, including restriction of apprentices. Schoeffler gave in to
their demands, and Madame Anneke was forced to transfer her paper
to the *Volksfreund* shop owned by Frederick Fratney. After publishing only six more issues, Madame Anneke moved her newspaper back
East.[8] The Typographical Union continued sporadically for a number
of years, but like many unions of the era, was more social than economic in character. In 1859 the Typographical Union achieved permanent status and became the first Milwaukee union to have national
affiliation when it joined the International Typographical Union as
Local 23, becoming the oldest union still in existence in Milwaukee.[9]

On July 11, 1853, between 300 and 400 Germans who had been
working on the La Crosse and Milwaukee Railroad came to Milwaukee to demand their pay. Their action was caused by the lack of
adequate laws to assure collection of back wages. They claimed that
the contractor, a Mr. Schultz, had promised to pay them but did not.
The men gathered about the entrance of the office of the company on
the southeast corner of West Water and Spring streets. The mayor, several aldermen, and a number of policemen went to talk to the men
and told them that they must look primarily to the contractor for payment, but that the company would attempt to protect them against
fraud by the contractor. The men were also warned against using violence. In the afternoon boys in the crowd broke into a barrel of sugar
in the dry goods and grocery store below the company office. The owner called a deputy sheriff to arrest a man who took some of the sugar.
When his companions, misunderstanding the cause of his arrest, attempted to rescue him from the officer, two were arrested. The entire
group, led by a man displaying a tricolor flag, hurried to the jail to rescue the prisoners. Sheriff Page met them and warned that any violence
on their part would be met by force. The fire department was called
out to direct water on the rioters and act as additional police, if neces-

sary. Mayor Walker again appeared and attempted to remove the flag, which was the rallying point of the rioters. When the mayor was hit on the side of the head with the blade of a shovel carried by one of the demonstrators, a riot started. The firemen turned water on the rioters who in turn threw brickbats at the firemen. Firemen and police charged the mob and drove them away; a number of persons were wounded. After the struggle the firemen and police were disbanded, but they and the military companies in the area were told to be ready for action. That night the mayor issued a proclamation, in German, that the company would pay the laborers out of money due the contractor. Eight men who had been arrested during the incident were released. The proclamation and the release of the prisoners sparked a parade by a large number of the men.[10]

The absence of adequate legal protection for collection of back wages inspired another incident in October, 1856, as reported in the *Daily Sentinel* of October 7. Four men, employed by the Cochrane and Hubbard Brick Company, were arrested after they tried to prevent teamsters from hauling bricks from the yard. They had also struck one of the owners of the yard because he failed to pay their wages on schedule. The men were brought to court on charges of disorderly conduct; two were fined $5 and the other two, $3. A similar incident occurred on September 15, 1858, when workmen in the lumber yard of Stronach and Company on Erie Street took direct action when they were not paid for their work. The company had gone into receivership after the death of one of the partners, and no one had paid the workers. The men assaulted the office, smashed the furniture, seized one of the partners, Nathan Engleman, and threatened violence if they were not paid. The men were soon arrested, but released when no one appeared to file charges, according to the *Sentinel's* account on September 17.

The first case of multi-employer bargaining was during the strike of journeymen tailors in 1853. On August 18, 1853, the journeymen tailors met at Military Hall to formulate a bill of prices. The employers, according to the *Sentinel* of September 3, agreed to increases of 25 to 30 per cent on many articles of clothing, but would not accept the entire bill of prices drawn up by the tailors. The tailors, therefore, went out on strike, and on September 2 about 120 tailors marched through the streets of the city, preceded by banners and music, to demonstrate their opposition to the position of the employers. A few days later the tailors appointed a "Committee of 18" to meet with the employers to seek a compromise. At the meeting the major point of difference was the demand of the strikers that those who worked by the week should receive a minimum of $7.50, claiming it was impossible to live on less. The employers contended that those who were hired during the busy season were often worth no more than $5 a week. The Committee of 18 reported back to the strikers at the City Hotel. The Committee maintained that the employers often took advantage of the foreign-born who could not speak English and consequently were hired for less than their worth. The tailors passed a resolution refusing to work until "two-thirds from Wisconsin Street to Walker's Point had signed the bill of prices." However, the employers refused to sign the bill, and the strike failed.[11]

The journeymen shoemakers were the first unionists in Milwaukee to strike over the issue of the closed shop. The shoemakers called a strike at Bradley and Metcalf's in January, 1855, because, although the company had reduced wages as agreed to by the union, it had not asked for proof of union membership when employing workers.[12]

Aside from the few strikes mentioned above, the efforts of the laborers in Milwaukee were sporadic. When the Association of Tailors was founded in 1850, they attempted to start a cooperative. Apparently nothing came of this, however, or of their attempts to regulate wages, hours, apprentices, and female labor. The Cigar Makers Union, organized in 1852, failed to obtain higher wages, abolition of the piecework system, or restriction of the number of women workers. Like many other unions of this period, the German Custom Tailors Union, organized in 1860, was largely a social organization.[13]

There were also a few attempts to establish, rather prematurely, a labor press. The *Workingman's Advocate,* founded in 1842, and the *Arbeiter,* founded in 1854, came to a Milwaukee unprepared for labor papers; each died within a year. The weekly *Workingman,* started in 1856, maintained its tenuous existence for two years. After that labor received only incidental support in Freethinker and Turner Bund publications.[14]

Unionism in the Civil War Period

The Milwaukee labor movement had been dormant between the years 1855 and 1860, but with the advent of the Civil War and the ensuing inflation, trade-union activity revived. During the early years of the Civil War, prices rose from 50 to 75 per cent although wages rose by less than half that amount. On August 15, 1862, the *Daily Sentinel* reported a shortage of labor among brewers and publishers as a result of enlistments in the Civil War. The inflation received new impetus in 1863 with the issuance of greenback currency by the federal government. For the first time in the history of Milwaukee, skilled labor began to organize into trade unions. Bricklayers and masons, custom tailors, and sailors were organized. Those unions organized before the Civil War discarded their benevolent role and assumed a more militant character. In 1864 and 1865 strikes became a common method of gaining wage increases. A fair number of these strikes, which usually involved only one enterprise, were successful. By the end of the war labor had secured wage increases of 60 to 75 per cent to compensate partially for the enormous price increases.[15]

An early manifestation of this new militancy was the strike of the journeymen tailors in July, 1860. Approximately 250 tailors demonstrated in the streets for an increase in wages. The journeymen designed their own price list and paraded the streets to induce the employers to sign the list. Fifteen did. In 1864 the custom tailors gained an increase of $2 a week without a strike.

The printers, organized before the Civil War, first reasserted themselves in a brief strike at the *Evening Wisconsin* and the *Daily Sentinel* offices, gaining a wage increase. But the shortage of male printers caused by the war again brought the problem of female labor to the sharp attention of the Typographical Union. Jermain and Brightman, the owners of the *Daily Sentinel,* had been considering the possibility of introducing female labor since 1861. Finally in January, 1863, the proprietors of the paper decided to employ a few female compositors. Local 23 of the Typographical Union held a special meeting on January 11 and adopted a resolution informing the owners that "the principles of our Union and the honor and integrity of its members, do not tolerate such help under any circumstances whatever." The owners denied that they intended to supplant the men with females, although they admitted that one man had been discharged as the result of the employment of females. The *Daily Sentinel* maintained that there was a shortage of printers and that many of the women employed were dependents of men now in the army. The paper also claimed that it had had letters from women all over the state anxious to learn typesetting. Further, the female compositors worked in a separate building from the males.

The union again pointed out that there had been no provision in its constitution for admitting females and that the quota for apprentices in the office was full. The union was determined not to concede; fourteen union compositors walked out. Mr. Jermain had evidently been prepared for the emergency. For several months prior to the strike he had had ten or twelve girls training in rooms outside the building. With the aid of these girls and a few "stray" compositors, the paper was able to continue publication.

The press of the state and of Chicago had a field day in denouncing the strikers. The Racine *Journal* exclaimed, "Such dictation as that of the Printer's Union, in this case is unreasonable and tyrannical." The Sparta *Herald* chided the union saying, "It is both ungentlemanly and unjust to attempt to curb Woman's sphere of usefulness in this arbitrary manner," and the Chicago *Post* cleverly chimed in, "The proprietors have certainly shown themselves more gallant than 'the boys,' who ought to be ashamed of themselves thus to strike women."

To replenish its labor force, the *Sentinel* advertised for compositors who would work with women, offering union wages. Some aid was given to the Milwaukee printers by union printers in Chicago in the form of an advertisement in the Chicago *Tribune* warning all printers not to work at the *Sentinel,* or to be prepared to bear the label of "rats."[16]

The striking printers were soon conscious that some new course of action was needed to be taken. Ferdinand Shurr, writing in 1886, gives this amusing account of their action:

The fourteen "prints," after walking out, met at the old rendezvous, "The Old Menominee Beer Hall," to discuss the situation. All went well for the first day; but on assembling on the second day they were politely informed by Peter Enders, proprietor [of the hall], that the "slate is broke."

Having an eye to business, he could tell for a certainty that as the point was not gained on the first day, the strike was lost.

The expression of the "slate being broke" opened our eyes to the fact that we were beaten as far as the strike was concerned, and being the aggrieved parties, we proposed to start a co-operative daily wherein we could mix our grievances with the news and at the same time bury the *Sentinel.*

After holding three or four meetings and counting what little money there was in the crowd, we made arrangements with Mr. Miller, the type founder, for an outfit, and actually succeeded in getting it. As a matter of course the types were not new, and by paying a little down we got six months time on the balance.

There never was a prouder set of men than those fourteen when the first number of the *Daily Union* appeared on the street—every one his own boss, every one a proprietor.

Not having any advertisements we worked day and night to fill the columns of the paper with the choicest and spiciest of reading matter, paying special rates for our telegrams—having the reports made up in Chicago and sent to us as specials—which made great inroads in our last assets.

Matters run on in this way for seventeen days and we had the *Sentinel* all but laid on the shelf, when the coal gave out. As printers are never known to set type in a cold room, we had no other alternative than to call a meeting and devise some means to replenish the fire.

As we had a circulation of over 900, and there had been no collecting done, we formed ourselves into a committee on collections.

Through some oversight there was no time set for the committee to report, and so I have been waiting all these years to find out whether our co-operation scheme really had "millions in it."

Mr. Miller was not slow in taking back his material and calling it square, and as we had to pay in advance for paper and presswork, the company, whenever it shall see fit to resume business, can do so with the assurance that there are no outstanding liabilities. . . .

Some of the boys drifted to Chicago, St. Louis and other places—some into the army, myself included, and some into that other world where strikes and co-operative newspapers are unknown.

When the remnant returned in 1865, T. P. Germain [sic] and Horace Brightman were amongst the first men to open their doors for work to the surviving co-operatives . . . if we could have had $2,000, or $1,000, the venture would have been a success and might have been alive and prosperous today.[17]

Because of the large number of their members who had enlisted in the army, Typographical 23 temporarily disbanded in 1864 but reorganized in 1865 or 1866, this time with women included as members. In 1866 the printers on the *Evening Wisconsin* successfully struck for a higher wage.[18]

Women workers were probably the group worst off during the Civil War era. In 1864 women tailors in Milwaukee received an average of only $3 a week, but had to work 11 hours a day and provide their own sewing machines. By 1867 the average wage for all women workers was $5 a week compared to the average wage for men of $13 to $14 a week. But it was to be a long time before the concept of equal wages for equal work would take hold.[19]

CHAPTER II

Union Activity After the Civil War

A S the war came to a close, union activity accelerated. During 1864 and 1865 there were strikes for higher wages by the printers, bricklayers and masons, iron molders and sailors in Milwaukee. The Boilermakers, Cabinetmakers, and Stone Cutters Unions were organized between 1865 and 1867. During this same time, there were important strikes conducted by the masons, bricklayers, printers, and coopers, as well as minor strikes for higher wages by the sailors and the bell boys at the Newhall House. Business and wages were good and unemployment rare. The *Daily Sentinel* in 1866 reported a shortage of labor and high wages in the building trades, and in 1867 it claimed that Milwaukee needed 5,000 to 6,000 more workers, with the promise of ready employment, high wages, and low rents. By 1867 the *Sentinel* was able to report the existence of sixteen local unions in the city. But the rapid growth of trade unions had by no means assured them the confidence of the community. The prevailing sentiment of the community was probably echoed in a *Sentinel* editorial of May 7, 1867, "There is . . . nothing wrong in workingmen's associations, in themselves considered, unless they are formed with the intention of forcing an unjust distribution of the general wealth . . ." or when they keep others from working.

The National Labor Union

The growth of unionism at the close of the Civil War brought about the formation of the National Labor Union. This was the second national federation of unions in America, the first being the National Trades' Union of the Thirties. The National Labor Union was a loose federation of national, city, and local union organizations, as well as various reform organizations. It had its first convention in 1866.

Milwaukee was represented at the national congresses of the National Labor Union in 1867, 1868, and 1869. In 1867 Richard Trevellick, one of the most prominent labor leaders on the national scene, met with the workingmen of Milwaukee at the City Hall. Trevellick reviewed the work of the 1867 Chicago convention of the National Labor Union, emphasizing the issues of greenbackism, cooperation, and the eight-hour day.

The first issue the National Labor Union stressed was the eight-hour day. The issue gained importance because of the unemployment that occurred at the time soldiers returned from the war.

The Eight-Hour Movement

As early as 1848 an effort to secure protective labor legislation had been made by the Committee of the National Reform Association in Milwaukee. This completely non-union organization had tried to get candidates in the November election to pledge their support for efforts to amerliorate "as far as practicable, the condition of the dependent landless laborer, till the restoration of the right of independent labor can be effected." One part of the pledge would have obligated candidates for office to support a law to limit the hours of labor to ten on public works and in corporations. In 1852 there had been an attempt to pass a law restricting workers' hours to ten per day on public projects. However, the movement for a shorter work day did not become important until the Civil War.[1]

The philosopher of the eight-hour movement was Ira Steward. Steward, a self-educated mechanic, believed that raising the worker's standard of living through a cut in the hours of work would compel employers to increase wages. Despite the absurd economic rationale of Steward's ideas, the demand for an eight-hour day struck a responsive chord among workers.

Steward believed political action was a more practical means of achieving the eight-hour day than trade-union action. In 1864 he created the first eight-hour organization in Boston, soon named the Labor Reform Association. The following year, a Grand Eight-Hour League was formed in Massachusetts. The movement soon swept the nation. On September 1, 1865, a Labor Reform Association was organized in Milwaukee, its chief objective being agitation for a shorter work day. In the fall elections of 1865, the Labor Reform Association (later, the Eight-Hour League) attempted to gain the support of legislative candidates for an eight-hour bill. The Democratic candidates for the Assembly in the Fourth and Fifth districts of Milwaukee, anxious to get labor's votes, according to the *Sentinel* of November 7, 1865, "made haste to avow their devotion to the Eight Hour system, that is being agitated throughout the country." The Eight-Hour committee pursued an avowed policy of supporting those candidates who endorsed the proposal, regardless of their political affiliations. The Association was successful in helping to elect endorsed candidates from the Fourth and Fifth Assembly Districts, A. R. R. Butler and C. H. Orton, respectively. Its control of 20 or 30 votes was generally believed to be responsible for Butler's election over Dewitt Davis, the Republican nominee.[2]

The agitation for an eight-hour system continued in the city, with appeals addressed from the national headquarters in Washington, D. C. Meetings of the Labor Reform Association were held in Milwaukee every Friday night. During 1866 and the early part of 1867, the General Eight-Hour League of Wisconsin, an outgrowth of the Labor Reform Association of Milwaukee, spread among the larger towns of the state, where it won limited support for its program. Early in 1866 the General League was reported to be considering the establishment of its own newspaper in Milwaukee. In 1867 it attempted to become incorporated under the state laws, but its bill was defeated in the State Senate.

As the April 1866 municipal elections approached, the Labor Reform Association of Milwaukee met and nominated candidates for alderman and councilor from six of the nine wards. It also endorsed the Democratic nominee for mayor, John T. Tallmadge, who had indicated his support by signing a petition asking the state legislature to pass an eight-hour law.

In January, 1866, Assemblyman C. H. Orton from Milwaukee's Fifth Assembly District introduced a bill into the Assembly to establish eight hours as the legal workday. Butler had been expected to introduce the measure. Orton's bill would have made it legal to enter into a labor contract specifying up to, but no more than, ten hours as one day's work, but it would have made eight hours the legal day's work if the number of hours per day were not specified in the contract. The bill was reported to have been received with "considerable favor by members of the legislature," but by February the proponents of the measure, in an attempt to have the bill reported favorably by the Judiciary Committee, asked that farm laborers be exempt from the provisions of the bill. At the end of March the Judiciary Committee finally reported a substitute measure modeled after the Ohio law. This bill, endorsed by the Judiciary Committee by a vote of 11 to 4, covered only women and children under 18 working in factories. Under the bill, employers could be prosecuted and fined $25 if they required or compelled women or children to work more than eight hours a day. However, if the woman or child "voluntarily" worked more than eight hours, there could be no prosecution. The bill further provided that eight hours would be the legal workday for women and children if the written contract was silent on the matter of hours. Opponents of the bill called it an unwise attempt to regulate labor, and argued that it would deprive the poor man of the rights to have his children work more than eight hours to provide food for the family. Finally, the opponents charged that the bill would discourage manufacturing in the state. Supporters of the bill made a strong plea for children who were compelled to work from daybreak to dark and asserted that the bill would reduce unemployment, a growing concern with the return of the war veterans. On March 28 the measure passed the Assembly by a vote of 50 to 36, but the following day it voted 54 to 42 to postpone the measure indefinitely.[3]

Although the bill was defeated in the 1866 legislative session, the Eight-Hour League passed a resolution stating it was not discouraged and would continue to fight for the law. The movement received new impetus in the 1867 legislative session when Governor Lucius Fairchild drew attention to the complaints of workingmen in his message to the legislature. He observed:" . . . to the men of the west, most of whom have at some time been laboring men, surely no argument is needed to show that those who create the wealth of the country, should be afforded every possible facility for participating in its enjoyment and non-producers should not enjoy all the luxuries of life, while the producers are awarded only the burdens."[4]

With this encouragement from Governor Fairchild, H. C. Hobart, Milwaukee Democrat in the Assembly, again introduced an eight-hour bill. The chief supporters of the bill were Hobart, C. E. Dyer of Racine, and James Coleman of Fond du Lac. This bill, similar to that rejected in 1866, was again rejected on March 8, 1867, by a vote of 47 to 43, but was reconsidered and passed by the Assembly on March 12 by a vote of 51 to 32. The bill was hotly debated in the Senate but passed on April 4, 1867, by a vote of 29 to 3, the Assembly later concurring with the Senate amendments. The amendments to the bill had so altered its character as to practically nullify it. The provisions of the law have been summarized as follows:

> The law finally passed in 1867 was far from the legislation advocated by the eight hour movement because general legislation, making an eight hour day for all occupations, was demanded by those who followed the leadership of Ira Steward. The Wisconsin law of 1867 was restricted, however, to the factories of the state and then applied only to women and children. Employers of women and children, under eighteen years of age, were not allowed to compel them to work more than eight hours per day. Children under fourteen were not to be permitted to work more than eight hours in any one day in any

factory or workshop. Violations of this section were to be punished by fines of from five to fifty dollars upon conviction. Only where a contract did not stipulate the number of hours, was the work day to be interpreted as eight hours, and then this section of the law provided that nothing of the second section should apply to contracts for labor by the week, month, or year.

No enforcement agency was provided by the law except by individual court actions. Clearly this law did not attempt to nullify any contract for work, a method commonly used in the lumber industry and in the construction of railroads in the state. Due to these limitations the legislation had been rendered almost worthless to the workman by the manufacturing, lumber and railroad interests of the state.[5]

An attempt was made to repeal even this ineffective law in 1868, but the effort failed.

The proponents of the eight-hour day also tried to get the city of Milwaukee to pass an eight-hour ordinance. In March, 1866, William A. Prentiss, then a member of the Board of Councillors and later mayor of Milwaukee, introduced a resolution holding that "a proper division of the twenty-four hours of each day should be made, so that portions thereof may be devoted to labor, intellectual and social improvements, and rest" and calling upon the Board of Aldermen to set eight hours as the legal workday for persons employed by the city of Milwaukee. His resolution, however, excluded operations where special agreements had been made or where the operations of a city department "require[d] more than eight hours each day to be devoted to the public service." This resolution was referred to committee but never reported.[6]

In spite of their weak victory in the state legislature, the workers were determined that the eight-hour law should be put into operation. In the spring of 1867 the Ship Carpenters and Caulkers, the Carpenters and Joiners, and the Machinists and Blacksmiths Unions adopted resolutions in which they proposed to accept proportionate wage reductions if the eight-hour system was introduced. All work over eight hours, however, was to be paid at time-and-one-half.

The *Daily Sentinel* reported on June 27, 1867, however, that after receiving a letter from William Goodnow, president of the Bay State Manufacturing Company, stating that the eight-hour system could not be instituted since firms in New York and New England worked ten hours a day, the Machinists and Blacksmiths Union, formerly chief proponents of the measure, resolved to postpone the enforcement of the eight-hour law "temporarily." A celebration, planned for July 4 when the law was to go into effect, was cancelled because interest in the eight-hour law was so reduced by the accompanying reduction in wages and by employer opposition. Only the Ship Carpenters and

Caulkers held a parade in the city streets that day. On the next day when the employers refused to grant the shorter workday, the workers struck successfully for an eight-hour day. But by July 8 most of the workers had become dissatisfied with the prospect of lower wages and many went back to the ten-hour day.[7] On July 15 the *Daily Sentinel* was able to report: "The eight hour system has seen its best days in this city, and is rapidly losing supporters among those mechanics who have applied the test .... Good-bye eight hour system."

Four states besides Wisconsin passed eight-hour laws in 1867: Connecticut, Illinois, Missouri, and New York. The following year, President Andrew Johnson signed an eight-hour bill for federal government employees. However, the movement collapsed in Milwaukee and Wisconsin after 1867, and the depression of 1873 brought an end to the scheme throughout the nation.

Milwaukee Labor Reform Assembly

The excitement over the eight-hour movement and contacts with the Congress of the National Labor Union stimulated the organization of a National Labor Union for the State of Wisconsin early in 1869 at Black River Falls. The Wisconsin branch of the National Labor Union invited all workers, regardless of their trade, to join and depend upon political action rather than strikes for results. Four months after its organization, the Wisconsin branch issued a call for a state convention of various labor associations and friends of labor at Watertown on September 30, 1869, to organize a State Labor Reform party. The convention lasted two days and embodied the views of the National Labor Union. Their state policy was: the assimilation of interests of different mechanical trades with all branches of industry, a uniform price for all types of labor, equal rights for all workers, the valuation of commodities by the amount of labor used in producing them, the marking of all manufactured articles to indicate the kind of material used, the establishment of contacts between laborers and farmers, and the passage of laws to give each person the full value of his work.

The convention was dominated by Milwaukee delegates and all officers elected were from Milwaukee: president, Thomas C. Tinker, Masons and Bricklayers Union; secretary, August F. Brunnotto, Tailors Union; and treasurer, Fred Treyser, Typographical Union. Milwaukee was made the headquarters of the Reform party and Watertown was designated the place for conventions.

A number of interested trade unions in Milwaukee held a joint meeting to receive and ratify the report and to organize the Milwaukee Labor Reform Assembly on October 8, 1869. On October 20, at the

second meeting, the Reform Assembly appointed committees to organize various wards in the city into Labor Reform Leagues. The political
reforms demanded in Milwaukee were the abolition of the caucus system and the opening of polls on election day from eight in the morning until eight at night. Thereafter, the state convention was generally
ignored in Milwaukee. The only known political effort of the Reform
Assembly in Milwaukee was the unsuccessful nomination of Robert
W. Travers for the Wisconsin State Assembly and G. W. Weis for the
Board of Supervisors. During the brief period of prosperity starting in
1871, the Milwaukee Labor Reform Assembly began to disintegrate.
The last report indicating its possible existence refers to 1874.[8]

Cooperative Movement

While in its 1866 convention the National Labor Union had
stressed the eight-hour day, in 1867 Greenbackism was the major issue.
While Greenbackism was essentially a cheap-money scheme, the labor
movement endorsed it so that it would be possible for workers to form
producers' cooperatives. The cooperative movement swept the nation,
reaching a peak in the post-Civil-War period.

As early as 1861 a strike of shipwrights and caulkers resulted in
the formation of the first successful producers' cooperative in Milwaukee. The Society of Shipwrights and Caulkers, founded in 1861,
soon grew to include nearly all the skilled men working in the ship-
yards. Evidently the union was a branch of an organization that embraced the Great Lakes. In December 1861 the Society demanded that
"barn-door joiners" (cheap labor) should not be hired. The employers charged that the union had been a "serious inconvenience" to
builders and sponsored an advertisement asking all shipyard builders
to refuse to hire any members of the Society. Thirty-nine owners and
masters pledged their support to the builders in "putting down the labor monopoly." The strike continued for over a month but was lost.

In early 1862 nine members of the Society became disheartened
over the constant bickering within the union on the question of non-
union labor. Consequently, they withdrew during the strike and started a cooperative shipbuilding association under the name of Allan, Mc-
Clellan and Company. Beginning with limited capital, they at first did
only repair jobs, constructing new ships if repair work was not available. The cooperative prospered from the beginning, but the more en-
ergetic members bought out the others and conducted the business on
a private basis. (The company eventually became the Milwaukee Dry
Dock Company on Jones Island.) However, the venture nearly
wrecked the union because the nine who withdrew from it were

among the best workers and leaders.

Although there were cooperative experiments in the beginning of the decade, such as those of the shipwrights and caulkers and the printers, the real surge of interest in producers' cooperatives did not develop until the Civil War had ended.[9]

The relatively prosperous period that had followed the end of the Civil War was succeeded by a depression lasting from 1868 until 1871. As strikes failed and unemployment was general, the economic conditions of the period turned labor's attention again to cooperatives.

The Carpenters Cooperative Sash and Door Company started with capital of $4,000 and was valued at $22,000; it employed 40 workers after being in business for two years. Low-cost houses were built outside the city limits by the masons and bricklayers. The enterprise was successful until some of the members organized a private company. Much less successful was the Badger State Carpenters and House Builders Cooperative, which failed to sell the houses it built. The houses were eventually occupied by the members themselvs.

The journeymen cabinetmakers started the Milwaukee Furniture Manufacturing Association in the late 1860's, making chiefly sashes, doors, and blinds. The first president of the Association was William Frankfurth, a prominent hardware merchant of the city. The twelve members of the cooperative got along well, but after two years they decided to sell out, realizing twice their original investment.

As the result of a strike the cigar makers, under the leadership of Henry Lecher, started the Cooperative Cigar Manufacturing Company. After a year and a half of fair progress, the cooperative was abandoned as a result of misunderstandings among the members. The German Tailors Union started a cooperative organization in 1871 or 1872 and advertised in the *Sentinel* of March 23, 1872, for 50 cutters and 150 sewing girls, but there is no report on the success of its venture.

Trade unions planning to start cooperatives found it desirable to incorporate under the laws of the state. In 1866 the Masons and Bricklayers, in 1868 the Cigar Makers and the Iron Molders, in 1869 the Machinists and Blacksmiths, and in 1871 the Milwaukee Tailors and the Bay View Sons of Vulcan sought, and were granted, legal recognition.

In some instances producers' cooperatives were used purely as a measure to force employers to grant union demands. The constitution of the Milwaukee Masons and Bricklayers Union, for example, provided: "In the event a strike shall be declared, and continue for the space of one week, the Board of Trustees . . . shall constitute the Board of Building Commissioners, and they shall figure on work, enter into contracts, and furnish bond for the completion of such work as they may obtain."

Although consumer coops were not significant in Wisconsin, Joseph Bennett, an eloquent English member of the Machinists and Blacksmiths Union who was familiar with the successful Rochdale system in England, preached principles of cooperation to his fellow craftsmen. In 1865 the union started a cooperative grocery store, arousing much interest. However, the store was conducted on too small a scale, refused to make deliveries, and was open only evenings when a committee of the union could take charge. The members tired of it and after six months it was abandoned.[10]

The Knights of Saint Crispin

Of the shoemaking industry, Merk reports:

> An interesting transition in the evolution of the factory system in the boot and shoe industry was represented in Milwaukee during the later sixties by an institution familiarly known as "Bradley's Barn." To this frame building, located in the Third Ward, approximately a hundred of Bradley and Metcalf's workmen brought and "worked up" each week the materials handed out to them at the central warehouse. They owned their own simple tools and devices and paid monthly a stipulated rent for the privilege of a working place. A similar institution, in which employees of Bradley and Metcalf and of Atkins, Steele and White were at work, was said to have been located near Fourth and Clybourne street.[11]

Thus a series of inventions and the huge demand for army shoes during the Civil War led to the replacement of one-man shops with factories. The Milwaukee *Sentinel* reported in 1869 that of the 450 men then employed at Bradley and Metcalf's boot and shoe factory "perhaps not more than ten were sufficiently skilled to have been of any service ten or fifteen years ago."

As a result of these changes in the industry, on March 1, 1867, the Order of the Knights of St. Crispin was organized at Milwaukee by Newell Daniels, formerly of Milford, Massachusetts, and six others: Samuel Wilson, W. C. Haynes, F. W. Wallace, Albert Jenkins, Thomas Houren, and Henry Palmer. Daniels was a boot treer by trade and while at Milford planned a national organization of boot treers. His move to Milwaukee delayed his plans and further reflection convinced him of the necessity of an industrial union of all shoe workers rather than a trade organization. The union, organized in the factory of Atkins, Steele and White, became Lodge No. 1. In the spring of that year, the German Custom Shoemakers Union of Milwaukee took the Crispin form of organization and became Lodge No. 2. The Milwaukee Knights did not resort to strikes, but operated three cooperative shops which competed with firms which did not comply with the demands of the union. For example, in 1869, twenty-one German Knights of St. Crispin organized the Milwaukee Boot and Shoe Manufacturing Association. They had enough capital to buy a complete set of machinery, and they were the most skilled workers in their craft. But after struggling for two-and-one-half years, the Association failed because of incompetent management and the hopeless attempt to compete with factory products when custom orders fell off. After 1871 the Crispins met a number of serious defeats in the East and the order virtually disbanded. During the panic of 1873, even the original Lodge No. 1 of Milwaukee was brought near death, and the Milwaukee shops were bought up by private interests.[12]

Trade Unions

During the post-Civil-War depression period, 1868 to 1871, the trade-union movement itself was notably unsuccessful. Working conditions deteriorated to the point where the Chicago *Workingman's Advocate* was prompted to say:

From a correspondent we learn that trade matters in Milwaukee are very dull; a large majority of the mechanics of the city are content with the offer of the bosses. Bricklayers who work up to their knees in water are glad to get $3.50 per day, while those who are employed on buildings average only $2.00. The wood-butchers are if possible in a still worse condition, while the plasterers take what's going. Won't some enterprising Milwaukeean contract for a load of coolies, as there is no danger of the mechanics of that city objecting to their introduction?[13]

With the return of prosperity, there was an upswing in trade-union activity. In 1872 there were, reportedly, at least fifteen strikes, not all successful. The strikes of the coopers, the printers, and the cigar makers were particularly long and bitterly fought in that year.

The Coopers

In the coopering industry, machine-made staves for flour barrels had come into general use prior to the Civil War. This displaced the most difficult and skilled part of slack-barrel cooper's work, leaving only the relatively simple task of "setting up." This change was not resisted by the coopers although it made the industry even more seasonal than before. Prior to the war, the millers in Milwaukee bought their barrels from small coopering establishments scattered over the city. However, the high war tax on the sale of industrial products led most Milwaukee millers to establish cooper shops as departments of their business. This change made union organization much easier, but the industry now became a succession of short periods of rush production and long periods of idleness. Each rush was a signal for a strike for higher wages, and after the rush the millers immediately cut rates to their former level.

On July 14, 1866, the *Sentinel* reported that the coopers of the city struck because of a reduction in wages. In September and October of 1868 the coopers struck to raise the rates from 15 and 20 cents for flat and round hooped barrels to 20 and 25 cents. The strikers, estimated at 2,000, had been getting the higher rates, and after a reduction they decided to quit work. The millers argued that the lower rates were adequate since the barrels were not made from machine staves and the coopers could work indoors. The coopers claimed they could not earn enough at the new rates since they worked only five or six months a year and were then idle. The strike ended unsatisfactorily for the coopers, with most of them going back to work at the lower rates. A number of millers agreed to a contract system which would provide year-round employment at 12.5 cents a barrel. However, the contract proved satisfactory to both parties—the millers found it difficult to get storage room for the barrels during the slack season, and the coopers revolted against low prices during rush seasons.

The cooperage trade in Milwaukee during the late 1860's and early 1870's was one of the most unstable and turbulent in the city. The coopers, who had organized a permanent local in 1867, joined the International Coopers Union in 1870 or 1871. In 1872 the union had a prolonged strike which ended disastrously, bringing the temporary dissolution of the local; it reorganized in June of 1873. During the 1872 strike there were reports of plans to bring in Chinese strikebreakers, although there is no evidence that this was done.

During the 1870's the Coopers continued their efforts to stabilize wages in the industry. In 1876 they fought a two-cents-a-barrel wage reduction. In October, 1877, they won an increase of three cents a barrel and successfully fought a reduction of two cents a barrel at the end of the same month. Despite the fact that the union included all but twenty-five of the coopers in the city, they lost battles against wage reductions on November 6 and December 26 of that same year. Their fortunes improved in October, 1878, when they won an increase of one cent a barrel. The union, burdened with the constant struggle against frequently fluctuating wage rates, disintegrated, and the membership lost interest. In 1879 only twelve coopers appeared when an attempt was again made to form a union.[14]

The Printers

In June, 1872, the printers presented a new scale of wages to the city newspapers fixing the rates for piece workers, foremen, and those employed by the week, regulating the number of apprentices in each office, and governing the distribution of copy among the printers. The newspapers refused the demands and the printers voted to strike at midnight June 30.

The employers involved—the Sentinel Publishing Company, Milwaukee News Company, German Printing Company, *Banner und Volksfreund,* and the *Seebote*—met the same day and formed an association "for mutual protection from the annoyances and impositions to which we are subjected from combinations of non-resident and irresponsible persons assuming to supervise our business and to determine for themselves our action, regardless of our ability to accede to their unreasonable requests."[15]

The newspapers of the city were aided by an offer from S. S. Merrill, general manager of the Milwaukee and St. Paul Railroad, to give free passes to strikebreakers. Out-of-town newspapers, such as the Janesville *Gazette* and the Whitewater *Register,* also aided the employers during the strike. The strike was hopeless and the union seriously hurt by the determined opposition of the employers.[16]

Depression Years, 1873–1878

With the Panic of 1873 trade-union activity in Milwaukee came to a virtual halt. During the following five years no union of lasting importance was founded, and the strikes reported were almost all lost, the employees often being replaced by others. The only efforts by Milwaukee workers that were noteworthy during this period were strikes by the Heaters at Bay View in 1873 and the Coal Heavers in 1876, and an unplanned demonstration by Negroes in 1877.

Typical of the poor personnel policies and ineffective modes of intraplant communication in the larger Milwaukee companies of the time was the incident leading to the strike of the Heaters Union at the Bay View plant of the Milwaukee Iron Works. In the evening of July 22, 1873, the heaters made two of the six heats required for a full day's work. Then nine of them left work, without telling the foreman, because of the unbearably high temperatures. Since their work was essential to the productive process, the plant had to be closed down. The company rules stated that the employees had to notify the company two weeks before they intended to leave. Hence, the company discharged the nine heaters, effective August 5. The Heaters Union questioned the right of the company to dismiss the men under the circumstances, but the company denied that the temperature in the plant had been too high and refused to reconsider. The union threatened to refuse to light the fires in the morning unless the discharge was revoked. The company evidently won, for the *Sentinel* of July 30 reported that the heaters "have taken a reasonable view of the position of the Company, and will resume work to-day."

The Coal Heavers' strike of 1876 was chiefly important because of the use of Polish workers as strikebreakers. In May of that year the coal heavers employed by Fette and Meyer struck to increase their wages from 30 to 50 cents an hour. The workers had received 40 cents an hour from 1867 to 1870, 60 cents in 1870, and 50 cents an hour until 1874 or 1875. But the coal dealers found that Chicago, Cleveland, Detroit, and Buffalo were paying only 30 cents and Racine was paying only 25 cents an hour. Consequently, in the spring of 1876 wages were reduced throughout Milwaukee's coal yards to 30, sometimes 40, cents an hour. The 200 coal heavers at Fette and Meyer's hoped to restore the old rates. Picket lines were placed around the yard, but a number of Poles refused to join the strikers and went back to work for 40 cents. Infuriated by the action of the Poles, the strikers hurled stones at the intruders and threatened to storm the yards and "drive the Polacks into the river." A police squad was called to quiet the demonstrators. Four days later, May 8, the coal heavers, reinforced by workers at other struck coal yards in the city, gathered on the south side of the city at various points along the docks, intending to force the Polish laborers at Fette and Meyer's to quit work. At the request of Mr. Fette a few policemen were sent to the docks but were laughed at by the strikers. Another call went out, more policemen arrived, and they rushed the crowd, arresting six or eight of the leaders. The strike ended unsuccessfully, but it enforced the belief in Milwaukee that the Poles were "cheap labor" who should be scorned, an attitude that became important during the riots of 1886.[17]

In 1877 another minority group in Milwaukee came into prominence, the Negroes. On July 31 Negro workers employed in rebuilding structures destroyed by fire on Market Street struck, protesting their treatment. The workers, apparently without any leadership, marched to the corner of Strand and Twenty-fourth Streets and induced another group of workers to quit. Negroes working at Levine's Picklery, Stump's planing mill, the freight depot, flour mills, and other places joined the demonstration. A strong detachment of police was sent to control the strikers, and the movement abruptly died. The *Sentinel* charged that the Negroes had been incited by "white demagogues," but no effort was made to organize the unhappy Negro laborer for many years.

Merk succinctly summarizes the status of the labor movement in the state, with equal applicability to Milwaukee's labor movement, saying:

The history of the Wisconsin labor movement during the years of the war and the years immediately following is thus a record of faint and uncertain beginnings. Wisconsin was still predominantly agricultural; her industrial population was too limited and scattered to permit of effective organization. The story of this first organizing of the wage-earning class in the State is interesting chiefly as it reflects the more significant movements that were going on in the larger industrial centers of the North.[18]

During the depression years of 1873 to 1878, it was the constant struggles of a few unions, such as the coopers', and a few incidental strikes, such as the coal heavers', that account for the little activity reported. Much more important during that time was the emergence of a Socialist movement in Milwaukee.

CHAPTER III

Early Socialism

THE basic factor contributing to the growth of a Socialist movement in Milwaukee was the migration of numerous Germans to the city. By 1850 more than one-third of the population was German-born. Immigrants who had come to Milwaukee after the 1848 revolutionary upheaval in Germany, the "forty-eighters," had a minority of skilled workers in their group. After the group had settled down in Milwaukee, these workers were generally excluded from the intellectual life of the middle-class forty-eighters. This exclusion induced the artisans to war against the *Geschwollenen* ("swelled ones") and to establish their own clubs. One branch of the Turners, the gymnastic club, was under the leadership of Heinrich Loose, the first in the refugee group to support the Communist Manifesto. The Arbeiter Gesang Verein, one of the singing societies among the forty-eighters, and the Verein der Arbeiter, one of the politically and intellectually oriented clubs, followed the teachings of Wilhelm Weitling. Weitling, who emigrated to America in 1847, advocated a bank of exchange as a replacement for capitalism.[1]

None of these groups, however, had any real connection with later Socialist movements. Rather, they represented opposition to the liberal bourgeois ideology of the majority of the forty-eighters. The anti-slavery movement and the Civil War absorbed the idealism of the early German immigrants, and the Socialist movement had to begin again in the Sixties.

Post-Civil-War Socialism was radically different from the old. It received its inspiration from two sources in Europe. One source was the International Workingmen's Association (the "First International") founded by Karl Marx in London in 1864 and the other was the teachings of Ferdinand Lassalle, embodied in his *Open Letter* to a workingmen's committee in Leipzig, published in 1863.

The International believed that trade-union organization must come before political action and that the trade union would be the basis of political victory. Lassalle, on the other hand, believed political action was the basis of Socialism; he tended to disparage the activities of unions.

An introduction to Marxian Socialism came to the Milwaukee Germans through the German-language newspaper *Phalanx,* edited by Gustav Grahl and published from 1865 to 1866. Unions such as the Cigar Makers, Brewers, and Carpenters, formed in the late 1850's and 1860's, often had exclusively German membership, giving them a strong political inclination. But the small amount of industrialization in the city and the emphasis upon non-Socialist objectives kept the Socialists hopelessly divided. It was not until industrialization had become more advanced and a depression had vitiated the efforts of the trade unions that the Socialists' ideology could take root—the period of the 1870's.[2]

During the early years of the International, the organization's only contact with America was through the National Labor Union. However, after 1870 the International established branches in nearly every large city in the United States, centering in New York and Chicago. The promotion of trade unionism by the International receded behind its propagandism of Socialism.

The International Workingmen's Association in Milwaukee

In 1874 a Milwaukee Branch of the International Workingmen's Association was formed and met at a place called Casino Hall. The following year Joseph Brucker began publication of *Der Sozialist* under the banner: "No master, no slave—the same obligation, the same rights!" Brucker, a young Austrian newspaperman and a convinced Lassallean, had come to the city about five years before and subsequently published the Milwaukee *Freidenker* for the *Freie Gemeinde,* and *Biron und Brucker's Sonntags Blatt.* The single-sheet *Sozialist* soon sold 2,000 subscriptions and became the organ of Section One of the International Workingmen's Association of Milwaukee. *Der Sozialist's* proclaimed purpose (November 15, 1875) was:

to make clear in a positive way the principles of a truly popular government of the people, to promote by way of teaching general education and, to show workers how they can liberate themselves from the shackles of private capital and make that capital useful to the common good.

. . . .

Thousands, yes, centuries, agree with us that the political decay in our republic has reached a point which makes us fear the worst. Thousands of wage workers are oppressed by the vampires of money and thousands go with us in the battle against the overgrown churches and sects. Therefore, it is our mission to unite those who are convinced of the necessity of building anew our social, political and religious relations. We believe that we can achieve that best by agitating for the positive ideas of a social-democratic state, and by encouraging education and enlightenment.[3]

Brucker's declaration of principles was significant in its omission of trade unionism. He and other followers of Lassalle's doctrine in Milwaukee seemed to despair of any worthwhile results emanating from the economic activities of unions. It was almost a year before the Workingmen's Association in Milwaukee made any real attempt to mobilize the latent force in the trade-union movement.

In the same year, 1875, Henry von Ende started an English-language counterpart of *Der Sozialist: The Social Democrat,* later renamed the *Emancipator.* The following year the movement began to make headway in Milwaukee. In February a second section of the Workingmen's Association was formed. The members began to collect statistics on wages and working conditions in the city for use in their agitational program. In April, 1876, about 500 working men and women attended the Stadt Theater in answer to an invitation by the Socialists. The speaker for the occasion was Peter J. McGuire, an itinerant agitator for the Lassallean Socialists. Later McGuire was to become the head of the Carpenters Union and the first secretary of the American Federation of Labor. The *Sentinel* (April 29, 1875) described McGuire as being "quite young, not very stylish, and tolerably incorrect of speech. He is a cabinet maker by trade, but now travels for the purpose of organizing Socialist clubs, and canvassing for a paper called The Socialist, of New York." McGuire, then only twenty-four years old and a convert to Lassalleanism for the past two years, contended the workers would be robbed by the "ruffianly capitalists" and that the "scattering Trades' Unions . . . will be crushed out by arrogant, brutal domineering, soulless capital unless [mutual] cooperation in this country becomes universal and all the workers in the land enlist under the banner of the Socialists."[4]

Among the speakers following McGuire was Gustav Lyser, an important figure in the movement. Lyser, a dogmatic Lassallean and hostile to trade unionism, had been editor of the New York *Sozial-Demokrat.* His outspoken opposition to unionism had proved untenable to the Social Democratic Party of New York after it established friendly relations with the National Furniture Workers Union. Consequently he was removed from the editorship by the executive board of the New York party in March 1875. When the party, in its July 1875 convention, went on record in favor of the preliminary organization of workers into trade unions, it also expelled Lyser from the party in punishment for his attacks on trade unionism. Evidently in the latter part of 1875 or early 1876, Lyser moved to Milwaukee to become active in the movement there. He also changed his position on trade unionism to a more acceptable one.

The May 13, 1876, issue of the *Sentinel* reported that 800 workers met at the North Side Turner Hall to hear Brucker, Lyser, and others talk on the current strikes of the coal heavers and wood handlers. Lyser talked an hour and three-quarters on the "workingman's woes, and the corruption of capitalists and the princely editors who live on the fat of the land and cry down the poor laborers."

About this same time, a committee which had been meeting at the office of the *Sozialist* reported the formation of an organization to be known as the Arbeiter-Bund ("Workingmen's League") of Milwaukee. The purpose of the Arbeiter-Bund was to "guarantee an existence that shall enable workers to attain a respectable standing in society" and to provide mutual assistance to further that aim. Through newspaper agitation, mass meetings, establishment of an "educational" fund, and opening the membership to every workingman who would enroll as a member, the Arbeiter-Bund hoped to achieve its objective. Organizationally, the Arbeiter-Bund was to be composed of sections of workingmen, such as the joiners, shoemakers, and masons, which would be eligible to elect one delegate from each section to attend a central committee. This central committee was to meet once a week and control the business of the organization.

Another mass meeting was planned for June 7, 1876, at the North Side Turner Hall. Delegates from the Carpenters, Shoemakers, Tailors, Masons, Furniture Makers, Printers, Machinists, Cigar Makers, Molders, and the Coopers Unions were instructed to take seats on the platform and present applications for affiliation with the Bund. At the meeting Brucker encouraged the organization of more trade unions and predicted, rather optimistically, that in a few years the solidarity of labor would give workers the balance of power. Brucker's long-range plan was first to organize all of Milwaukee's labor, then to send speakers throughout the state and encourage unions in every village and city and in other states to follow Milwaukee's example. After a sufficient number had joined unions, a national Bund would be formed for political action and the existing political parties would fade away. Brucker cautioned the members to remain independent of political action, for the present at least, and concentrate upon the organization of unions instead.[5]

The attempts to interest more workers continued, and by the end of the month the Bund had secured the support of some English-speaking workers, represented by a delegation headed by Patrick Mc-Manus, P. J. Quinn and C. P. Southwell. The emphasis of the group turned now towards immediate political action. Brucker declared it would be futile to break the power of the capitalists through strikes, consumer cooperatives, and savings banks. Instead, he maintained, the workers must gain control of Congress and the state legislatures to free them from the power of the capitalists. Brucker urged his ideas be propagated to other unions without regard to language or nationality.

In July another mass meeting was held at the North Side Turner Hall with a disappointing attendance of 300 persons. On the stage sat such prominent men in the movement as Leopold Ries, H. Hoffman, Oskar Lincke, Joseph Brucker, and Gustav Lyser. The stage was appropriately decked with a red banner, ten by four feet wide. Brucker, dubbed by his opponents as the "fierce and fearless Apostle of Non-sense," spoke first, denouncing the Democrats for allegedly favoring slavery and having an alliance with Rome. He regarded the Republicans as somewhat better, but dominated by "bond-holders, profligate pastors and monstrous monopolists." Brucker urged the people to stay away from the voting polls until the Socialists were strong enough to elect their own candidates.

Lyser spoke on the topic: "Can Socialism Prevail Without a Revolution?" He concluded that the freedom of the workers was only on paper but that equality could be achieved through the ballot box without a physical battle. Brucker then read a "Modern Declaration of Independence" adopted July 3 by 5,000 Socialists of Chicago at a meeting attended by Lyser. In fiery words the declaration proclaimed:

The history of the present competitive system, extending back to the middle ages, is a history of oppression, robbery, and despotism, compelling the great mass of producers to waste their lives in misery and degradation, toiling for the benefit of the few, who by taking advantage of their necessities, enforced ignorance and obtained control of all means of production, and through pretended competition with each other, in which the suffering workers are the real competitors, have put a premium upon selfishness and crime.6

Five days later, the Bund elected Gustav Lyser to represent it at the Union Congress to be held in Philadelphia on July 19, 1876. The Philadelphia Congress, including delegates from the International, the Labor Party of Illinois, the Social Political Workingmen's Society of Cincinnati, and the Social Democratic Party brought an uneasy truce between the Lassallean and International factions. Immediately after the Congress, the Workingmen's Party of the United States was organized.

In August the Milwaukee Socialists responded to the political action decree by denouncing the faithlessness of the professional politicians and resolving to start an independent political movement. The political demands of the new party (*Sentinel*, August 25, 26, 1876) were: sanitary regulations, stringent legislation against food adulteration, laws to protect the health of factory workers, safety legislation for factories, banishment of factory employment of children under fourteen and improvement of the courts of justice. Although the party, later named the Social Democratic Party, did not intend to enter the fall elections of 1876, it urged the workers not to vote the Democratic or Republican tickets.

On September 17 the Milwaukee Arbeiter-Bund held a picnic and parade to celebrate the unification of the trade unions into one central body. Among the participating organizations were the Turnverein Sokol, Bohemian Benevolent Association, Coopers, Carpenters, Printers, Tailors, Shoemakers, Masons, Machinists, Furniture Makers, Book Binders, Hand Workers, Bricklayers Unions, and Section One of the Social Democratic Party (at this time still called the Workingmen's Party). Shortly thereafter the Social Democratic Party was united with the Arbeiter-Bund. This merger brought the complete submission of the few Socialists who advocated trade-union action to the dominant political-Socialists. In the months that followed the only reported nonpolitical activities of the Socialists were a discussion of plans to help the unemployed workers and their families during the winter of 1876-1877, and a futile attempt to incorporate a newly formed tailors' union into the Socialist Party. After October 31, 1876, *Der Sozialist* no longer carried news about, or mentioned, trade unions in Milwaukee. The workers complained that long speeches were interfering with business proceedings and nothing important was being accomplished. The great loss of interest and membership, particularly among the English-speaking workers, soon led to the disappearance of the Bund.[7]

The Social Democratic Party

The Social Democratic Party was pleased with the results of the spring election in 1877. Advocating public ownership, political reform, cooperatives, and labor welfare measures, the party received about 1,500 votes and elected two aldermen, two supervisors, and two constables.

The increased activities of the Socialists and the great railway strikes throughout the nation in mid-1877 aroused much concern in Milwaukee. During the time of the strikes, Mayor Butler and Chief Beck enrolled the active Turners in the city as Minute Men in case of trouble. Sheriff Sanger listed one hundred "trusty citizens" who could be relied upon, and the Sheridan Guard was readied. Many of the breweries and larger factories in the city doubled their night watch. On July 26 Mayor Butler issued a proclamation urging that no one incite violence. The Socialists declared they would start no trouble, and discounted reports that Socialists in other cities had been involved in the violence. The U. S. War Department sent instructions to Milwaukee to send reports to Washington every six hours. Despite the alarm and the elaborate precautions, the only "uprising" (so called in the *Sentinel* of July 27 and 30, 1877) was the visit of a committee of machinists, blacksmiths, and boilermakers working on the St. Paul Railway to discuss several grievances amicably with General Manager S. S. Merrill.

The party continued to grow during the summer, and in August the Milwaukee party had German, English, Scandinavian, and Norwegian sections. That fall the Social Democratic Party won significant votes in Chicago, Cincinnati, Buffalo, New York, New Haven, and Detroit, as well as in Milwaukee. The platform of the Social Democratic Party in the city remained about the same but added a demand for a state bureau of labor statistics.

In the 1877 election another competitor for labor's support was the Greenback Party. E. P. Allis, head of a large steel processing firm (later to become part of Allis-Chalmers), was its candidate for governor. The Greenback Party was not primarily a labor party, and despite the efforts of Robert Schilling (then living in Cleveland), a leader of the Knights of Labor and later prominent in Milwaukee labor circles, the party was unable to overcome its primarily agrarian appeal in that year. The Social Democratic candidate for governor, Colin M. Campbell, received 1,403 votes to 1,064 for Allis in Milwaukee County. Henry Smith, candidate for the State Assembly from the Sixth and Thirteenth Wards, received a clear majority over his Democratic and Republican rivals to become the only successful nominee of the Socialists.[8]

Despite the auspicious beginnings of the Socialist political movement in Milwaukee in 1877, the efforts did not bear fruit in future years. In late 1877 the name of the party was changed to Socialist Labor Party, and the 1878 spring election saw the Socialists endorse some candidates of the old parties for alderman, supervisor, and constable—more often Republicans than Democrats—but they failed to endorse any candidates for the general elective offices.

The Socialist press in the city similarly declined. *Der Sozialist* began to lose ground, and its editor, Joseph Brucker, joined the Repub-

lican Party. A New Jersey Socialist who had assisted him, Herman Si-
gel, took over the paper as the *Vorwaerts*, but soon needed financial
help from some brewery owners. After two more changes of name, the
paper merged with a German Republican daily. The English-language
Emancipator died after only a few months. More permanent results
came from the establishment of the weekly *Arminia* by Michael Biron
in 1880. Biron, a former Roman Catholic priest, had been associated
with Brucker in editing the *Freidenker* in 1872 and had founded
the short lived *Arbeiter-Zeitung* in 1879. The *Arminia* was the principal voice of the Socialists during the followng years. When Biron's
interests became absorbed in his anti-clerical paper, *Lucifer*, Paul
Grottkau took over as editor of the *Arminia* in 1886, changing its name
to the *Arbeiter-Zeitung* (not to be confused with the *Arbeiter-Zeitung*
founded in 1879) and launching a new era in Socialist activity in
Milwaukee.

The Socialist movement in Milwaukee undoubtedly suffered a
blow when Gustav Lyser, a leading spirit, moved to Chicago in 1877 or
1878 to become editor of the *Vorbote*. An eight-hour demonstration by
the Socialists at Quentin's Park in 1879, featuring Paul Grottkau and
J. Belaratsky of Chicago as speakers, drew only 300 participants. The
Socialists continued to court the trade unions, particularly those
formed during 1879, and whenever possible condemned the misman-
agement of public institutions. However, the revival of trade-union activity with the return of prosperity temporarily stifled their efforts on
the labor front. They were reduced to working with the Greenbackers
in 1880 and following the political lead of local labor leaders from
1880 through 1886.[9]

CHAPTER IV

The Birth of a Labor Movement

The Revival of Unionism

THE return of prosperity in 1878 brought a revival of unionism throughout the nation. After unemployment and wage reductions in the mid-1870's, workers were now passionately interested in a return to union activity which would recoup their losses and raise wages to new heights. This change in attitude, made possible by a more favorable economic climate, was signaled in Milwaukee by the strike of the flour millers in 1878.

The flour-mill workers had been forced to accept a reduction in wages in June, 1878. In July the employers resolved to reduce wages another 24 per cent because wages were allegedly lower in Minneapolis and St. Louis. The workers, while at first reluctant to strike or to form a union, successfully resisted the reduction and went back to work at the old rates.

The activity of the unions increased slowly, but in 1879 took a more aggressive turn. The coal heavers throughout the city struck for a 25 per cent increase in wages in June, 1879. Despite the presence of the police (a not too unusual occurrence during the times) the employers were unable to get the workers to return to work or to find replacements. A strike of the tanners in July for an increase of 10 per cent was similarly successful. An unusual feature of this strike was the charge of Milwaukee firms that Chicago tannery owners had sent a delegation to Milwaukee to organize a union, hoping to raise Milwaukee wages to the Chicago level and eliminate a "competitive disadvantage."[1]

Iron and Steel Workers

Probably the strongest union in Milwaukee during the period of the revival was the Amalgamated Association of Iron and Steel Workers founded in 1876. The union had two lodges with 800 members located in Bay View. In 1880 the union gained a daily wage ranging from two to eight dollars a day, rejecting a company counter offer of a 25 per cent increase. But not all workers at the Bay View plant of the North Chicago Rolling Mills were content with merely the increased wages. In 1881 the 450 puddlers working at the mill were angered by the long hours they often labored because the previous shifts were unable to complete their work on time. The day shift started at three-thirty in the morning. By one o'clock in the afternoon, they usually had completed four of the five required "heats." However, a break would often occur or the machinery would be out of order, and it would be impossible to complete the five heats within 12 hours. Consequently the first shift, often working 15 and 16 hours before the furnaces, would still be on the job when the next shift came to work. The puddlers therefore demanded that each shift be restricted to 11 or 12 hours. These workers gained some changes in working hours the following June when the Iron and Steel Workers won another wage increase during the course of a nation-wide strike involving 35,000 men in six states.[2]

The Waterfront

Another important scene of renewed union activity during the economic revival of 1878-82 was the waterfront—with a notable lack of success. The dock laborers had been angered by the employers' practice of deducting wages for time lost while making repairs during the unloading of the vessels. The laborers hopefully appealed to the courts. In April, 1880, 75 dock workers struck when the agent of the Anchor Line, D. M. Brigham, refused a demanded increase from 20 to 25 cents an hour. The strikers attempted to keep replacements from working, but were dispersed by the police. Another strike in August to gain a wage increase to compensate for their irregular employment also failed. Despite the organization of the Milwaukee Dock Laborers Union that followed, two strikes in 1881 for wage increases—one of them including 300 men—also failed.[3]

More successful was the Milwaukee Branch of the Chicago Seamen's Union founded in 1880 or 1881. This union soon grew to include 250 men. The primary incentive for its organization was the competition of unskilled laborers, including skilled workers of other trades who frequently came to the lake for employment during their slack seasons. Though beset with frequent, and sometimes violent, strikes between the owners and workers and frequent encounters between the seamen and non-union workers, the union was able to minimize the competition of the unskilled and established benefits for its sick and disabled members.[4]

Railroad Employees

One of the most publicized disputes of the time occurred among railway-yard employees. In 1878 workers in the yards of the Chicago, Milwaukee and St. Paul Railroad quit work for three days in protest against a rumored (*Sentinel,* August 12) reduction of working hours and wages. In the *Sentinel* of August 14 the rumor was denied by the company manager, Sherburns Merrill. In the summer of 1880 the machinists and blacksmiths employed in the St. Paul railway shops presented a list of grievances to the management. The workers demanded immediate full wage payment upon termination of employment, a revision of prices in the "tool list" so a worker was charged no more than the replacement cost of a lost tool, and a 10 per cent increase in wages. The company agreed to the first two demands and granted a wage increase putting wages at the St. Paul yards on a par with others in the West. On August 26 the management called workers into the office and presented statistics purporting to show that their wages were higher than in any other company in the West. However, the management indicated they would be willing to grant a small increase to a few skilled mechanics.

The workers claimed the cost of living was higher in Milwaukee and pointed out that they had previously accepted a 5 per cent reduction when business was poor. Further irritated by the removal of the company's shops to the Menomonee Valley, making it necessary to carry cold dinners and ride in unheated boxcars to get to work, and by the "tyrannical spirit" of Superintendent William C. Van Horne, the workers refused the offer of the management and voted to strike. The company posted notice that the 260 strikers must return to work by August 27 or be peremptorily discharged. The company also demanded that the workers turn in their keys and checks. The workers refused to comply. Superintendent Van Horne then reported that the company would not compromise with the strikers and had made arrangements to hire men from out of the city to replace the strikers. When the strikebreakers came to the city, they were met by committees of the strikers and induced to leave. The committees were sometimes misled by the claims of tramps. Under the pretense that they were strikebreakers hired by the company, the tramps took three dollars apiece from the strikers to pay their transportation out of the city, using the money to buy liquor.

Between 100 and 200 workers remained on the job, claiming the strike vote had been pushed by a few younger members and denying there were arbitrary or obnoxious rules in force in the shop. The strikers denied the allegation, charging they had been forbidden to talk to coworkers while on the job and accusing those who remained on the job of being the original strike agitators. As the strike dragged on, the men received financial support from the employees of E. P. Allis and from the Mechanical Engineers Union. There were threats to spread the strike over the entire line.

Finally on September 7 the men decided to go to the shop in a body, demanding their wages due and severing all connections with the company. However, the general manager and the superintendent appeared before the meeting of the strikers, asked them to return to work, and promised that wages would be raised to the level in Chicago. The strikers countered with a proposal to return, provided wages were immediately increased 10 per cent. The issue was finally compromised by appointing a committee of two strikers and one manager to go to Chicago to report on wage levels. After the report of the committee, the strikers returned to work, accepting a scale similar to that paid in three leading railway shops of Chicago.[5]

The gains made during the two-week strike of late 1880 did not long satisfy the desires of the men, who were conscious of the increased business of the railroads. By April, 1881, the painters at the shops of the Chicago, Milwaukee and St. Paul Railroad were demanding increases in pay, and the following month a strike broke out that involved most of the employees of both the St. Paul and the Chicago and Northwestern railroads. On May 2, 42 of the 54 employees in the freight sheds of the Chicago and Northwestern sent a petition to the local freight agent, C. E. Moody, asking for an increase from $1.20 to $1.50 a day and one hour's call-in pay. The petition denied, the men struck on May 5, refusing a company offer of $1.35. Because two of the strikers returned to work, the men decided to accept the company's offer the following day, but one of the leaders in the strike was not re-hired.

On the same day the freight-house employees, the switchmen, yardmen, and brakemen struck at both railway companies. The brakemen, who had to pay for their own food and lodging while on the road, demanded an increase of $5 a month. The yardmen demanded a $10 increase. While the brakemen and yardmen soon won part of their demands, the switchmen fared much worse. Encouraged by the strike and subsequent wage increases of the railroad workers in Chicago, the switchmen had sought an increase averaging 57 cents a day. The St. Paul Road notified the strikers to collect any wages due and refused to listen to their demands. Both the St. Paul and the North-western roads required brakemen and conductors to replace the switchmen, though six brakemen were fired for their refusal to scab. The switchmen had added to their claims a demand for double time on Sundays, asserting that during the winter they had worked seven days a week but were allowed only one-half day's wages for Sunday and were often compelled to work nights for nothing. The switchmen induced the night shift to join the strike. When the employers began to hire green hands on a permanent basis, the switchmen attempted to gain the support of other workers in the area.

The strike of the switchmen took a new turn at midnight on May 9 when a bomb, loaded with glass and slugs, was thrown at Michael Kaiser, a foreman who had been riding a switch engine. Fortunately he was not hurt. Later it was contended that the bomb had been intended for H. L. Teal, a foreman the strikers loathed. The St. Paul Company immediately hired detectives and placed guards on the bridges leading out of the Menomonee Valley. Despite a resolution of the Switchmen's Mutual Aid Association that "we have not so far and do not [now] sanction any such acts or proceedings," the incident served to reinforce the position of the company. It adamantly refused to discuss the issues further. By May 16 the strike was near an end, with many of the older workers willing to return at former wage levels.[6]

The Printers

Even more noteworthy were the strikes and boycotts of the printers in 1882 and 1884. During the depression following the Panic of 1873, wages of printers in the city were reduced several times. At the time no union in the city included a majority of printers, and the only existing body of printers agreed to the reductions. With the return of prosperity in 1878-79, wages were not restored, although prices rose. In April, 1881, a meeting was held to reorganize the union. Before the union, which hoped "to protect just and honorable employers from the unfair competition of greedy cheap-labor huckstering rivals,"[7] had become a full-fledged branch of the International Typographical Union, a strike started. The Cream City Typographical Union, as the local was called, demanded an increase from 33 to 38 cents per thousand ems. The strike involved the *Sentinel, Republican and News,* and the *Evening Wisconsin.* The *Evening Wisconsin* acceded to the demands of the printers prior to the strike, contingent upon the acceptance of the new rates by the *Sentinel* and the *Republican and News.* Despite the efforts of the newspapers to run the papers without the aid of the compositors, and later to bring recruits from Chicago and New York (who joined the strikers upon reaching the city), the strike continued successfully. The union was encouraged when it was able to get nine women employed by the *News* to join the strike. At about the beginning of May the strike was settled, the union winning a compromise of 36 cents per thousand ems.

However, conflict continued with the *Republican and News*. At the end of the strike the *Sentinel* had recognized the union, but the *News* announced its hostility to the union and refused to recognize it. Some of the *News* printers belonged to the union, but a considerable number did not. Since the paper was not organized, the union could not establish a grievance committee to take complaints to the owners. One of the principal problems at the *News* was the attitude of the foreman, Andrew C. Macrorie, who had been brought from Chicago during the strike. The foreman was an avowed and bitter enemy of the union and asked the remaining union compositors to renounce the Typographical Union if they wanted to keep their jobs. The paper also formed a Printers Protective Association to defend the interests of the non-union employees. Because of the unsure position of the unionists, they appealed to the Cream City Typographical Union for help, "and the Union made their cause its own."

In the beginning of August a strike was launched against the *Republican and News,* the principal demand being the replacement of Macrorie by a union foreman. The union forbade its members to work at the paper and, with the aid of its newspaper, the *Printers Bulletin,* brought out at the beginning of the April strikes, launched the first boycott in Wisconsin's history. The boycott received the whole-hearted support of the Milwaukee trade-union movement. Within a few weeks the *News* lost over 700 subscribers and was forced to offer former subscribers free issues for one month if they would again take the paper. In its eagerness to make the boycott successful, the union extended it to cover the Quiet House, a gathering place of printers. Because the owner, Adam Roth, had refused to drop his subscription to the *News,* the union resolved to fine any member five dollars if he patronized Roth's place.

The boycott against the *Republican and News* continued until May, 1882, when the *News* purchased the *Sentinel,* forming the *Republican-Sentinel.* The *Sentinel* had been unionized, but the new owners decided to take their old non-union employees into the new office. The owners offered to operate an open shop, but the union insisted upon a completely unionized shop. The strike and boycott continued, now in opposition to the policies of the *Republican-Sentinel.* When, about two months later, the Buffalo (New York) *Courier* had a strike and offered free transportation to non-union workers who would move to Buffalo and replace the strikers, several of the employees of the *Republican-Sentinel* left and union printers were hired to replace them. Later, the printers marched into the office in a group, took possession of the type cases, and demanded 38 cents per thousand ems, the rate received by non-union employees. The employers conceded and the boycott was ended, eleven months after it began.

Two years later on February 2, 1884, a second major strike and boycott by the Typographical Union began, now against the *Evening Wisconsin*. The union demanded that women compositors on the paper receive the same wages as men. The owners claimed there was no discrimination against women other than during the apprenticeship period. The union conceded the point but wanted the office reorganized and the strikebreakers replaced. To make the strike more effective, the printers reissued their *Printers Bulletin* and asked organized labor to boycott anyone who subscribed to or advertised in the *Evening Wisconsin*. Boycott resolutions were adopted by the Machinery and Stove Molders, Bricklayers and Masons, Cigar Makers, Seamen's, Blacksmiths and Machinists, Plasterers, Boilermakers, Upholsterers, and Broommakers Unions and the Milwaukee Trades Assembly. The boycott was formally lifted in April, 1886, when all men employed by the *Evening Wisconsin* joined the union.[8]

The Milwaukee Trades Assembly

The upward trend of the labor movement after 1879 brought a rapid growth of city federations throughout the nation. In July, 1880, three unions in Milwaukee started the Milwaukee Trades Assembly. Shortly afterward, it was incorporated under the state law. The principle of the organization was "that wise concert of action on their [the unions'] part can secure the redress of any abuses of which members of their class may be subjected." The Trades Assembly said it would have nothing to do with the internal affairs of member unions, but instead sought "to put an end to a condition of affairs that fosters the employment of cheap and incompetent labor for the production of low-priced and illegitimate goods which demoralize the market for good work."[9]

For almost a year after its formation, the Trades Assembly was little known in the city. But in 1882 it gradually gained more and more member unions. When, on September 4, 1881, the Trades Assembly held its "First Annual Picnic and Festival" at the Milwaukee Garden, it was able to report the participation of the Cigar Makers, Iron Molders, Horse Shoers, Amalgamated Iron and Steel Workers, St. Paul Railway Shop Employees, Cream City Typographical, German Typographia, Pressmen's, Trunkmakers, Stone Cutters, Bricklayers and Masons, Hod Carriers, Lathers, Flour Barrel Coopers, Tight Barrel Coopers, Seamen's, Tanners and Curriers, Brewers, Carpenters, and Shoemakers Unions.

Over 2,000 persons participated in the demonstration. Fred W. Leiff, president of the Trades Assembly, disclaimed any political objectives and instead stressed trade-union activity and the use of the boycott. However, F. Bakeman, while supporting union organization and the use of arbitration and the boycott, also encouraged political organization, denouncing corporate monopoly as "the blighting scourge and common enemy of our country, . . . the relic of barbarianism and the feudal ages . . . ." Richard Powers, of the Lake Seamen's Union in Chicago, and Gustav Lyser, who had moved back to Milwaukee, were also there to encourage the new Trades Assembly. The following day (September 5) the Milwaukee *Sentinel* commented: "No such demonstration has ever before been made in this city which could be compared in magnitude with the first annual gathering of the Trades Assembly of this district and they were congratulated by all those interested in the objects which they have at heart for the perfect good humor and quietude which marked their entire proceedings."

The Trades Assembly maintained the interest expressed by the Milwaukee unions. In November, 1881, it was one of eleven trades assemblies present at the founding convention of the Federation of Organized Trades and Labor Unions of the United States and Canada (which became the American Federation of Labor in 1886) held in Pittsburgh.

The contacts with other unions produced a new *élan* within the movement. As one member of the Trades Assembly later reported: "After working for more than twelve years in this city, five years ago I hardly knew any craftsmen except those working with me in the same shop. To-day I am personally acquainted with four-fifths of all the men engaged at my trade, and everybody seems to know me. This fact I appreciate more than almost anything connected with my social position."[10] The purely economic character of the Milwaukee Trades Assembly was not to last long. The prolonged strikes of the printers and the cigar makers (discussed in the next chapter) led to a rise in political activity.

Political Action

Although there had been an abortive attempt to start a "People's Ticket" by the Socialists and others in 1880 and although the Brewery workers had allegedly cost the successful Republican nominee, Thomas H. Brown, some 600 votes, the trade-union movement as a whole did not follow the lead of these groups.[11] However, concrete grievances brought the question of politics to a head in 1882.

During the Cigar Makers' strike of 1881-82, there had been a number of clashes between trade unionists and strikebreakers, resulting in the arrest and conviction of a number of union members. The Cigar Makers Union denounced violence on the part of strikers and attempted to retaliate by securing warrants for the "arrest of employers who committed gross outrages upon the laboring classes." Municipal Court Clerk Julius Meiswinkel refused to issue the warrants, incurring the hostility of the unions. The union charged that a number of men had been arrested and sentenced by Judge James Mallory simply for having had the audacity to pass Asherman's cigar manufacturing company.

A mass meeting of the striking cigar makers and other laboring men in February, 1882, was attended by 1,800 to 2,000 people. Meiswinkel was denounced for his refusal to issue warrants against the employers and for his allegedly promiscuous issuance of warrants against workers. The *Sentinel* reported the speaker "denounced Meiswinkel in so unmeasured terms that decency forbids a repetition of them." Fred Leiff, president of the Cigar Makers and of the Milwaukee Trades Assembly, urged the workingmen of the city to organize thoroughly, "and if they could not get justice in the courts they should get it at the ballot box." This, plus the prolonged struggle of the Typographical Union against the *Republican and News,* was the signal for the Trades Assembly to enter the spring municipal elections.

On March 1 the Trades Assembly decided to enter a full ticket in the spring elections and made preliminary nominations. At the end of the month, the nominees were formally announced. John M. Stowell, sometime Democrat known for his fair treatment of workers at the Cream City Iron Works which he headed, was nominated for mayor. Henry Smith, sometime Socialist, Greenbacker, and Democrat, was the nominee for comptroller. Smith was known to the laborers for his fight in the state legislature, against a "tramp law" which would have defined a vagrant as any person who refused to work for the usual and common wages given to others in the area and for his opposition to the exemption of certain railway lands from taxation. Smith, at the time a member of the city council, had also fought to enforce a bill prohibiting child labor in factories and against renewal of the city's unpopular contract with the Milwaukee Gas Light Company for the lighting of city streets. The other nominees were August Kieckhefer, then alderman of the Seventh Ward and private contractor sympathetic toward labor, for treasurer, and P. J. Somers, a Democrat, for city attorney.

The platform of the Trades Assembly proclaimed:

We believe ourselves, first of all, citizens of a government under whose constitution and laws, all men are free and equal, and that whether native or foreign born, we owe to that government our warmest love and allegiance.

We believe in a just, impartial and efficient administration of law and of every public trust.

We believe that honesty and capability should determine tenure of office, regardless of politics.

We believe that labor, being the foundation of all wealth and the only security of our national prosperity, should have the fostering care and protection of our laws, to the end that laboringmen have an equitable share of the fruits of their labor.

We maintain the inalienable right of workingmen of every trade or condition, in common with other classes of citizens, to organize for mutual aid and protection. . . .

. . . .

We do not oppose the legitimate *use,* but the licentious *abuse* of capital, that abuse which profanes justice in her temple, and defiles law by corrupting the law-maker; that abuse which makes beggary and want where nature brought forth plenty; which makes a wanton trade and commerce, breeding at will financial panics, commercial depression, and all the evils that result from the speculation of moneyed fools and the manipulation of moneyed knaves.[12]

The platform was notable for its implicit disavowal of any radical approach to American political institutions, the appeal to "good government" reformers, and its quasi-greenback, antimonopoly sentiment. To attract the support of workers, the platform specifically called for the elimination of prison and child labor, restriction of Chinese immigration, and compulsory school-attendance laws. Demands for the reorganization of court procedures, strict economy in public improvements, reform in the methods of assessing and collecting property taxes, elimination of "ring rule," and rigid enforcement of laws relating to bribery in elections were designed to enlist the support of all Milwaukee's citizens. The platform chided public officials who "insolently discriminate between rich and poor in the discharge of the functions of their offices" and criticized "executives who will . . . prostitute the police or military to coerce and intimidate workingmen from exercising the common rights and constitutional privileges of citizens."

Actions of the Republicans and Democrats raised the workers' hopes for victory. Thomas H. Brown, the victorious nominee of the Republicans in 1880, was opposed by the stalwart faction of the Republican Party because of his appointment of Democrats and his gen-

eral independence in office. Comptroller George Paschen was determined to block the renomination of Brown. Consequently, the Republican convention became a struggle between E. R. Paine, president
of the Board of Aldermen, and Harrison Ludington, mayor of Milwaukee during the 1870's and former governor of the state. Ludington
was nominated, but this victory of the stalwarts over Brown alienated
some Republican voters. The Democrats, hoping to capitalize on the
dissatisfaction of a number of Republicans with the nomination of
Ludington, considered fusion with the dissident group, but resolved to
remain independent. As late as March 21 the managers of the Democratic Party announced they still intended to nominate a slate independent of any group, even of the workingmen. However, a few days
after the nominations of the Trades Assembly were formally announced, the Democrats also endorsed Stowell, Smith, and Somers.
The only disagreement between the Trades Assembly and the Democratic Party centered about the nominee for treasurer. The Democrats
nominated Peter J. Stamm, who was obnoxious to labor for his opposition to the formation of a Tinners Union in Milwaukee and his aid to
Asherman and Company during the strike of the Cigar Makers.

The Trades Assembly made almost professional plans in entering
the campaign. A campaign committee of 11 members was appointed,
and committee chairmen were named for 11 of the 13 city wards. Also,
poll watchers were appointed for every precinct of the city on election
eve. The ticket of the Trades Assembly did not, however, please all its
members. Some Republican members asked why the Assembly did not
have a ticket independent of the Democrats, although the officers denied there had been a deal with the Democrats. A few workers were
displeased with Stowell's opposition to protective tariffs, but generally
there was harmony within the Assembly during the campaign.

The campaign was vigorously fought, the Republicans charging
the Trades Assembly had demanded money from the Democrats.
There was an alleged fund of $4,000 presented by various manufactur-
ers in the city to the Republican Party. The Trades Assembly charged
that Ludington was backed by "ring politicians" and monopolists.
Further, it claimed he was a former Know-Nothing and hated German
immigrants. While governor in 1877, Ludington allegedly kept workers from striking by sending a letter to Washington asking the veterans in the Soldiers' Home be armed and put at the state's disposal.

The election resulted in the victory of Stowell over Ludington by
a vote of 9,635 to 7,321 and similar margins for Smith and Somers. An
indication of the voting strength of the Trades Assembly ticket may be
gathered from the vote for treasurer. The Trades Assembly nominee

received 3,787 votes, the Democrats 5,528, and the Republicans 7,311. The Democrats gained control of the Common Council and the Board of Supervisors. Generally the Trades Assembly was pleased with the results, although some would have preferred to win on an independent ticket.[13]

The success of the spring campaign encouraged the Trades Assembly to enter the fall elections. The local assembly of the Knights of Labor, still a small group, also decided to enter the fall campaign and cast its support for the platform and nominees of the Trades Assembly. The President of the Assembly, then Mike Walsh, optimistically announced that the combined Trades Assembly and Knights of Labor would control 6,000 votes, exclusive of Democrats or Republicans. The Assembly later endorsed the Democratic candidates for sheriff and county treasurer and nominated George B. Goodwin for Congress in the Fourth Congressional District. The platform called for: (1) equal justice for all, (2) legal protection for labor, including a national and a state bureau of labor, (3) sanitation laws in industrial establishments, (4) abolition of prison labor, (5) enforcement of the eight-hour laws of Congress and the states, (6) enforcement of the law prohibiting children under fourteen from working in factories, (7) compulsory and free education for all children from eight to fourteen years of age, (8) the end of free land grants to railroads, (9) life imprisonment, without parole, as punishment for defalcation by a public official, and (10) a graduated tax on incomes.

The endorsed candidates for sheriff and county treasurer won, but in a three-cornered race for Congress, the Trades Assembly candidate received only 10 per cent of the votes cast. Their only notable success was the election of two assemblymen, D. D. Hooker and M. P. Walsh.[14]

Disintegration

The romance of political action began to wear thin, and the trade-union support of the Assembly began to decline. In January, 1883, eighteen unions were still affiliated with the Trades Assembly, a drop of only two unions since 1882, but the decline began to gain momentum. In 1882 much of the $1,200 in the funds of the Trades Assembly had been used to inaugurate the *Volksblatt,* soon under the control of the Knights of Labor faction, contemptuously referred to as the "Schilling People." This expenditure aroused great dissension within the Trades Assembly. Robert Schilling and his followers left.

Trade unions began to withdraw from the Assembly, some because of the recession beginning in 1883 and some because they believed there had been "undue political agitation." In 1884 the Trades Assembly showed some signs of revival, but the temporary treasurer, Hillig, absconded with approximately $1,500 (the proceeds of the annual summer picnic) leaving the Trades Assembly with a debt of $900. George W. Mackie, president of the Assembly in 1884, worked assiduously to eliminate the debt and revive union interest in the Assembly, and by October 3 a special committee on indebtedness was able to report all bills paid. The end of the Assembly's perilous financial problems did not, however, bring a revival in its fortunes. January, 1885, saw only twelve unions still affiliated with the Assembly, and by midyear a member reported the once powerful Assembly on the verge of dissolution.15

Lack of attention to the economic needs of its member unions and political action without any ideology that could unify the demands of the still-emerging labor movement with the vicissitudes of party politics led to the decline of the Assembly. The financial loss incurred during the summer of 1884 and a subsequent depression were facilitating factors in its early end.

The depression of 1884 seriously weakened Milwaukee unions and brought a low point in trade-union activity. The problem was further complicated by the heterogeneous group of workers in the city. This was not at all uncommon in the United States at the time, for a distinguishing characteristic of the labor unions was the predominance of foreign-born workers. The Illinois Bureau of Labor, for example, estimated that only 21 per cent of the union members in that state were American-born. The predominance of foreign-born workers in the labor movement was a result of the breakdown of the apprenticeship system. As a consequence, the United States drew its supply of skilled labor from abroad.

The heterogeneity of labor had its effect on unions. The Hod Carriers Union in Milwaukee, for example, found that the organizing of campaigns was made more than usually difficult by the number of workers of different nationalities who were unable to speak or clearly understand any language but their own. The Tanners and Curriers witnessed dissension by the English-speaking members, partly because the meetings were conducted in German. Discrimination against the foreign-born was not uncommon. Wages of printers in German shops were reportedly 30 per cent lower than those in English offices. The Wisconsin Bureau of Labor and Industrial Statistics reported that some manufacturers entered a "bonus agreement" with foreigners and minors. Under the agreement, the employee would get a bonus, usually $1 a week, if he worked for the company a full year. Often the employers would fire the workers before the end of the year for some allegedly good cause, thus saving the price of the bonus.[16]

Recovery, beginning in 1885, brought a sharp upswing in strike activity, though few ended in a clear-cut victory for the unions. A number of trade unions were organized or revitalized. Most significant was the appearance of the Knights of Labor as a dominant force in Milwaukee.

The Knights of Labor

The Noble Order of the Knights of Labor, founded in 1869, did not become important in the labor movement of the United States until after 1873. Secrecy was used to provide protection from employer harassment. During its first nine years the Knights made slow growth. In 1878 it abolished secrecy under pressure of public opinion caused by the Paris Commune of 1871, the great railway strikes of 1877, and the terrorist activities of the secret Molly Maguires in the anthracite coal fields of eastern Pennsylvania.

At the same time the Knights abandoned secrecy it adopted a new Preamble (the "First Principles"). The Preamble advocated a union of all workers, education, and the establishment of producers' co-operatives as the ultimate goal of workers. With the return of prosperity in 1879, the Knights of Labor, despite its ideal of cooperation, was forced to concede to the demands of its members for strike action. Along with the trade unions, the Knights grew steadily and rapidly. Its membership of 20,151 in 1879 expanded to 51,914 in 1883. The high turnover of its membership meant the number of persons brought under its influence was even greater. Extensive publicity in newspapers and a host of lecturers sent out by the Knights added recruits and made the Knights of Labor a well-known organization.

Robert Schilling

The most prominent figure among the Knights in Milwaukee and in the state of Wisconsin, was Robert Schilling. Schilling had been president of the Coopers International Union and in 1873 and 1874 headed the Industrial Congress. Impressed by what he considered the inadequacy of the existing basis of the labor movement, Schilling in 1874 wrote a preamble for the Industrial Brotherhood. The document so well stated the demands of labor at the time that it was adopted as a preamble, with modifications, by the Knights of Labor at its first national convention in 1878.

Schilling's interests soon turned to political action. In 1874 he was one of the two laboring men present at the founding convention of the

Greenback Party in Indianapolis. A week after the great strikes of 1877, Schilling began publishing the *Labor Advocate* in Cleveland and vigorously agitated for a workingman's party. His work bore fruit with the formation of the Greenback Labor Party in 1878.

About 1880 Schilling moved to Milwaukee. Whether this move was caused by contacts with Milwaukee delegates to the Industrial Congresses or with Milwaukee locals of the Coopers Union, or his acquaintance with Edward P. Allis (both were delegates to the 1878 Greenback Labor Party convention) is unknown. In Milwaukee, Schilling became editor of the *National Reformer,* a Greenback paper founded in 1880, and became active in Knights-of-Labor circles. At first he urged all workers to join a union, not necessarily the Knights. Schilling idealized the labor movement, hoping it would, through the formation of debating societies, become a "training school in intelligence for [its] members."

As was previously mentioned, Schilling and his followers first came into conflict with the trade unions on the issue of spending money for the *Volksblatt.* This led to his withdrawal from the Trades Assembly. Schilling also alienated some trade unionists by his consuming and lifelong interest in politics. Doubtlessly his work contributed to the rise of the Greenback Party presidential vote in Milwaukee county from 76 in 1880 to 901 in 1884.[17]

The Knights of Labor had been present on the Milwaukee scene since 1880, but its members played no decisive role in public affairs. In 1882 it was proposed to induce every trade union to join the Knights, but the venture had no important results. A nation-wide strike of the Brotherhood of Telegraphers in 1883 was backed by the Knights of Labor. The sudden and disastrous end of the strike brought the Order into disfavor in Wisconsin, despite denials of any connection between the Knights and the strike. As a consequence, the two local assemblies of the Knights existing in Wisconsin disbanded.

The depression year of 1884 brought failure in strike activity throughout the nation, but the business revival beginning in 1885 brought a renewed effort. The outstanding event of the year was the successful strike of the Knights of Labor against railroads controlled by Jay Gould. Victory over the most powerful capitalist in the country brought exaggerated claims about the strength of the Knights. Unskilled workers, who had been particularly affected by the depression of 1884, flocked into the Knights.

Reports from all over the country telling of the phenomenal growth of the Order led to renewed interest in Wisconsin. During the winter of 1885/86, two or three local assemblies were established in Milwaukee. Schilling was appointed state organizer. Local assemblies began to appear everywhere, and some old trade unions were abandoned, members joining the Knights of Labor. By May, 1886, there were forty-two local assemblies with over 12,000 members in Milwaukee and 25,000 members in the state. New assemblies were organized daily. The local assemblies in Milwaukee joined to form District Assembly 108 of the Knights. By early 1886 this upturn had made Schilling the pre-eminent labor leader in the state and the Knights the dominant organization.[18]

CHAPTER V

Riot!

The Cigar Makers

MORE than any other group, the cigar makers mirrored the struggles and conflicts of the pulsating period of the early 1880's. The Cigar Makers Union had, like other trade unions, declined during the 1870's, but in October, 1877, the union was reorganized and affiliated with the Cigar Makers International Union. On October 1, 1881, the Cigar Makers demanded a 10 per cent increase in wages. The demand was approved by the International Union. A strike committee headed by Fred W. Leiff, president of the local, was appointed to visit the manufacturers. The union, which included about 700 out of 900 cigar makers in the city, was successful in gaining the reluctant consent of all the cigar manufacturers but Asherman and Company. The union immediately began a strike against Asherman. Strike benefits of $4 a week, paid by the International, plus 10 per cent of the wages of other union cigar makers working in the city were given to the men on strike. Asherman began to employ girls and boys to replace the union workers and threatened to bring a number of Bohemian families to America to replace the strikers.

On November 25 the strike of the cigar makers became a general lockout by the cigar manufacturers. The owners who had previously conceded banded together to form a manufacturers' association. The association started a lockout to enforce the following rules: no smokers (free cigars) would be given to the workers; no worker would be allowed to leave the shop without the permission of the foreman; no worker would be allowed to smoke during working hours; team work would be allowed only by permission of the manufacturer; prices for special work would be agreed upon between the worker and the employer, and prices for all types of work were to be agreed upon between the employer and employee, not the union.[1]

The union, incensed by changes which took away time-honored privileges (such as the right to damaged cigars free of charge), interpreted the rules as an attempt to break the unions. A meeting was called by the union, and 700 members unanimously resolved not to submit to the owners' rules. The strike continued with vigor. The union claimed. "The bad example set by the manufacturers of Milwaukee, if followed by the manufacturers of other cities [would] reduce the 40,000 cigar makers in the United States to a more abject state of slavery than ever existed in the South."[2]

On December 4 Fred W. Leiff and George Winter, of the local union, arrived in New York at the request of the International. A mass meeting in New York and later one in Chicago brought national support and publicity to the Milwaukee strikers. Weekly payments from the regular dues of the few unionists still at work and contributions from unions in Milwaukee, New York, and Chicago brought strike benefits of $3500 to $4000 weekly. Adolph Strasser (president of the International Cigar Makers), Richard Powers (president of the Chicago Seamen's Union) and Form (of the Detroit Trades Assembly) came to Milwaukee to encourage the striking cigar makers. Strasser said he had come to conciliate the differences but would not give in to the owners' "unreasonable demands." However, the manufacturers' association informed Strasser that it "had no desire to negotiate with him as 'a power behind the throne,' but . . . each individual firm would be willing to see him . . . and listen to his story of alleged grievances."

Despite the continued efforts of the International Union to aid the strikers, including a special assessment of 25 cents on all its members, there was little hope of success. The manufacturers had not been idle. They sent agents to New York and other cities to recruit women and children to replace the strikers. Agents were even sent to Europe to enlist cigar makers with promises of steady employment and better wages. A number of these immigrants joined the strikers upon arrival in Milwaukee, but in the end, the labor supply was sufficient to defeat the strikers.[3]

In the fourteenth week of the strike, a meeting was called and attended by 350 strikers and members of other trade unions in the city. The history of the strike was reviewed, the position of the manufacturers denounced, and a plea was made for public support of a cooperative shop to employ the 400 workers still out of work—a proposal previously sanctioned by the International.[4]

In May 1882 the Milwaukee First Cooperative Cigar Manufacturing Company was incorporated by Otto Krueger, Frank Hirth, and

Calvin W. Styn, members of the union. The capital stock consisted of 1,000 ten-dollar shares. By June $2,970 had been paid in on shares subscribed, and business began with fourteen cigar makers. The president of the cooperative, Emil Block, soon gave notice that a change of financial management was needed, and in November a meeting of the shareholders was called. Accusations by some employees, charging that union men had been fired and girls hired to replace them, turned the meeting into an uproar. Petty jealousies, such as Block's disgust over the failure of the Milwaukee Trades Assembly to nominate him for sheriff, further complicated the issues. A resolution was introduced suggesting that $2,900 in cash and goods on hand be given to the stockholders and the factory closed. It was voted down. Consequently, the president and a majority of the board resigned, but the stockholders voted to continue operations. The superintendent of the company reduced the number of workers to four and moved the factory to cheaper quarters. It was soon discovered that one agent had defrauded the factory of $1,000 and another agent, $280. Because of this additional financial strain, the factory was sold for $835.85 with outstanding debts of $378.85. Thus on January 1, 1883, the experiment failed ignominiously.

The union dwindled from its original membership of 700 in 1881 to 150 in 1884 and to 40 in January, 1886. The cigar manufacturers continued their vigilant watch against renewed union activity. For example, in 1883 the manufacturers imported a number of New York tenement-house cigar makers, who had been thrown out of work, to guard against the possibility of strikes by the regular workers.[5]

Boycott

The notable failure of strike action in 1884 brought into use another weapon of labor—the boycott. An important example of the use of the boycott grew out of the strike of the cabinetmakers and joiners beginning in February, 1886. To enforce the strike, the cabinetmakers began a boycott against the employers and also began a boycott against *Der Herold* because the newspaper had carried an article about the strike that the union members considered insulting. The boycott against the company ended when the strike was won. The boycott on *Der Herold* was ended on the condition that the newspaper became unionized and paid the costs of the boycott. This action indirectly forced the German newspaper offices of Milwaukee to recognize the German Typographia Union.

Not all boycotts were similarly successful. The Barbers Union was unable to secure the abolition of Sunday labor through the boycott.

April 17, 1886, the journeymen bakers of Milwaukee struck for a ten-hour day and the abolition of the boarding system, which they claimed reduced them to "white slaves." Adolph Feinhold, a baker of the city, became exasperated with the boycott that accompanied the strike and had August Seidel, who had distributed the boycott handbills arrested; the man was fined $25 and court costs. The strike and boycott were never formally settled; the men returned to work on the old terms after four or five weeks.

The boycott, however, was not a one-sided weapon. In April, 1885, the Journeymen Plumbers Union went on strike against fifteen master plumbers. The union had withdrawn its three members from the shop of Richard Finn when he refused to fire a man who had failed to account for a number of tickets he had sold for the union's anniversary ball. Since the organized master plumbers had agreed not to hire anyone who could not produce a certificate from his last employer, the three men from Finn's shop could not get new jobs and the union called a strike which dragged on for two months.

Settlement of the strike seemed impossible. The Plumbers International Union advanced funds to the local to start cooperative shops, and the headquarters of the president of the International, Patrick Coyle, was moved to Milwaukee to assist the proposed movement. On June 22 four cooperative shops were opened in the city, employing 35 journeymen and 7 helpers. But on June 23, 1885, the National Master Plumbers Association met in St. Louis and adopted boycott resolutions against the cooperators designed to make it difficult for them to obtain materials. Milwaukee manufacturers of cement sewer pipes were asked not to sell goods to the coops, but they refused. Subsequently, the Master Plumbers Association organized a sewer-pipe association among themselves in order to boycott dealers and maunfacturers, especially in Milwaukee. Despite the efforts to eliminate the cooperatives, they temporarily enjoyed success. In 1886 it was reported that the concerns were out of debt and had $10,000 in cash and good accounts.[6]

Undoubtedly the most important boycott of the mid-1880's involved a struggle between Cigar Makers Local 25 and Cigar Makers Assembly 5,354 of the Knights of Labor. A visit to Milwaukee in late 1885 by an officer of the International Cigar Makers Union, Bisbing, failed to revive interest in the union. The Knights of Labor claimed they had tried to help Bisbing, but were unsuccessful. Contrarily, the union charged that Schilling had worked behind the scenes to undermine the union. A number of cigar makers expressed interest in joining the Knights. Many were admitted to already existing assemblies and then formed their own local assembly in February, 1886. The union charged that the persons joining the Knights were the individuals who had, during the 1881 strike, received "about $75,000 in strike benefits, turned traitors and did their utmost to destroy the very source that furnished them shelter and bread to eat. The same mal-contents who [had] turned scabs. . . ."[7]

The conflict was further intensified when the Knights began to distribute a cigar label, printed on white paper, which was to substitute for the well-known label of the Cigar Makers International, printed on blue paper. The controversy stimulated interest in the Cigar Makers Union in Milwaukee, and the local grew from almost nothing to over 550 members. The Knights claimed approximately the same number. The contention between the two was so great that it was difficult to have members of both factions working in the same factory. Herman Segnitz and Company, the largest cigar manufacturer in Milwaukee, found it necessary to close the factory until the factions could settle their differences. Rather than diminishing, the struggle grew more intense when the General Assembly of the Knights of Labor discarded the white label and began printing one on paper the same color as the International Union used.

Subsequently, both the Knights and the union submitted a new scale of prices to Segnitz and Company. Segnitz and Louis Kindling, another manufacturer employing sixty persons, decided to sign the union's price list. The scales were approximately the same, the Knight's being slightly higher. According to Herman Segnitz, the union was preferred over the Knights because of the absence of "arbitrary rulings." The Knights charged that the manufacturers had previously agreed to have their men join the Knights, but had failed to keep their pledge so that they could take advantage of the union's allegedly lower rates. Segnitz denied the accusation and charged that the Knights had been "guilty of double-dealing and prevaricating . . . ."

The Knights claimed they had attempted to end the dispute by offering to endorse the union's label if the union would reciprocate. "The offer," the Knights maintained, "was refused by the union, and its members not only insisted that we should endorse their label, but not use ours at all, and, in addition, that all our members should join the International Union." The Cigar Makers Union charged that inability to reach agreement was caused by the contemptuous behavior and arbitrary demands of the Knights. "The dirty work here experienced," they added, "has been done in other localities. Not alone has the International Union suffered at their hands, but every National Union in the country has cause for complaint."

With no hope for an amicable settlement, the Knights, in March,

1886, began a boycott against Segnitz and Kindling. The Knights charged that the companies had violated an agreement to sign the Knights' scale and had discharged employees who belonged to the Order. The union retaliated with a plea to the public not to buy cigars with the Knights-of-Labor label. Segnitz, charging that the Knights' boycott resulted in a loss of business, started suit against the executive board of District Assembly 108 of the Knights. The issue was brought to a head when the city was at fever pitch over the eight-hour-day riots in early May (see below, pages 57 ff).

Schilling, despite the opposition to boycotts by Terence V. Powderly, national head of the Knights, declared "a man was either a knave or a fool who opposed boycotting for certain purposes." For their admitted support of the boycott, Schilling and others were indicted by a grand jury and tried. The boycott continued, but the union eventually won the struggle. Many members of the Knights refused to support the boycott financially and were suspended; they joined the union.[8]

The Central Labor Union

Conflict between the Knights of Labor and the trade unions in Milwaukee led to the formation of the Central Labor Union on March 31, 1886. Delegates from the Metal Workers, Hod Carriers, Coal Heavers, Carpenters, Butchers, and Custom Tailors Unions adopted a constitution and launched the organization. The Central Labor Union was the successor to the almost defunct Milwaukee Trades Assembly. The meeting was addressed by Paul Grottkau of Chicago, who moved to Milwaukee and became the leading spirit of the Central Labor Union.

Grottkau, born in Berlin, had been a convinced Lassallean. Fleeing to the United States after the German anti-Socialist law of 1878, he settled in Chicago. For four years, he edited the *Arbeiter-Zeitung* of that city, becoming prominent in the Socialist movement there. He was later expelled from Socialist ranks for his opposition to the Socialist-Greenback compromise of 1880. As editor of the *Zeitung,* he became associated with August Spies, a leader in the Chicago anarchist movement. Grottkau also became German secretary for the Information Bureau of the International Working People's Association (Black International). As an advocate of vigorous trade-union action, however, he finally broke with the anarchists.

After this break, Grottkau came to Milwaukee at the instigation of Valentine J. Blatz, prominent Socialist and Milwaukee brewer, to organize the workers under the Socialist banner in opposition to the

Knights of Labor and especially to Robert Schilling. The Social-Democratic *Herald* later described him as a "natural orator . . . being considered by many the peer of Carl Schurz. There were few who could get hold of people in the way that he did. His elegant but simple German had a power that was marvelous."

In Milwaukee he became editor of the old *Arminia*, which was renamed the *Arbeiter-Zeitung*. Published under the banner "The same right for everyone!" the paper was made the official organ of the Central Labor Union on May 1, 1886. The paper received the whole-hearted support of the Milwaukee Socialists, about 140 members, but not the anarchists. The latter were a small group of 40 members who had received their inspiration from Johann Most when he spoke at the Robert Chivas Post Hall in May, 1884. The anarchists were bitterly opposed by Valentine Blatz and other Socialists.

The conflicts between the Socialists and anarchists did not, however, dominate the Central Labor Union. Instead, the controversy with the Knights of Labor received the vigorous endorsement of the trade unions. Within a few months, the Central Labor Union had added the Painters, Custom Shoemakers, Cigar Makers, Bookbinders, Hardwood Finishers, Bakers, Lumberyard Hands, Brickyard Laborers, Plasterers, and Tailoresses Unions to their ranks. Charging that the Knights of Labor was under the direction of persons unacquainted with local conditions and claiming it could serve the workers better, the Central Labor Union and its affiliated trade unions soon grew to include 5,300 members.[9]

Temporarily obscuring the conflict between the Knights and the unions was the culmination of the struggle for the eight-hour day.

The Rallying Cry: Eight Hours!

The Federation of Organized Trades and Labor Unions, established in 1881, was a loose federation of unions emphasizing purely legislative goals. Within a few years, it was evident that the Federation was a failure as a legislative organization. To infuse new life into the group, the Federation, in 1884, passed a resolution calling for the adoption of the eight-hour day by May 1, 1886. This position was reaffirmed in 1885, but a circular issued by the Secretary of the Federation, W. H. Foster, in January, 1886, urging unions to take action received no attention from the dying Milwaukee Trades Assembly.

However, support of the Federation's position by the General Assembly of the Knights of Labor in 1885 led to noticeable activity in the ranks of the Knights in Milwaukee. In the middle of February, 1886, an Eight-Hour League, composed of three delegates from each assembly of the Knights, was formed. When the Central Labor Union was organized a month later, the League delegates were also admitted. A mass meeting of 3,000 persons met in the West Side Turner Hall to press for action by the city's aldermen on a pending eight-hour resolution and to create a general eight-hour boom. The action of the League induced the Milwaukee Common Council on March 16 to adopt, with one dissenting vote, an ordinance fixing the working day at eight hours for municipal laborers. The action of the Council gave renewed vigor to the eight-hour agitation.

The appeal of the eight-hour day brought a rush into the ranks of the Knights of Labor across the nation. From a membership of 104,066 in July, 1885, the organization mushroomed to 702,924 a year later. The national leadership of the Knights was not, however, enthusiastic about the eight-hour issue. Rather, they used it as a slogan to recruit members.

A letter issued by Grand Master Workman Powderly urging the Knights of Labor to use caution in the movement was ignored in Milwaukee. The continued agitation served to swell the ranks of both the Knights and the trade unions. Within a few weeks after the adoption of the eight-hour ordinance by the Common Council, a new Plasterers Union with 100 members was organized, followed by a Teamsters Union of 60 members. The Planing Mill Assembly of the Knights admitted 150 members; the Tanners and Curriers Assembly added 200 to its 1,000 member group; 70 tobacco company employees made an application to join the Knights in a body. The Reliance Assembly initiated 618 Polish laborers in one day and reported 300 applications pending, making it the largest assembly in the Order with a total membership of 1,600.[10]

Adoption of the eight-hour day, without a reduction of pay, by all tobacco manufacturers of Milwaukee gave further stimulus to the plan. The Knights of Labor was determined to gain the eight-hour day at the Reliance Works, owned by Edward P. Allis, before May 1. It hoped small concerns would follow the example. On April 3, Allis granted the eight-hour day but also reduced pay. The pay reduction, accepted by the negotiating committee of the Eight-Hour League, precipitated the denunciation of the League and Allis by 600 employees who were determined to have the reduced workday without pay cuts. The intensity of the demand for eight hours made it impossible for one manufacturer to inaugurate a profit-sharing plan; the labor movement feared the plan would hamper the drive.

The Commissioner of Labor and Industrial Statistics reported, as the beginning of May came near:

... the agitation [for the eight-hour day] permeated our entire social atmosphere. Skilled and unskilled laborers formed unions or assemblies. Men, and even women, contributed money and time to its promulgation. It was *the* topic of conversation in the shop, on the street, at the family table, at the bar, in the counting rooms, and the subject of numerous able sermons from the pulpit.

Columns upon columns in daily newspapers showed the varying phases of the movement in different sections of the country, and long editorials and literary contributions from learned men were given to the public from day to day. Everybody claimed to thoroughly understand the subject, and appeared prepared for its consummation.[11]

The general excitement was raised by the appearance of unexplained signs (actually the signs used by the Knights to call meetings) that appeared on fences, sidewalks, and cellar doors throughout the city. Their unusual appearance gave rise to the conviction that they were the "signal for inaugurating a general reign of butchery and destruction...."[12]

May Day

During the month of April, representatives of workers in 200 workshops and factories in Milwaukee made the demand for the eight-hour day. Twenty-one firms granted the concession, but some asked for more time to consider, some closed down, and some refused. The reluctance of employers to concede precipitated a wave of strikes in the city. May 1 found 7,000 people out of work, including shop tailors, bakers, carpenters, joiners, cabinetmakers, planing-mill hands, brewers, and common laborers. This large number of idle workers—soon to swell to 16,000—coupled with the announcement of a parade to be held on Sunday, May 2, unnerved a number of Milwaukee's citizens.

The mayor of Milwaukee told the military that all second-hand arms in pawn shops had suddenly been sold and expressed his alarm. When Governor Rusk came to Milwaukee late in April for the four-day session of the Scottish Rite Masons, certain prominent citizens of the community told him of their apprehensions. Rusk returned to Madison and had ammunition ordered for the National Guard. The ammunition was shipped to Madison, repacked in dry-goods boxes, camouflaged with blankets, overcoats, and similar items and sent to Milwaukee. Thus, without public knowledge, 31,000 rounds of ball cartridges were added to the vaults of the newly-built armory on Broadway Street.

Four companies of infantry and artillery and the Light Horse squadron were alerted to be in position to move at a moment's notice.

The entire police force was put on duty, comprising, with the military, a force of 600 men that could be readied instantly.

The parade of May 2 was planned by the Central Labor Union with the cooperation of the Eight-Hour League. Twenty-five hundred men participated in a demonstration headed by the red flags of the Socialists and the tri-color flags of the Eight-Hour movement. With bands and drum corps to attract attention, the laborers displayed various mottoes, some of which declared "Eight hours! Our password and battle-cry." The slogans expressed the grievances of various groups of laborers in the city. Those dissatisfied with the work of the Eight-Hour League asked, "Where is the Eight-Hour League? She works still for ten hours." "One cause of bad times: Stock gambling and speculation in general," proclaimed the money reformers. "The boycott," said its defenders, "is an American institution. One hundred years ago it was called embargo. Only the name is changed." A few still held that "Cooperation must take the place of wage slavery." The bakers asked all to boycott bread without the union label, and the cigar makers' factions disputed the policies of H. Segnitz and Louis Kindling. Despite the presence of members of the Knights of Labor, their leader was denounced with the placard: "Humbug, your name is Robert Schilling." Most seemed to subscribe to the idea "Political without economic freedom is a lie." The parade, without provoking any incident, culminated in a picnic at the Milwaukee Gardens.

The parade was but a prelude to the demonstrations of the following days. On Monday morning, May 3, crowds gradually gathered on street corners, especially in the manufacturing district, and rumors of strikes filled the city. At seven in the morning, the brewery workers—all members of the Gambrinus Assembly of the Knights—who were on strike for a general increase in wages, met at the headquarters of the Assembly and decided to march to the Falk Brewery to persuade or force the men, who had accepted a compromise offer of the employer, to quit work. About 1,000 men approached the brewery, but Falk's employees refused to strike unless ordered by the District Assembly. About noon, the men returned with the order, and the Falk men, after long protest, struck.

At eleven o'clock the same morning, a group of 300 or 400 Polish laborers marched down the tracks of the Milwaukee and St. Paul Railroad and forced shovelers in the coal sheds to quit work. The group, constantly reinforced by more men, went on to drive the molders out of the company's foundry, "hustled and yelled" until the men in the machine shop quit, and forced the men in the paint shop to strike. The sheriff and five deputies then arrived and persuaded the men to leave the premises. An order went out to close the shops for the day. The crowd, swollen to 1,300, then marched toward the city, compelling all employees on the way to quit work, until they reached the Prairie du Chien yards. Here a fight started when the crowd attempted to compel 20 men to quit work. A patrol wagon was called and the crowd gave way. When the police left, the crowd tried to capture the largest warehouse in the yards, but the foreman closed and barred the doors.

The mob, electrified by its success in closing down the railway yards, marched towards the Reliance Works of the E. P. Allis Company. Allis, forewarned of danger, had his employees armed with hammers and clubs and prepared water hoses to turn on the rioters. When the crowd appeared and attempted to enter the main gate, it was repulsed by streams of water. The attackers then went to another door, massed and rushed, and three hundred entered the gate. The shop employees drove them into the streets. Twenty policemen stationed in the South Side station across the street from the plant joined the defenders. The crowd fell back and began to fire rocks at the police and the Allis employees. The police captured four or five of the leaders, but the mob rescued all but one. When an east-side patrol wagon appeared, the crowd scattered; but lines were reformed, and the strikers marched south, gathering additional support from workers at the Chicago Rolling Mill in Bay View. A little after four in the afternoon the crowd dispersed.

Because of rumors that the mob would return the next day, Allis asked the mayor for armed guards in the plant. The mayor declined, and Allis closed the factory, putting more men out of work. Meanwhile Governor Rusk was summoned to Milwaukee. At 10:30 that night, Rusk, Adjutant General C. P. Chapman, Colonel Lewis of the First Regiment, Mayor Wallber, Sheriff Paschen, and Chief of Police Ries met at the Plankinton House. Roswell Miller, general manager of the St. Paul Railway, was present and demanded military protection for his shops. However, local officials insisted that forces at their disposal were able to maintain order and protect property. They refused to ask the governor for troops. The meeting ended at midnight.

Early the next morning, members of the Polish Assembly of the Knights met near St. Stanislaus Church. Informed that the Reliance Works of Allis were shut down, they decided to march through the valley, shutting factories and workshops on the way, to the Chicago Rolling Mills in Bay View. Sheriff Paschen and Chief of Police Ries were notified that a mob was moving through the valley and sent a force of seventy-five policemen, who proved unable to quell the disturbance. The sheriff then signed a request for the National Guard to move in. Excitement ran high and was further increased when fire-alarm bells began ringing, a signal for the military forces in Milwaukee to assemble.

By the time it reached the offices of the Rolling Mills, the crowd had grown to over 2,000. A delegation was sent to confer with Superintendent William B. Parkes and other officers of the company about the demands of the mill workers for an eight-hour day and a daily wage of $1.50. Parkes contended that the company could not grant the eight-hour day and wages must vary with the output of the company. A. Bonzel, head of the Polish Assembly, explained the company's position to the workers, noting that the company was willing to confer on other complaints of the men, and asked, "Does this satisfy you?" The tumultuous crowd roared back, "Eight hours!" Attempts by company officials to explain were shouted down. Finally Parkes suggested another conference, and leaders of the group, accompanied by Robert Schilling who had appeared during the demonstration, went in to confer. Schilling (who years later claimed he had been sent by the mayor and the chief of police to disperse the mob and prevent an outbreak) came out and spoke to the crowd in English and German; Bonzel spoke in Polish. Schilling counseled moderation and said the officers of the company were willing to discuss the grievances with a shop committee or a committee of the Knights.

After the committee had returned to the plant again, the arrival of the Sheridan and Lincoln Guards and the South Side Riflers temporarily scattered the crowd. Two companies of guards marched to the gates of the plant and the Lincoln Guard to the front office. Shortly afterwards, trains arrived bringing the Kosciusko Guards and other soldiers to the scene. The Kosciusko Guards, composed exclusively of Poles and commanded by Captain Borchert, were first cheered by the crowd as members of the same nationality, but the attitude soon changed. The crowd yelled "Rats!" and threw stones at the Polish guards. Captain Borchert was hit on the head by a rock but was not seriously hurt.

The committee of workers then reappeared and said the local officials of the company were unable to grant the concessions asked, but had telegraphed Chicago asking for instructions. The confused mob cheered and then jeered the news. Ten minutes later news came that Chicago had refused permission to make concessions. The crowd, incensed by the long and disappointing wait and by the appearance of the militia, set up a howl and threw more stones at the soldiers. At the same time, men still working for the company decided to strike.

Meanwhile, as the result of consultation between Parkes and other company representatives and Major George P. Traeumer, who was in charge of the troops, the soldiers were moved inside the company grounds. The crowd took this as a sign that the militia had weakened and again began throwing stones. The Kosciusko Guards were the last to pass through the gates and received most of the blows. Unable to endure their treatment any longer, two members of the Kosciuskos bringing up the rear of the column turned and fired above the heads of the mob. The mob retaliated by throwing more stones, but most ran away. Then nearly all the Kosciusko Guards turned and fired 25 or 30 shots into the air. The crowd took refuge behind piles of pig iron and kept up the fusillade; no one was injured. A few minutes later the plant was shut down, putting 1,800 men out of work. The crowd quieted and gradually moved away.

While the demonstration was going on at Bay View, Paul Grottkau was addresing a mass meeting of 1,500 laboring men, mostly members of the Central Labor Union, at the Milwaukee Garden. Grottkau, as he later related the incident, advocated the creation of a central executive board composed of the officers of the various trade unions and assemblies in the city to deal with the employers while others worked to keep the men off the streets and out of trouble. Grottkau hoped it would be possible to dispense with the services of the National Guard and to ask the governor to withdraw the troops. Grottkau's speech was delivered in German and was later interpreted by reporters, who did not understand the language very well, as a call to violence. After Grottkau left the meeting, a motion was made to march to Brand's stove factory and compel the workers to strike. Consequently, 1,000 men marched to the stove works and forced the men to join them, despite the fact that the firm had already granted the demands of the employees. A shout then arose to move on to the bakeries, but action was deferred. About six o'clock in the evening, the crowd dispersed with plans to meet the next day.

Earlier that afternoon, Mayor Emil Wallber has issued a proclamation calling upon "all unlawful, disorderly or riotous assemblages of persons of every kind" to disperse and return home. The executive board of District Assembly 108 of the Knights, anxious to avoid all connections with the riots, voted to call upon all members of the Knights to assist the authorities in the crisis and aid in the restoration of law and order. The Knights further volunteered their services to act as special police for the protection of life and property. As a condition for their cooperation, the military was to be immediately withdrawn.

By nightfall the number of Wisconsin National Guardsmen on

duty in Milwaukee was over 800. Reinforced by troops from Janesville and other points in the state, the soldiers settled down for an uneasy night. Throughout the city, men in small and large groups met to discuss the day's events and make plans for the next day. A Milwaukee *Journal* reporter who spent the night of May 4 with the rioters reported, "They have no organization or leaders, and act merely under pressure of momentary excitement." The Polish workers, frequently taunted with being cheap laborers who injured their fellow workers, were determined to gain the eight-hour day. The rioters were incensed, claiming skilled laborers had started the labor movement but were leaving the onerous tasks to fall upon the common laborers after the manufacturers had granted concessions to the skilled.

That same night an event took place in Chicago that shook the labor movement throughout the nation and destroyed the eight-hour movement for that year. A mass meeting to protest against shooting by the police was held in Haymarket Square at 7:30 P.M., May 4. After several speeches most of the crowd left, dispersed by a threatening storm. When the police advanced on the remaining crowd, a bomb was thrown, killing one policeman and hurling sixty to the ground. The Haymarket Affair opened a reign of terror in Chicago and spread fear across the land.

In Milwaukee, the tumultuous series of events reached a climax on Wednesday morning, May 5. The mob that had disbanded in Bay View on Tuesday again gathered near St. Stanislaus Church, reportedly armed with sticks, knives, pistols, and stones. The mob of 1,000 again headed for the Bay View Rolling Mills, carrying the Eight-Hour flags. As the crowd appeared near the mills, Major Traeumer telephoned the governor. According to the recollection of General Charles King, it was Governor Rusk who gave the order, "Fire on them!" Traeumer ordered the mob to halt, but the noisy group was 1,000 yards from the soldiers and probably did not hear the order. Two more warnings were given and ignored, or, more likely, not heard. Traeumer then ordered the soldiers to fire on the demonstrators and nine persons were killed or wounded, among them a man feeding his chickens and a twelve-year-old boy on his way to school.

Action then shifted to the Milwaukee Garden. There, when police and the Sheriff attempted unsuccessfully to disperse a mass meeting of workers, mainly Germans, troops under the command of General King were called in, and a number of persons arrested.

The riot of 1886 had ended in Milwaukee. In the nation the demand for the eight-hour day involved an estimated 340,000 men. Perhaps 190,000 actually struck, 42,000 with success. An additional 150,-

000 secured the shorter workday without striking, though few retained their gain for very long.[13]

Reaction

After the riots, a few employers decided to prevent further trouble by adopting the eight-hour day, but after a few weeks, many had returned to the ten-hour system. By the end of the first week of May, all public agitation for the eight-hour day had died. On May 13 the last company of militia was withdrawn. By the middle of the month, all factories in the city had resumed work. The trade unions and local assemblies ended all strike activities and were anxious to disassociate themselves from any responsibility for the riots. But there was no serenity in Milwaukee.

The general opinion of the people of Bay View was that the action of the militia was hasty and bloodshed could have been prevented. Individual members of the Kosciusko Guards involved in the Bay View affair had their businesses boycotted. Captain Borchert, head of the guards, reported his law practice was almost ruined. Alderman Hanizjewski, Supervisor Schubert, Thomas Jasiek, a grocer, and a Mr. Kubal, an undertaker, similarly suffered. The Carpenters and Joiners Union expelled one guardsman, Alexander Gilinski, from their ranks.

Labor spoke with one voice in its condemnation of the affair. "The firing," said Robert Schilling, "was unjustified and cruel, and to say it in plain German, it was cowardly, premeditated murder. The most guilty man is the Old Knownothing Jerry Rusk, by the grace of the ignorant people, Governor of Wisconsin." The Central Labor Union resolved that the action of the governor and the militia was "unjustifiable and damnable." In July a political convention of the Knights of Labor at La Crosse "greeted with cheers" a resolution that condemned the action of the public authorities "in firing upon unarmed and defenseless citizens without any notice of the intention so to do . . . as unlawful and inhuman."[14]

Not all persons condemned the actions of the militia and Governor Rusk. After the riots of 1886, Rusk received many letters and telegrams approving his action. In replying to ex-governor Edward Salomon, Rusk wrote: "I am in receipt of your very kind letter of congratulations on the successful suppression of the Milwaukee riots. It is very gratifying to me to receive the approval of the people for performing a plain duty." The Milwaukee City Council passed a resolution thanking Rusk for his prompt action which had "saved the city from total destruction . . . ." Mayor Wallber struck a discordant note by vetoing the measure. General King reports in his autobiography:

And then and there began, most deservedly, the boom for Uncle Jerry's third and triumphant term as governor. He was in the heyday of his fame and reputation when he went with his state officials, his military staff, and his Grand Army attendants to the funeral of General Grant in New York City, probably the greatest pageant of the kind the metropolis had ever seen. Everybody had heard of the Wisconsin governor who had "knocked the backbone out of anarchy with a single volley" . . . and even on so solemn an occasion, the dense crowds in places showed a disposition to applaud him.[15]

The Republican state platform of 1886 expressed strong approval of the "prompt and effective action of Governor Rusk in suppressing the riotous mobs instigated by anarchist agitators." As late as 1888 Rusk received twenty-five votes for the presidential nomination of the Republican Party, more than just the votes of the Wisconsin delegation.

The foreign-born and radicals were indiscriminately denounced for their alleged inspiration of the riots. "Can not all the demonstrations in America against law, society, property, government and peace be traced to foreigners," raged the Commissioner of Labor. "It will be far easier to keep out characters so dangerous and wicked that they can not be controlled in their own country, than to . . . Americanize them here."[16] Even the pro-labor Milwaukee *Labor Review* on May 8, 1886, editorialized that the events of early May "must have opened the eyes of business men and manufacturers to the danger of a policy pursued in importing foreign labor . . . ." The Milwaukee *Daily Journal* of May 10 reported that Polish laborers employed in the shops of the Chicago, Milwaukee and St. Paul Railway were discharged and their places filled by men of other nationalities.

The city council repealed the eight-hour ordinance it had passed, and, effective July 14, city employees again worked from seven in the morning until six in the evening. Alderman Chase introduced a "Red flag ordinance" to ban the activities of radicals; the judiciary committee reported a substitute that was substantially the same as the state law designed to quell riotous assemblages. Because the boycott of the Cigar Makers Assembly was prominent at this same time, Chase also introduced a measure calculated to make boycotting a criminal offense.[17]

A special committee of the Common Council charged that Alderman Theodore Rudzinski, who had publicly denounced the handling of the rioters by the militia, "did, at various times . . . willfully utter and make use of seditious and inflammatory words and speeches intended and calculated to incite certain persons to commit acts of riot, disturbance, disorder and breach of the peace . . . ."[18] After a protracted investigation, Rudzinski, a leader in the Polish community, was censured by the council, and his commission as notary public was re-

voked by Governor Rusk. The censure of Rudzinski seemed provoked less by any alleged inflammatory act he committed than by his
open contradiction of the efforts of certain persons "who sought to
quiet the popular tumult and excitement by justifying to the rioters
the actions of the authorities."

On the same evening the riot ended, May 5, the police decided to
arrest every man in the city known to be an "agitator" against whom
"evidence could be had that would tend to convict of inciting a riot or
taking part in the demonstrations of the past two or three days." On
these broad grounds twenty men, including Paul Grottkau, were immediately taken into custody. The next day, at the request of District
Attorney W. C. Williams, Judge James A. Mallory called a grand jury
to convene on May 18 to consider the cases of the men under arrest for
inciting to riot or for rioting and set bail at not less than $5,000 each.

Meanwhile, a coroner's jury had been selected to evaluate the actions of the militia. On May 7 and 8 the jury handed down verdicts
that the killings were accidental and the militia had performed an un-
pleasant duty. The jury went on to commend the militia for having
ceased firing when it was apparent the crowd had stopped advancing.

When the grand jury met near the end of May, Judge Mallory
charged it to investigate the acts of the labor organizations and determine whether "anything in any of their constitutions, or in any oath
which any officer or member is required to take, binds officers or
members to resort to violence or other unlawful means for the purpose
of accomplishing the objects sought to be obtained." The Judge out-
lined the law on riots and instructed the jury to investigate the boycott
of the Cigar Makers Assembly. Mallory ruled that if "two or more
persons conspired together for the purpose of boycotting a man, with
intent to injure or destroy his business, they may be indicted for a conspiracy . . . ."

On June 2 the grand jury indicted 5 men, including Grottkau, for
conspiracy to riot, 25 for riot and unlawful assembly, 3 for intimidat-
ing witnesses and conspiracy, and 16, including Robert Schilling and 3
members of the executive board of the District Assembly of the
Knights, for conspiracy to boycott. Schilling was also indicted for sending a "threatening communication" to Segnitz and Company during
the cigar makers' boycott.

When the trial was about to begin, the lawyers for the defendants
filed an affidavit of prejudice against Mallory for his outspoken opposition to unions. The defense hoped the case would be moved to another jurisdiction. Their plans were dashed when Judge Mallory replaced himself with Judge A. Scott Sloan of Beaver Dam. The defense

then asked for a dismissal of the charge of sending a threatening letter against Schilling on the grounds that the physical property of Segnitz was not damaged. However, Judge Sloan ruled that property included not only physical goods but also profits or income of the business. "His honor," wrote the Milwaukee *Labor Review* on June 26, 1886, "was of the opinion that all organizations seeking to interfere with the management of business were unlawful." With this definition of the term property to include not only physical but intangible assets, the trial continued.

On July 1 the jury reported that after twenty-three hours' deliberation it had been unable to agree on the guilt of Robert Schilling. However, three men were found guilty of conspiracy to riot and sentenced to nine months in prison. These cases were immediately appealed to the Wisconsin Supreme Court on the grounds that Judge Sloan did not have jurisdiction in the Milwaukee courts. This took the trials from the Milwaukee scene for the rest of the summer and early fall, and allowed labor to turn its attentions to another field.[19]

The People's Party

At the end of May, 1886, the Merchants Association held its ninth annual banquet at the Plankinton House. A number of speeches were made denouncing the rioters and the unions. Judge Mallory talked on "Law and Order vs. Boycotting." The nature of the speeches provoked the Central Labor Union to resolve that:

The participants of the banquet had a perfect right to mutual admiration. They have, under the existing unjust social system, the legal right to champion their morally untenable interests . . . but they have not the right to publicly slander, to defame the working class which created their wealth, and to brand the exercise of their rights and liberties . . . as criminal.[20]

Resentment over treatment by the courts, provocation by speeches of the conservative members of Milwaukee's society, and most important, the deeply-held belief that the acts of the militia and the governor of the state had been unnecessary if not criminal, united the laboring people and caused them to take action. As Robert Schilling wrote: "The poor victims are dead and buried. They shall be revenged. Not by making blood flow; not through force. The intelligent citizens have a weapon mightier than the ball or the bayonet—the ballot."[21]

A parade of 5,000 members of the Knights of Labor on May 23 was but a prelude to a more important meeting of 400 people at the Robert Chivas Post Hall on June 13. The meeting, dominated by adherents of the Knights of Labor, adopted a resolution calling for the appointment of a committee to arrange meetings throughout the city which would elect delegates to a convention in La Crosse and help to organize a party in the county.

The July meeting in La Crosse was dominated by delegates from Milwaukee. These delegates formed the People's Party and adopted a platform calling for the prohibition of child labor, a graduated income tax, the establishment of a national monetary system, and other middle-class reforms of the period. Because of the unrepresentative character of this group in La Crosse, a new convention met at Neenah on September 18 to nominate a full slate of candidates for state offices, headed by John Cochrane, candidate for governor. The slate was notable for the absence of any worker as nominee for a principal office.

Prior to the nomination of candidates for office in Milwaukee County, both the trade unions and the Knights participated in a Labor-Day parade displaying the slogan: "When Bad Men Combine, the Good Must Associate," and advertising: "We Shoot Ballots, not Bullets." On September 20 the People's Party in Milwaukee met to nominate candidates for the county elections, including Newell Daniels, former head of the Knights of St. Crispin, who was nominated for sheriff, and Henry Smith, ofttimes candidate on labor tickets and recently elected State Master Workman of the Knights, who was nominated for Congress.

Although the party and the campaign were primarily the offspring of the Knights, many persons, including Grottkau and Juliet H. Severance, a suffragette and advocate of labor's cause, worked for victory. While the platform appealed to various reform elements in the community, it was undoubtedly opposition to the re-election of Governor Rusk and outrage over the shooting in early May that served as a cohesive bond and gave the political movement its emotional impact.

The upheaval of 1886 gave birth to a political labor movement in many places in the nation. In New York City Henry George, the internationally famous advocate of the single tax, was nominated by a labor party for mayor. In a climactic campaign, George polled 68,000 votes to 90,000 for Abram S. Hewitt, the Tammany nominee, and 60,000 for Theodore Roosevelt, then a young politician. In Chicago, a labor ticket received 25,000 out of a total of 92,000 votes.

The People's Party in Milwaukee was victorious in the November elections far beyond the expectations of most observers. The entire slate of county officers was elected, Smith was sent to Congress, and the party sent one state senator and six of the twelve assemblymen, including former Alderman Rudzinski, to Madison. The People's Party in Milwaukee County received 12,500 votes to 10,700 for the Republicans and 8,100 votes for the Democrats. But if their principal objective had been the defeat of Rusk, the People's Party would have done well to endorse the candidate of the Democratic Party, thus securing Rusk's defeat. After the election, the *Daily Journal* observed, on November 1, 1886, that immediately after the May riots:

A separate labor ticket had not been spoken of. The Schillings, Smiths and Grottkaus had relapsed into an unwonted silence of days and weeks after the rattle of musketry at Bay View.

The "issue" was made by the panicky monopolist, boastful after the reaction of fear. It was made by sleek capital bellicose *post facto*. Judicial dicta from the stump made it. Merchants' banquets made it. Advertisements in the papers: "Knights of Labor need not apply," made it.

Then came the indictments against boycotting.

Labor began to talk of a labor ticket to show that the shorn Samson still had some strength. . . .

Labor had won a stunning victory. For the first time in Milwaukee, a labor ticket had won major elective posts without the aid of the Democrats or the Republicans. Instrumental in this success was the vigorous work of Robert Schilling, much more a middle-class, reformist politician than a labor leader. Having temporarily won on the political front, labor once more shifted its attention to the courts and the remaining cases of the indicted men.

On November 13 the Wisconsin Supreme Court ruled that Judge Sloan did have jurisdiction to try the cases; consequently trials were again held in late 1886 and early 1887. Of the 49 men indicted, 7 were imprisoned, 2 fined, 7 given suspended sentences, and 9 acquitted, 14 cases were dismissed and the outcome of 10 cases is unknown. The indictments for conspiracy to boycott against Robert Schilling and members of the Knights of Labor were among those dismissed on motion of the district attorney, John W. Wegner, recently elected by the People's Party. The strongest penalty, one-year's imprisonment, was placed on Paul Grottkau. Grottkau, convinced his treatment resulted from the machinations of Schilling and Wegner, swore vengeance on what he believed were vindictive acts.

Hardest hit by the riots of early May and the subsequent political activities were the Socialists and the Central Labor Union. Deprived of the leadership of Grottkau, who was publicly excoriated for his implication in the riots, the Central Labor Union was reduced to a corporal's guard. The Socialists, who regarded the newly-elected slate of the People's Party as mere money-reformers and political hacks, also suffered from public condemnation. Visits to Milwaukee in November, 1886, by William Liebknecht, leader of the Socialist Party in the German Reichstag, and Dr. and Mrs. Edward Aveling (Karl Marx's daughter) failed to rouse the Socialists to new levels of action.[22]

The first round in the renewed struggle between Schilling and Grottkau and between the Knights of Labor and the trade unions had been won by the former. But the next few years saw the downfall of reformist politics and the Knights of Labor.

CHAPTER VI

The Triumph of Trade Unionism

The Union Labor Party

THE upheaval of 1886 gave birth to a number of labor parties. The United Labor Party in New York City, the Central Labor Union ticket in Boston, the Industrial Party in Baltimore, the Union Labor Party in Chicago, and the People's Party of Wisconsin were but a few of the labor tickets found in the fall election. The unexpected success of the labor tickets, though nowhere as spectacular as in Milwaukee, gave rise to demands for a permanent organization to unite these new political parties.

The Chicago *Express,* at the behest of 500 petitioners, issued a call for a national convention in Indianapolis, which in turn called for another convention in Cincinnati on February 22, 1887. The Cincinnati convention, dominated by farmer delegates, organized the National Union Labor Party. In the Midwest, organized labor merged its political movement with the new party. Though conflict between the Union Labor Party and the pro-single-tax United Labor Party caused the Milwaukee group to change its name back to the People's Party in July, the name was again Union Labor by the spring of 1888.

In the spring of 1887, labor tickets were on the ballot in at least 59 locations. In Milwaukee the Union Labor Party, a composite of money reformers, trade unionists, the Knights of Labor, and Socialists, backed the candidacy of Newton S. Murphy for circuit judge and Peter Rupp for superior judge. The successes of the preceding fall prompted the Democrats and Republicans to join in support of a Fusion ticket. Fears of further political victory by the new party prompted the Milwaukee *Journal* to editorialize on April 4, "Shall Grottkau and his kind rule in Milwaukee?" The newspaper claimed the political battle in Milwaukee was "one between American citizens of whatever extraction and the imported demagogues and agitators whose avowed purpose is the destruction of American institutions." The *Nation* magazine on April 7, 1887, also vastly overestimated the radical nature of the party by referring to its leaders as "cutthroats and anarchists."

The power of the new political forces represented in the Union Labor Party was enough to carry the city by almost 1,500 votes, but the rural areas of the county were lost by approximately 3,000 votes thus costing the party the election. However, nine of the fourteen aldermen elected that year—three supervisors, two justices of the peace and four constables—were candidates of Union Labor. It was significant that while the labor vote was 100 less than the preceding fall, the Fusion vote was 4,000 less than the combined vote of the Democrats and Republicans in the fall elections of 1886.[1]

The narrow defeat in the spring of 1887 by no means diminished the political efforts of the new party. Interest was further stirred by an address by Henry George at the New Academy shortly after the spring election. Accompanied on the stage by Henry Smith, the labor congressman, W. H. Park, editor of the *Daily Review,* and Robert Schilling, George spoke on the "crime of poverty" emphasizing the evils due to land monopoly. While the single-tax concept was not a rallying call for action in Milwaukee, the appearance of this famous man did serve to increase the efforts of the labor politicians. Pride in the victory of 1886 and the near victory of 1887 brought a suggestion from Robert Schilling that the national convention of the new Union Labor Party be held in Milwaukee in the spring of 1888. However, the national convention was ultimately held in Cincinnati.

The Milwaukee party entered the mayoralty campaign of early 1888 with high hopes for victory. After all, they had carried the city in 1887 against the Fusion forces. On March 20, 1888, a convention of the Union Labor Party was attended by such prominent leaders as Schilling, John Jacques, leader of the cigar makers and recording secretary of the newly-formed Federated Trades Council, Alvord Curtis, Juliet Severance, Val Blatz, Colin Campbell and A. Bonzel. Nominated by the convention were Herman Kroeger, a German Catholic, for mayor; W. C. Powell, a native of Ohio, for comptroller; Edward J. Kelly for treasurer; and Peter Rupp for city attorney. The Union Labor Party endorsed public ownership and management of municipal improvements, establishment of public baths, taxation in the interests of the common man, and a provision that municipal officers be subject to recall.[2]

The Socialist Bolt

The Union Labor Party did not, however, reckon with the action of the Socialists, who withdrew their support from labor tickets in the spring elections of 1888. Unable to gain converts to Socialism by working within the labor parties, the Socialists split away in Chicago, Kansas City, and Milwaukee.

Headed by Paul Grottkau and Valentine Blatz, the Socialists bolted the Union Labor Party and set up an independent ticket, the Socialist Labor Party. Convinced of the necessity of a Socialist ticket and irked by the middle-class reformism and the personality of Schilling, Grottkau denounced both Schilling and the Union Labor Party. Nominating a ticket headed by Colin M. Campbell, the candidate for governor on the Social Democratic ticket in 1877, the Socialists advocated paying salaries to aldermen, the abolition of child labor, equal and uniform taxation, uniform lighting and street cleaning in the poor as well as the rich sections of the city, strict factory inspection and safeguards, the eight-hour day on public works, promotion of education, safeguard of personal liberty, disposal of industrial waste without injury to the public health, erection of city meeting halls, sale of wood and coal to citizens at cost, and the recall of municipal officials.

The Union Labor group charged that there had been a "deal" between the Socialists and the Fusion Party leaders, that the Fusionists had given free beer to the Socialists, bribed Grottkau, and illegally offered to facilitate the naturalization of Grottkau Socialists so they could vote in the election. This split in the ranks of labor aided the opposition who had entered the election under the banner of the Citizens Ticket. Conservative German-Americans, the remnants of the liberal bourgeois "forty-eighters," conservative Polish Catholics and business interests stood solidly against the laboring forces. Judge James A. Mallory, remembered and hated by labor for his role in the trials of 1886, was chairman of the Citizens' committee. He argued the election of Kroeger would discredit the city and turn away capital.

The election of April 3 resulted in 15,978 votes for the Citizens' candidate, 15,033 for the Union Labor candidate, and 964 votes for the Socialists. Thus but for the defection of the Socialists, labor might have been able to elect a mayor by the slender margin of nineteen votes. Although labor did elect 10 of the 36 aldermen and 8 of the 25 supervisors, the loss of the chief city offices was a bitter blow.[3] After the results of the election were known, Robert Schilling appeared before a gathering of Labor Party workers and said, "Gentlemen, it is evident that Paul Grottkau has won a victory. He has proved a traitor to the cause of Labor and the finger of scorn should be pointed at him

wherever seen, for if he had not bolted the party and sold out to the
Fusionists the Labor ticket would have been elected . . . ."⁴ The day
after the election, the Federated Trades Council unanimously voted to
tell Grottkau to take from the masthead of his newspaper, the *Arbeiter-Zeitung,* the words "Organ of the American Federation of Labor."
Although the action proved ineffective and was later rescinded, Grottkau's activities in the election only served to further alienate the Socialist movement from the trade unions.

Grottkau's case in connection with the riots of 1886 had been
fought through the courts for almost two years. The day following the
election, he appeared in court to be sentenced by Judge Sloan. In passing judgment, Sloan noted he was compelled to sentence Grottkau but
added: "If it was in my power I should feel disposed to remit the sentence of Mr. Grottkau for the great good he has done to the people of
Wisconsin in the last election and I hope that the governor will par-
don him." To the Union Labor Party this seemed to be the final evidence of betrayal on the part of Grottkau. Schilling, who was in court
at the time, denounced the remark as the worst political speech he had
heard a judge make while on the bench.

At the end of May, Grottkau was released from prison on technical
grounds; the judge ruled that the time Grottkau was out on bail while
his case was appealed was part of his one-year sentence. Grottkau
vowed he would stay in Milwaukee until he had squared himself with
Schilling and District Attorney John W. Wegner. Unquestionably
Grottkau's intense dislike of Schilling had motivated his disavowal of
the Union Labor Party, but it is equally true that the reformism of
the Union Labor group was incompatible with the class consciousness
of this German Socialist.⁵

The End of Union Labor

After the election of early 1888, Schilling had said, "This defeat will
purify the party a great deal, but let us take heart anew and go fresh
at work for the next campaign, which is of more importance than the
present one." Though Schilling and his followers did not realize it, the
Union Labor Party had passed the pinnacle of its power. Despite elaborate preparations for the fall campaign when Henry Smith would be
a candidate for re-election to Congress, the work of the party resulted
only in a humiliating defeat. Although the Democrats endorsed the
candidates of the Union Labor Party that fall, the Republican county
ticket won every office but county treasurer, and the Labor-Democratic
coalition elected but one person to the state legislature. A. J. Streeter,
the Union Labor candidate for President of the United States, received

4,494 votes, slightly more than 10 per cent of the total vote cast in Milwaukee County. Milwaukee was the only large city in the country where the Union Labor Party showed any strength. But this vote for the man who, according to the Milwaukee *Labor Review,* could "save this country from the inevitable destruction which has overtaken every nation dominated by a monied plutocracy," was not enough to stem the decline of the party.

In the spring election of 1889, the party elected only two aldermen in Milwaukee, and the small vote they received almost cost the party the patronage privilege of appointing election inspectors and clerks. In the mayoralty campaign of early 1890, the party contented itself with endorsing a Citizens Ticket headed by N. S. Murphy, which came in last in the field of three parties. The time had come for the reorganization of the political forces of the reformers in Milwaukee.

In October of 1889 the *Seebote* reported a move to unite the Union Labor and Socialist parties on the basis of the "great economic truths" set forth in Edward Bellamy's famed utopian novel, *Looking Backward.* No "Nationalist Party" was formed as a result, but the efforts to find a new basis of political support continued. District Assembly 108 of the Knights of Labor on June 14, 1890, discussed the possibility of joining with the Farmers Alliance of the state to form a new party. Finally in August, Schilling, who was also the chairman of the state central committee of the Union Labor Party, issued a call for a state convention of the party and independent voters in Milwaukee on September 5. Each county had two delegates and two additional delegates for every hundred votes or greater fractional part cast for A. J. Streeter in 1888. Also, every Farmers Alliance, Knights of Labor assembly, trade union, National Club, or "other progressive commercial, agricultural or industrial organization" was to be entitled to one delegate.

This odd assortment of individuals, not all well represented, met in Milwaukee and nominated Reuben May, a wealthy farmer from Vernon, for governor. The convention almost split over the issue of the Bennett Law, which required every school to teach all subjects in English. The fact that the majority of the delegates favored the law served to weaken the political appeal of the Union Labor Party in the fall election. A month later the Union Labor Party also nominated a county ticket headed by Schilling as candidate for Congress. The election was almost disastrous, Schilling and May received only 3 per cent of the total vote cast in Milwaukee County. Despite the defeat of the party, Schilling continued to work to organize a political party around the Farmers Alliances. The Socialists refused to have anything to do with the proposal because they "wanted to tear away from Robert Schilling and his political manipulations."

By May of 1891 Schilling was able to assemble a delegation, including Henry Smith, State Senator Herman Kroeger, Herman Freihube, George Streichel, William Crass, Theodore Prochnow and W. H. Park, to go to Cincinnati to aid in the organization of a new political group, the People's or Populist Party. On November 29, 1891, the Union Labor Party officially changed its name to the People's Party— thus signalling a shift in Milwaukee labor politics.[6]

The Federated Trades Council

The convulsion of 1886 brought the Knights of Labor to its pinnacle of power. With 700,000 members, the Knights dwarfed the trade unions with their 250,000. After the events of May, 1886, the conflict between the two groups intensified. The aggressive spirit the Knights adopted in 1886 caused the trade unions to draw together to form a new central organization. In December the Federation of Organized Trades and Labor Unions became the American Federation of Labor. Whereas the old Federation had emphasized labor legislation above all, the AFL stressed the economic objectives of its member unions.

Unlike the highly centralized government of the Knights, the AFL was but a weak federation of national unions. While the Knights sought to enroll skilled and unskilled workers alike into a common organization, the AFL insisted upon the organization of only skilled workers into separate unions representing the various crafts. The Knights of Labor was willing to tolerate high membership turnover, but the AFL made a fetish of membership stability. Even more basic, the Knights of Labor was committed to its "First Principles" with their emphasis on producers' cooperatives. The AFL, on the other hand, pursued the more conservative goal of winning wage increases and improvements in working conditions within the existing economic order. These many and basic differences inevitably meant that the Knights of Labor and the trade unions led by the AFL were to become bitter and irreconcilable enemies.

In January, 1887, the remnants of the Central Labor Union in Milwaukee collapsed. The trade unions found it necessary to organize a new central organization to coordinate their activities on the local level. Consequently, on January 23 a meeting was held to organize a new city central, and on February 20, 1887, a Federated Trades Council was formally organized by Molders Local 66, Typographical Local 23, and Cigar Makers Local 25. The FTC received a charter from the AFL in August. The charter was granted to Emil Applehagen, George

Wiggins, William Crass, John Stippick, D. D. Shur, Barney Wiener and Henry Siever.

Because of the reaction against over-involvement in politics, the constitution of the new organization banned political discussion, although many of its members were active in politics as individuals. Emphasis of the new organization, in the words of its constitution, was to be on "unity of action and organization among working people . . . to combat the evergrowing encroachments of organized and consolidated capital." The function of the FTC was to deal with the "many questions affecting the welfare of the working class which cannot be dealt with in special and separate Trade or Labor Unions . . . ."

Despite predictions by Paul Grottkau that the FTC would soon include most of the unions in Milwaukee, under the leadership of Emil Applehagen, it continued a precarious existence during its first years of life. The council suffered from attacks by its enemies in both trade-union and Knights-of-Labor ranks. At the end of the first year, there were only six unions represented in the council, and the situation looked discouraging.[7]

Conflict with the Knights

Within trade-union ranks there were conflicts over political action and policy towards the Knights of Labor and between the small group of Socialists and the non-Socialists. The primary problem for the trade unionists was, however, their relationship with the declining but still powerful Knights of Labor. Although the Knights numbered 48 local assemblies in its ranks in Milwaukee in mid-1887, it had lost its fighting zeal. The problem to many seemed to be a demarcation of jurisdiction between the Knights and the unions. Although the FTC itself attempted a policy of conciliation, marked by a joint celebration of Artisans Day in September, Paul Grottkau, through the pages of the *Arbeiter-Zeitung,* was untemporizing in his denunciation of the principles and policies of the Knights.

The *Labor Review,* generally friendly to the Knights, attempted to steer a middle course between the state socialism advocated by Grottkau and the cooperatives advocated by the national leadership of the Knights. The *Labor Review's* economic doctrines, it claimed,

do not differ radically from those of the *Arbeiter-Zeitung.* Even casual readers of both papers must . . . realize that both are *opposed to industrial depotism,* i.e. the current wage-system, which deals with labor as though it were a mere commodity; and that both are trying to emancipate the wage-slave, i.e. *achieve industrial democracy.* Therefore [we differ] not in theory but in practice.

.   .   .   .

For it is only by *patient diplomacy alternating with* SUCCESSFUL *coercion* that industrial despotism (the wage-system) can be dethroned and a limited industrial monarchy (corporate co-operation) can be established in its place, as an interregnum, till the times shall be ripe for industrial democracy (state socialism).[8]

The *Labor Review* suggested that the Knights of Labor should be primarily concerned with economic and political education, and "the wage question" should be left to the unions. The simple dichotomy of functions seemed reasonable since the local Knights' leaders emphasized political action while the trade unions were reluctant to become involved in politics. However, the suggestion overlooked the real conflict between dual organizations of the Knights and the unions. Both organizations claimed locals among the boot and shoe workers, cigar makers, painters, coopers, and seamen. Although the Knights of Labor soon lost the unskilled members recruited during 1886, the conflict between the craft assemblies and the trade unions continued. Despite the fact that the Knights had declined to a membership of 2,000 in Milwaukee by 1889 with less than sixteen local assemblies, the fight was not abated.

Discrimination by employers against the re-employment of trade union members after a coopers' strike in 1890 only intensified the feeling between the two contending parties. The following year, differences between the Lake-Faring Men's Assembly of the Knights of Labor and the Milwaukee Branch of the Chicago Seamen's Union flared into open fighting on the Milwaukee waterfront. The continuing struggles between the Knights and the unions and the over-emphasis on politics led to a decline in membership in both groups.[9] By 1888 the Commissioner of Labor and Industrial Statistics was able to write: "The numerical strength as well as the influence of labor organization has been steadily on the decline in Wisconsin . . . . From some localities they have entirely disappeared, and everywhere the life and spirit of 1886 have departed from such unions and assemblies as still remain . . . ."[10]

Resumption of the Eight-Hour Movement

The decline in activity was arrested by the resumption of the struggle for the eight-hour day. In December, 1888, the AFL convention decided to make a general demand for the eight-hour day to become effective May 1, 1890. By early 1889, John Stippick, the new and more vigorous president of the FTC who had succeeded Emil Applehagen in early February, was able to claim that unions in Milwaukee were gaining strength because of interest in the campaign. Prior to that time, Stippick pointed out, "interest in labor organizations lagged amidst the hurrah and speechmaking [of politics]."

The eight-hour movement, a local paper declared, became the "means of harmonizing to a large extent the once discordant trades council [FTC] and district assembly [of the Knights]." In June, 1889, a committee from the Knights' District Assembly attended a meeting of the FTC to discuss the movement and the advisability of forming an eight-hour league composed of both Knights and FTC members. Henry Smith, the former congressman and now head of District Assembly 108 urged a united movement composed of all interested people in the city; the suggestion was adopted. Ten days later, about 100 representatives of the Knights and the unions met to complete plans for organization of an eight-hour league.

Some trade unionists, led by Anton Rozanski of the Cigar Makers Union and J. D. Harrison of the Typographical Union, feared that the movement would be used to boost the lagging fortunes of the Union Labor Party. Henry Smith further antagonized the unionists by disparaging the efficacy of either the Knights or the unions and putting emphasis upon political action. After a long and heated discussion, a motion to form an eight-hour league was passed overwhelmingly. Nine union members, Frank Wagner, Charles Scheel, Jacob Urban, Joe Bessa, J. D. Harrison, Frank Lux, George Moerschel, John Jacques, and Anton Rozanski, voted negatively and walked out of the hall.

Despite the defection of these important union leaders, the eight-hour movement continued to grow. The Milwaukee *Daily News and the Daily Review* of November 11, 1889, reported:

For a long time the unions were at a standstill, there being but few members added to the list and the suspensions were many. In consequence, the unions were constantly losing ground and the workmen were gradually drifting from the nine-hour system into the ten-hour rut again. But a reaction has set in. New life is beginning to show itself and at every meeting being held new members are being proposed and initiated, and the expelled members are paying up their back dues and being reinstated. The old aggressive spirit is again beginning to manifest itself.

The recently-organized Carpenters District Council, composed of Locals 30, 228, 290, and 318, voted on November 9, to stand out for the eight-hour day in May. To attract new members, they decided to reduce the initiation fee from $5 to $2, the lowest amount allowed by their constitution, until March 1. All of the building trades were expected to combine their efforts through the FTC and stand by each other in the eight-hour movement.

The FTC appointed committees to agitate for the eight-hour movement; an ordinance was drafted to submit to the Common Council to establish the eight-hour day on all city work; halls were rented and English and German speakers selected. Demands poured in from unorganized laborers seeking to be formed into unions. To finance the campaign, all unions affiliated with the FTC voted to pay a ten-cents-a-member assessment. A mass meeting on February 22, 1890, brought hortatory speeches from Stippick and Smith. Paul Grottkau, now an eight-hour agitator paid by the AFL, pleaded eloquently for unity in the movement. On April 17 the Common Council passed the eight-hour ordinance. Four days later Samuel Gompers, president of the AFL, came to Milwaukee to advertise the eight-hour day as a means for providing "more and steadier employment to the toilers . . . ."

On direction of the AFL, the Carpenters Union was chosen to be the first to demand the decrease in hours. In Milwaukee the union served notice it must be granted the shorter day on May 2. Within a few days, all but a few small contractors had granted the eight-hour day with an increase in wages; no strike was necessary. Under the influence of the movement, the carpenters' unions in Milwaukee expanded from four to six locals, adding one English and one Polish local, and from a membership of barely 400 to over 1,400. Wages of carpenters were increased from $17\frac{1}{2}$ cents an hour for the ten-hour day to $22\frac{1}{2}$ cents an hour for the eight-hour day.

Other unions also benefited from the drive. The Masons and Brick-layers Union increased its membership from 100 to 600, the Hod Carriers from 200 to 700, and the Cabinetmakers from 12 members to 300. New unions were organized among the painters, plumbers, marble workers, car drivers and conductors, machinists, tin, sheet-iron, and cornice workers, wood turners, boot and shoe workers, steam and gas fitters, and coremakers. The Machinery Molders were reorganized, and older unions were revived. Many unions, including the German Printers, the Plumbers, and the Marble Workers, reduced the work week and increased wages.[11]

The Milwaukee *Daily News* on November 15, 1890, accurately described the situation as follows:

The past year has been a remarkable one in the history of trades unions of this city The growth of the various organizations has been phenomenal, and that it has not been of the mushroom order can not be gainsaid. Not only have the old and established unions gained greatly in membership, but new unions have been organized and all are in a healthy condition.

There were now 52 trade unions in the city with memberships ranging from 50 to 700.

The End of the Knights

The organizing device of an eight-hour movement had proved to be a great success. The new found *élan,* buttressed by stable organizing, served to put the trade unions and the FTC upon a sure and enduring foundation. The drive had also sealed the fate of the Knights of Labor in the city.

Even though they had cooperated with the movement, no traces of the Knights could be found in Milwaukee after 1896. The few assemblies that remained in 1890, joined the trade-union ranks or dissolved. The leaders of the Knights, with the exception of the few who entered unions, were hereafter primarily concerned with political action. Robert Schilling was amazingly oblivious to the changes going on about him. As late as June, 1891, he wrote to Terence V. Powderly that the AFL was "traveling to oblivion as fast as Hell," and "in two years . . . will be forgotten."[12] If Schilling's prediction had been applied to the Knights, he would have been more nearly correct.

The New Pattern of Unionism

National Affiliation

The decline in the national membership of the Knights of Labor from 700,000 in 1886 to 100,000 in 1890 had paralleled an even-more-precipitous decline in Milwaukee. The eight-hour movement of 1890 ended the Knights; the trade unions, led by the AFL, were now the dominant force. However, action by local trade unions became increasingly circumscribed by the gradual centralization of power within the labor movement and the emergence of national trade agreements.

Prior to the 1880's, Milwaukee connections with national unions had not been supremely important. However, as more and more local unions became affiliated with their respective nationals, the consequences of the relationship became more obvious. The locals of the Amalgamated Association of Iron and Steel Workers had almost from their beginning been greatly affected by national policy, but the stove molders' strikes of 1887 were perhaps the first clear indication of this intimate relationship.

There were many stove molders' strikes during the 1880's, and in 1886 the national union began to give effective aid. In the same year, the employers in the industry formed the Stove Founders National Defense Association to combat the demands of the workers. The great battle between the union and the employers was fought the following year.

In March 1887 the employees of the Bridge and Beach Manufacturing Company in St. Louis struck for higher wages. The issue immediately involved the International Union and the National Defense Association. To defeat the union, the St. Louis' company began to send its patterns to foundries in other areas belonging to the National Defense

Association. Two of the foundries involved were Brand's Stove Works and Dutcher's Stove Works in Milwaukee.

Following the policy of the International Union, the 100 union members in the two companies refused to work on the patterns. After a three-week strike, the matter was temporarily settled on the basis that the apprentices, over whom the union had no control, would do the work on St. Louis' jobs. But after one week the stove molders again struck because Dutcher, under the terms of the National Defense Association's agreement, had had to accept more patterns from St. Louis. The union members, who were not required to do the work, began a strike which lasted another three weeks. The issue ended in June, when the patterns were recalled, the National Defense Association having supplied a sufficient number of strikebreakers to the St. Louis company.

The dispute ended in a stalemate that year, both sides claiming victory. But significantly, the Defense Association and the International Union finally signed a national trade agreement in 1891 providing for continuous collective bargaining and a grievance procedure for the adjudication of disputes. This agreement marked the beginning of the widespread use of collective bargaining agreements. The labor movement had found a new means of securing its objectives. Producers' cooperatives and other panaceas were now a thing of the past.

Another example of the centralization of the struggle between employer and union occurred in 1888 among the brewery workers. In that year, the recently-organized Brewery Workers Local 9, had demanded an increase from $55 to $60 for thirty days' work. Negotiations between the union and the Milwaukee Maltsters Association proved futile, and a strike was ordered by the national executive board of the union. The strike, endorsed by both the District Assembly of the Knights of Labor and the FTC, involved only 83 men. The brewery and malt-house owners decided to break off all relations with the union and began the systematic discharge of all active union members. In retaliation for the lockout, which had become nation-wide, the executive board of the national union declared a boycott against Milwaukee beer. Consequently in January 1889, the employers told all their men to quit the union within two days or be discharged. As a result 140 unionists, in addition to 210 previously laid off, were fired. It was generally believed that Milwaukee delegates to the brewers' national convention in St. Paul had been instrumental in barring any brewery hiring union workers from membership in the national body. The national boycott lasted fourteen years, but the conflict failed to destroy the union or to keep it from growing.[13]

The Building Trades Council

In addition to the obligations of national affiliation, another problem for the growing trade-union movement in Milwaukee was jurisdiction between and cooperation among the building-trades' unions. In January 1891 the FTC voted to call a meeting of all building trades to form an organization to provide assistance in case of a strike or lockout. Subsequent meetings of the building trades resulted in the formation of a "Building League" under the jurisdiction of the FTC. The League, composed of carpenters, stonecutters, bricklayers, gas and steam fitters, painters, cabinetmakers and cornice workers, was to consist of two delegates from each of the affiliated locals. Only the plumbers refrained from joining, but they promised their moral support. All disputes in the building trades were to be referred to the Building League, but in case settlement was not reached on any question, the matter was to be referred to the FTC.

The building-trades' unions had a combined membership of 5,000. After organization of the League, the plasterers were locked out by sub-contractors who refused to pay the union scale. The carpenters immediately passed resolutions endorsing the stand of the plasterers. Demands for wage increases, averaging five cents an hour, resulted in a lockout of stonecutters, masons and bricklayers, and hod carriers on April 1. The contractors insured joint action by requiring each employer to put up a forfeit of $500. They began to hire non-union workers, causing 200 carpenters to strike rather than work with non-union bricklayers and hod carriers. With 1,500 men already on strike, the movement gradually spread with some painters and more carpenters leaving work. On April 18, 130 plumbers were told to quit the union or be discharged. Two hundred additional carpenters struck to enforce a demand for wage increases on May 1.

The first of this wave of strikes to be settled was that of the stonecutters. The union gained the demanded wage increase, but the employer was allowed three apprentices for every ten or more men employed. The employers proposed in early May to end the long strike of the masons and bricklayers. The terms of the employers were: the union was to withdraw from the Building League, agree to handle any building materials no matter where prepared, place no obstacles in the employer's way in using two apprentices in addition to his sons, agree to work with non-union masons and bricklayers, and make no demands in the future except by mutual agreement between the union and the employers' society. In return the employers agreed to an increase in wages and agreed to allow the union to use "honorable means" to induce the non-union workers to join the union. The union overwhelmingly rejected the offer because it was obviously designed to destroy the union, and further, it conflicted with an agreement with the stonecutters and hod carriers. Lack of cooperation between the Masons and Bricklayers and the Hod Carriers Union and the refusal of the Masons to join the international union undermined the position of the union. On May 16 the union was forced to accept the offer of the employer. The Plumbers Union was more successful, and in early June ended its seven-weeks-old strike, winning wage increases and recognition of the union.

On the whole, the strike of the building-trades' unions ended unsatisfactorily. Cooperation between the unions proved only half-hearted, but the need for an organization to coordinate their activities continued. This need, plus the desire for a greater voice in the affairs of the AFL, led to the formation of the National Building Trades Council in 1897. Some of the Milwaukee unions formed a local Building Trades Council independent of the FTC and, although the powerful carpenters' locals remained aloof from this organization, it proved to be an irritation to Milwaukee unionists until it merged with the FTC in 1907.[14]

The Street Railway Workers

On the national scene, the two most spectacular strikes of the 1890's were the Homestead and the Pullman strikes. The Homestead strike of 1892 pitted the Amalgamated Association of Iron and Steel Workers against the giant Carnegie Steel Company, and the Pullman strike of 1894 involved the American Railway Union against twenty-four railroads centering in Chicago. In both cases, the union lost and was virtually destroyed. Neither of these famous disputes had any direct effect in Milwaukee, but the running fight between the street-railway company and its workers held center stage in Milwaukee.

As early as 1888 the street-railway men had been organized into an assembly of the Knights of Labor. The assembly had enjoyed fair relations with the street-railway companies despite the fact that outsiders had to be chosen as officers so they would not be discharged by the company. Wages at that time averaged $10 a week for the first three months. The workers successfully resisted a wage reduction, primarily because of strong public sentiment in their favor, but the organization then folded.

While the workers had previously dealt with independent and separate street-railway companies, the introduction of electric street railways necessitated an organization capable of financing this development. Consequently, in December, 1890, the Milwaukee Street Rail-

way Company was organized, acquiring at various times the Milwaukee City Railroad Company, the Cream City Railway Company, the
West Side Railway Company, the Milwaukee and Whitefish Bay Railway Company, the Milwaukee Street Railway Company, the Edison
Electric Illuminating Company, the Badger Illuminating Company,
and the Milwaukee Electric Light Company. Controlled through the
Wisconsin-Edison Company by the North American Company of New
York, this consolidated company represented a much more formidable
foe to the workers.

In 1893 the workers were slowly organized into Division 15 of the
Amalgamated Association of Street Railway Employees. Despite its
poor timing—1893 brought another financial panic—the union made
slow but steady headway. The first incident to engage the attentions of
the new union occurred on February 4, 1895. The morning was unusually cold, 16 degrees below zero. Motorman John Kennedy was piloting
car number 16 over the Russell Avenue line. The streetcar came to the
bridge on Kinnickinnic Avenue. The bridge was opened to let a fire
boat through. The bridge tenders gave three warning bells to stop the
streetcar, but the car did not stop. It plunged into the river killing
Kennedy, a young school teacher, and a widow. Eleven others including
the conductor, were saved.

In those days the vestibule where the motorman stood was not enclosed. Subsequent investigation brought out the fact that Kennedy,
who was vice president of the union, had been over eight miles of the
road earlier that morning and had complained before the trip of being
so cold he would have to leave. When he did, however, make the fate-
ful run he bundled his head tightly because of the extreme cold, a
circumstance quite possibly explaining his inability to hear the warning bells.

The coroner's jury found Kennedy guilty of negligence for not stop-
ping his car fifty feet from the bridge and not holding his car in proper
control. However, the jury went on to recommend that all electric
railway cars should be provided with enclosed vestibules to protect the
motormen in extremely cold weather. The jury believed Kennedy's
lack of caution was largely due to his exposure to the weather. The
union immediately began to lobby for a compulsory closed-vestibule
law. International Union President Mahon came from Detroit to add
his pleas before the state legislature and, despite the opposition of the
company, the bill was passed. The first closed-vestibule car went into
action that same year. The protection given was little more than a
windbreak, but it was a beginning.[15]

The struggle between the union and the company over the passage of the closed-vestibule law was but a prelude to the major strike of 1896. On May 1, a committee of the Amalgamated Association of Street Railway Employees sent a letter to the company making a number of demands. The company, named the Milwaukee Electric Railway and Light Company after another financial reorganization, replied the next day. It contended that the committee did not fairly represent the employees and that the demanded increase of 1 cent an hour could not be paid since the company had granted a penny increase in 1893 and had not reduced wages despite the Panic of 1893 and the financial reorganization. Finally, the company argued that the demand for arbitration of grievances by an impartial board would, in effect, "yield the ultimate right of deciding for ourselves all questions as to the executive management and policy of our company."

A conference was arranged between the company and the union for Monday morning, May 4. However, the the preceding Sunday, the union learned the company was importing cots, cooks, and cooking utensils at the North Avenue barn, presumably to feed and house strikebreakers. When the union called one of the directors of the company, Henry C. Payne, and asked for a conference that night, Payne's refusal convinced the union that the company planned to lock them out.[16]

On Monday morning, 700 employees of the company went on strike. The company barricaded its property and brought in hundreds of strikebreakers. The sympathy of the public was overwhelmingly on the side of the union, and a mass boycott against the company began. One newspaper correspondent, exaggerating the picture, described it as follows:

This boycott is a marvel. . . . Its like has never been seen before in this or any other country. The condition into which it has thrown a big, busy city stands unique in the history of the world to-day. King Boycott is absolute master in Milwaukee. The 200,000 and more human beings who live and toil in this city are subject to his scepter. The first blow was aimed at the street railway company and nobody cared. The sympathetic people walked or rode in nondescript vehicles, called omnibuses, and suffered inconveniences uncomplainingly. The next blow hit officers of the street railway company through their private enterprises, and only those directly interested suffered. Then the ban was placed on all who might offer aid and comfort to the enemy by riding on cars, doing business with its officers, or doing business with those who had ridden on the street cars. The final blow reached all walks of life, all enterprises, all avocations, and was extended even into the third and fourth generations and to relatives by marriage. In Milwaukee every man in the service of King Boycott is a spy upon his neighbor. The result is virtually a reign of terror. Business is throttled almost to the point of complete strangulation.[17]

On May 9 Mayor William Rauschenberger of Milwaukee notified the recently-created State Board of Arbitration and Conciliation of the strike, noting that "street car traffic in this city has been greatly interfered with and the business of the merchants of the city largely diminished, and has further been the cause of the assembling of crowds, and of more or less riotous behavior." On arrival in Milwaukee, the State Board conferred with the mayor and the strike committee. The union told the board it would be willing to end the strike if the company would rehire all of the strikers. However, the company refused the suggestion of the union since it had promised to retain the strikebreakers but indicated there might be room for about 250 men, especially those with families. After more conferences, the strikers decided to refuse the counter offer and hold out until the company agreed to rehire all of the men.

The long and bitter strike, called by Samuel Gompers " a strike without parallel in the labor world," ended about a month after it had begun. The unsuccessful struggle resulted in the destruction of the union. International President Mahon attributed the ill-will between the company and the union to the closed-vestibule law gained the previous year. The strength of this utility monopoly, the employment of strikebreakers, and the arrogance of the company officials served to overcome the relatively puny strength of the union, despite the early and vigorous support of Milwaukee's citizens. Another forty years lapsed before the company was successfully unionized.[18]

Wisconsin State Federation of Labor

Although Milwaukee workers concentrated primarily on union action, legislative activity was also important. Had the Milwaukee unions wanted to remain aloof from this field, the passage of conspiracy laws in 1887 as a result of the riot of the preceding year would have ended such an attitude. In September, 1888, the FTC pointed out that "while we are opposed to entering any political party as a body, we declare it our duty to use our influence with the law-making power to secure" certain legislation.

The legislative accomplishments of the late 1880's and the 1890's were not particularly notable. There was some improvement in safety legislation, an ineffective law requiring payment of wages in cash rather than script, laws fixing the liability of railroads toward injured employees, and protection against infringement of the union label. The use of Pinkerton detectives in the Homestead strike brought the passage of a law in 1893 prohibiting the use of armed men who were not authorized by state law. However, the use of deputized strikebreakers during the street-railway strike of 1896 demonstrated to labor the weakness of the law which had been hailed as a great triumph.

The state also created a three-man State Board of Arbitration and Conciliation in 1895. It had no power to compel settlements, and its members worked only part-time. The board had an auspicious beginning by bringing an early end to a strike at the Glenwood Manufacturing Corporation in Glenwood, Wisconsin, but it proved ineffective in many other cases, notably the Milwaukee-street-railway strike and a dispute involving members of the Oshkosh Woodworkers Council in 1897. The board continued to exist until 1911, but it was seldom used.

The increasing importance of state labor legislation was one of the primary reasons motivating the formation of the Wisconsin State Federation of Labor. While moves to organize a state federation had begun as early as 1888, it was not until June, 1893, that an organization could be formed. Invitations were sent to all labor organizations in the state, and in June representatives of labor unions of Milwaukee, Madison, Marinette, Oshkosh, West Superior, Racine, and Ashland met at Fraternity Hall in Milwaukee. The constitution adopted by the new organization called for universal suffrage, enforcement of child labor legislation, protective legislation for men employed in factories, mills, and other places, a shorter workday, the repeal of the anti-boycott law, and the freeing of charitable, penal, and educational institutions from political control.[19]

The creation of the State Federation was primarily the work of Frank J. Weber, state organizer of the American Federation of Labor. Weber, born in Wisconsin, had been sailor, school teacher, and ship carpenter. A former member of the Knights of Labor, he helped organize a carpenters' union in Milwaukee, taking a leading part in the carpenters' strike for the eight-hour day in 1886. During the 1890's, Weber was employed as an AFL organizer in the coal-mining regions of West Virginia and among longshoremen in Southern ports. Weber was head of the legislative committee of the Wisconsin State Federation of Labor from its organization until 1920. Later, 1902 to 1934, he served as chief officer of the FTC. Like many unionists of the time, he was active in the Populist Party. Again like others, he was soon to enter the ranks of the growing Socialist movement.[20]

CHAPTER VII

The Alliance with Socialism

DESPITE the increasing opposition of the American Federation of Labor, third-party movements were not unusual in Milwaukee. The attitude of Milwaukee unionists towards the older parties was expressed in a satirical want ad that appeared in the 1894 *Artisan Day Souvenir* booklet.

WANTED.

An unlimited number of male human beings, called "men" by the superficial, who are willing to march through mud, sleet and snow, and break one another's head. Must be poor and have mortgaged homes and farms. Unemployed also desired. Must be well trained to talk about the tariff. Must understand the great benefits of our national banking system, and must stand steadfast for a money of intrinsic value that will be good for Europe. No person who uses his brains for the purpose of thinking will be admitted. Brains were made for the use of brigands and cut-throats only. Upon the acceptance of applicants they will be divided into two hostile camps and labeled "democrat" and "republican," and while their wives bend over the washtub, and their babies cry for bread, they will be fighting one another, when they are not searching for work, or when not engaged in picking the scraps from slop barrels. Address all applications to Demo-Repo Executive Committee, Wall St., New York.

The ad suggests that the allegiance of the majority of the Milwaukee unionists was to the Populist Party. Although the Socialists had been active in the city since the mid-1870's, their sectarian views and emphasis upon long-run objectives had failed to win the support of the trade unions. Only Paul Grottkau had any appreciable influence in these groups.

The increase in the influence of the Socialists was facilitated by changes in the number of pro-labor newspapers in Milwaukee. In the latter part of the 1880's, the *Daily Review* (later called the *Daily News and the Daily Review*) covered labor news, particularly in the field of politics. Although emphasizing political action and at times demonstrating a pro-Knights-of-Labor bias, the *Daily Review* was endorsed by the FTC as "the only English daily . . . [that] is cordially recommended to the kindly consideration of all union men and organized labor generally."[1] However, with the decline in power of the Union Labor party, the *Daily Review* covered labor news no more adequately than other, general, English-language papers.

In the field of German-language papers, the *Arbeiter-Zeitung* was supported by the FTC as a newspaper which had "proven itself the steadfast champion of the principles, aims, and objectives of the American Federation of Labor . . . ."[2] The *Arbeiter-Zeitung* grew steadily with the decline of the Knights. Under the management of Simon Hickler, who took over the paper after Grottkau left Milwaukee in 1888, the paper was able to absorb the *Reformer* and the *National Advance,* two competing labor papers under the control of Robert Schilling. By the beginning of 1893, the *Arbeiter-Zeitung* was the only paper in the city of Milwaukee that could be considered pro-labor. In that year, the *Zeitung* was taken over by Victor L. Berger who changed its name to the Wisconsin *Vorwärts*. The *Vorwärts,* already the official organ of the AFL, was made the official newspaper of the FTC in May, 1893, and of the Wisconsin State Federation of Labor in 1894.[3]

Victor L. Berger

Born in Austria-Hungary in 1860, Berger migrated to the United States in 1878. For a while a cowboy in the West, then a metal polisher in New York, he settled in Milwaukee in 1882 and became a public-school teacher. According to legend, Berger, originally a single taxer, was converted to Socialism as a result of his studies in preparation for a debate with a Socialist. For some time Berger belonged to the "Cincinnati persuasion" group within the Socialist movement. The "Cincinnati persuasion" followers advocated immediate political action and were silent on the subject of trade unions. Subsequently, Berger became convinced of the necessity of working within the framework of the AFL.

Berger was of above average height, had a solid frame and a round, full face. His heavy German accent and faltering English emphasized his awkward gestures. Despite his almost uncontrollable temper, he was friendly and courteous. He resigned from teaching in December, 1892, and devoted himself to Socialist activities. Adopting an evolutionary Socialism not unlike the revisionism of Eduard Bernstein in Germany, Berger was able to gain influence within the labor movement.

About the time Berger took over the *Arbeiter-Zeitung,* he organized a loose Socialist group called the Sozialistischer or Sozial-Democratischer Verein, composed largely of German-speaking Socialists who had abandoned or refused to join the local of the Socialist Labor Party. The society attracted men who were leaders in the trade unions—John Doerfler, Emil Seidel, Jacob Hunger, George Moerschel, Karl Kleist, Frederick Brockhausen and Richard Elsner. The Verein formed a wing of the local Peoples Party, not as Populists but as recognized Socialists. As Olson writes: "The thirty or so members struggled along without friends or even converts except those picked up occasionally by word of mouth, but to have been one of them proved later to be the open door to party office and public candidacy."[4]

The Socialist-Populist Federation

On the evening of October 9, 1893, representatives of the Verein, the Socialist Labor Party, the People's Party, and the FTC met as a group to organize for the approaching municipal campaign. While differing on many points, a coalition committee of fifteen finally agreed on a cooperative ticket and adopted a platform influenced by Socialist thought. The alliance with the Populists was made possible because the People's Party in Milwaukee was more radical and more inclined toward Socialism than the national party. This cooperation served to present the Socialists in a good light to the unionists and gave them a means of winning the workingmen over to their beliefs.

A step preliminary to the growth of Socialist influence in the FTC was the elimination of the office of president. Since its founding in 1887, the FTC had elected a president. Under the rule of John Stippick, the office was used as a means of dealing with minority dissension and informally tying the Council to the Populist Party. In 1891 the FTC adopted a constitutional provision that the president would be elected for six months and could not succeed himself. Finally in 1893, on the motion of Frank Weber, then president of the Council, the office of president was abolished and the custom of electing a chairman for each meeting began.[5]

While the Socialists had strength in the Council, the brewery workers and cigar makers alone contributing about twenty Socialist delegates, the radical Populists remained the dominant group in 1893. The constitution adopted by the FTC in October, 1893, reflects the Socialist-Populist admixture. The "Declaration of Principles" eschewed the earlier reluctance of the Council to enter politics and declared: "Our only hope of industrial emancipation lies in alliance with the progressive political forces of the times. Our greatest error in the past has been in the support of parties pledged to the perpetuation of an industrial system which has produced an arrogant plutocracy and impoverished the common people."

Political activity was necessary, the constitution proclaimed, because the "ruling moneyed class has . . . obtained legal sanction to wring from the workers all the benefit that strikes and resistance gained . . . ." This the wealthy did by charging high rents, through costly transportation, "gigantic" corners in grain and provisions, and by monopolizing the issuance of money—distinctly a Populist explanation.[6] The constitution of the FTC adopted such demands of the Socialists as direct election of the President and State senators, federal ownership of communications, railroads, and mining, and municipal ownership of public utilities. The central demand of the Socialists was the gradual nationalization of the means of production and distribution, but the constitution of the FTC put as its first and most important demand the Populist plea for the abolition of national banks and the issuance of all money directly by the government to break the grip of the "moneyed class."

Despite the differences that existed between the Socialist and Populist factions, these parties, with the FTC, entered the municipal elections of early 1894 under the banner of the Cooperative Labor Ticket. The executive committee of the fusionist organization was composed of Berger, Schilling, and S. L. Wiemar. After attempting to nominate such prominent figures as Henry Smith, Victor Berger, and Frank Weber, the group finally settled upon John Ulrich, an elementary-school principal, as their candidate for mayor. The Cooperative Labor Ticket polled 3,583 votes, a little less than 8 per cent of the total.

The alliance between the Populists and the Socialists was not an easy one. At the June convention of the Wisconsin State Federation of Labor in Oshkosh, Schilling led those who favored endorsement of the Populist Party and Berger advocated the establishment of a separate Socialist Party. Since the Populists had already called a convention, the State Federation decided to cooperate by sending delegates and requested the Socialists and the trade unions of the state to do the same.

When the Populist convention met in Milwaukee the following month, there was a great debate over the admission and right to vote of delegates who had been chosen by local Socialist organizations and the trade unions. Schilling, chairman of the Populist state central committee, led the fight against the admission of these "irregulars," asking whether Berger would support the Populists if the Socialist planks were not included in the platform, Berger said the Socialists would support the Populists only if the political platform of the American

Federation of Labor was accepted. The AFL had adopted a platform that year calling for the collective ownership of all means of production and distribution. Schilling refused the terms, and when the convention supported him twenty-four Socialists and trade unionists led by Berger withdrew from the convention. But the convention reconsidered its motion and the "irregulars" again took their seats. As finally written, the platform showed the influence of the Socialists. The convention endorsed the Omaha platform of the Populists and the 1893 proposals of the American Federation of Labor political program.

As a result of this uneasy truce, the *Vorwärts* in the congressional campaign of 1894 endorsed the Populist ticket, which polled 10,000 votes—the best showing ever made by the Populists in Milwaukee. Berger claimed he would continue the alliance if the coalition moved in the "right direction." In the municipal campaign of 1896, the fusion movement again received about 10,000 votes. But when in the fall of that year the Populists endorsed the Democrat William Jennings Bryan for President, the Milwaukee Socialists broke away and endorsed Charles H. Matchet, candidate of the Socialist Labor Party. However, the Socialist Labor Party was not a suitable permanent home for the Milwaukee Socialists. The SLP had come under the domination of the dogmatic Daniel DeLeon. The narrow, sectarian outlook of that group, plus its disastrous sponsorship of the Socialist Trade and Labor Alliance in opposition to the AFL, had made it suspect to the growing trade unions. The SLP lost such Milwaukee labor leaders as Carl Minkley and George Moerschel to Berger's ranks and gained no new ones.[7]

On January 15, 1897, the *Vorwärts* expressed dissatisfaction with the present state of affairs and urged independent political action by the Socialists. Thus ended the Socialist-Populist partnership and began Socialist ascendency. The break between the former allies precipitated a bitter struggle for supremacy in the Federated Trades Council.

The Social Democratic Party

After the break between the Populists and the Milwaukee Socialists, a new home had to be found for Berger and his followers. The Social Democratic Party, created by Eugene Debs from the ashes of his American Railway Union, was the center of the new movement. On July 7, 1897, Debs, introduced by William Beimdicke, organizer of the Federated Trades Council, made a speech for the new Social Democrats at the West Side Turner Hall before a large and tumultuous audience. Two days later, Branch One of the Social Democratic Party was formed in Milwaukee and the "independent class-conscious state" of the Socialist Party in Milwaukee had begun. On August 5 the FTC unanimously passed a resolution endorsing the new party. After that action, however, the Socialists began to lose ground in the Council. Conflict on the national scene between Socialists who favored the formation of a cooperative commonwealth in the West and those who favored political action made the new party lose some of its early glamour.

The following year marked a period of uncertainty and hesitancy in the policies of the FTC caused by the internal strife between the Socialists and the Democratic-Populist elements. In early January, 1898, the FTC elected five delegates to the first city convention of the Social Democratic Party to be held on February 1. The Brewery Workers, Brewery Teamsters, Cigar Makers, Coopers, Blacksmiths, Joiners, and the Hod Carriers Unions also sent delegates. The municipal platform of the party emphasized the importance of immediate improvements. The candidates nominated for the municipal election in April were intimately connected with the Milwaukee labor movement. The Socialist vote was less than 2,500, the German wards giving the only significant vote to the party. After the election, the Socialists claimed that the leaders of the FTC and the independent trade unions had conducted a secret, but effective, agitation against the Social Democrats in favor of the fusionist (Populist-Democratic) candidates, thus cutting down the vote that could have been expected.

Although prominent Socialists participated in the Labor-Day celebrations of the FTC in 1898, and although the United Brewery Workers' Hall served as party headquarters in the election that fall, the struggle for supremacy in the labor movement was not ended. The *Vorwärts* in March, 1899, complained that the FTC was virtually in the hands of anti-Socialist labor leaders. The paper charged that leaders of the FTC were striking bargains with other political parties to deliver the labor vote. Every now and then a new central body, such as the North Western Advisory Committee of the Trade Union, would be organized for the obvious purpose of selling its services to the old political parties. The Building Trades Council was noted for the vehemence with which it fought the Socialists, and the Carpenters Council went so far as to declare a boycott against the *Vorwärts* for attacking respectable (*i.e.,* anti-Socialist) labor leaders.[8]

Victory within the FTC

The fight within the ranks of the FTC was resolved in favor of the Socialists in December, 1899, when a meeting of the FTC elected, by a large majority, an executive committee composed exclusively of Socialists, including Victor L. Berger. After the election, the *Vorwärts* warned that:

It is the duty of the Socialists in the Federated Trades Council to use their success with wise moderation, and not to forget for a single moment that, although a trade-union is a proletarian class organization . . . yet a trade-union must never be dragged into a purely political struggle. Democrats, Republicans, Populists and Prohibitionists must all alike belong to the trade-union, else the latter fails to fulfill its purpose. However, the seventy trade-unions affiliated with the Federated Trades Council offer us a broad field for our socialistic agitation of the Social-Democratic type of socialism.[9]

In early February, 1900, Berger proposed a resolution that the FTC elect delegates to the city convention of the Social Democratic Party. After much wrangling, the motion was carried by a vote of 63 to 35, and Robert Schroeder, Frederick Brockhausen, and Charles Kunds were chosen to represent the FTC. Many individual trade unions were also represented at the party convention. All told, 67 of the 147 delegates were members of trade unions, and only trade unionists were nominated for office. The convention also adopted a curious resolution urging that its members join a union, but indirectly censuring those labor-union leaders who opposed the efforts of the Socialists to get the labor vote.

On February 23 the delegates to the municipal convention of the Social Democratic Party read their report to the general meeting of the FTC and, by a vote of 53 to 23, the candidates of the party were endorsed. About a dozen anti-Socialists demonstratively left the meeting in protest, and nine of them ultimately resigned from the Council. The action of the FTC was appealed to the executive board of the American Federation of Labor. The AFL, replying through its state organizer, Frank Weber, said that no notice would be taken of the appeal because it had not been properly addressed to the executive council and the appeal had to have the endorsement of the local and national organizations to which the appealers belonged.[10]

The revisions made in the constitution of the Federated Trades Council that year, when compared with the constitution of 1893, reflected the changes brought about by the victory of the Socialists. While in 1893 the primary national demand of the Council had been the abolition of national banks and the issuance of all money directly by the government—the Populist program—the constitution framed in 1900 placed as the foremost demand the "collective ownership by the people of all the means of production and distribution, and all means of communication and transportation." Proportional representation, which would give the small Socialist Party more seats in the legislative assemblies, was also advocated, as was the important right of minorities to "use . . . halls in all municipal buildings . . . free of charge . . . for the discussion of public questions." The state militia, excoriated in 1893 as an "engine of destruction" used by the "plutocracy" for the subjugation of the people, was in 1900 denounced as a weapon of "capitalism." The Socialist influence was also expressed in the advocacy of a system of public works for the employment of the unemployed, national insurance for working people against accidents, unemployment, and want in old age, and the brave demand for the "abolition of war and the introduction of international arbitration."[11]

While the constitution did not explicitly endorse the Social Democratic Party, it did proclaim that to prevent the constitution from being "merely an idle declaration, but . . . have force and power for good in the fight of labor for the fruits of its industry, we charge all members of this parliament of labor, and all affiliated bodies, to actively support, with their ballots and otherwise, the political party whose platform is nearest to the . . . declaration of principles and the . . . demands."[12] It took no particularly perceptive person to see that the trade-union movement in Milwaukee had found a new friend in the Social Democratic Party. Within the next few years, the victory of Socialism was repeated in the councils of the Wisconsin State Federation of Labor.

The Interlocking Directorate

The trade-union movement and the Social Democratic Party in Milwaukee were separate movements. One did not dominate the other. But there was in effect, as Marvin Wachman put it, an "interlocking directorate." While some trade-union leaders had been active in the Populist movement of the 1890's, by the first decade of the Twentieth Century men prominent in the ranks of the FTC and the Wisconsin State Federation of Labor, such as John J. Handley, Frederick Brockhausen, Frank Weber, and William Coleman, were also active as members, officers, and candidates of the Social Democratic Party.

In virtually every political campaign, the FTC appointed committees to visit the local unions to urge support of the Social Democrats. When dignitaries of the Social Democratic Party, such as Eugene Debs, came to Milwaukee the FTC would march in a body to greet them. The enemies of the Social Democrats became the enemies of the FTC. David G. Rose, Democratic mayor of Milwaukee and consistent opponent of the Socialists, was once denounced for using language which, according to the FTC, was "ungentlemanly, blasphemous and smacking of the 'red light district,' and not in keeping with the dignity of the office of mayor . . . ."[13] It was the FTC that defended the right of the Socialists to be recognized in the selection of jury commissioners, and it was also the Council that arranged for the courts to hold night sessions to enable the immigrant workers, who were more apt to vote Socialist, to get their citizenship papers.

No less important to the success of the Socialist Party was the financial support given by the Federated Trades Council. In the beginning of the decade, the amounts donated to the Socialist campaigns were small, $25 or $50. Because even these small amounts caused reaction among the non-Socialists in the FTC, Berger on one occasion turned down an offer of $100 and instead asked, on behalf of the Socialist Party, for the "council's good will." After a heated debate, the FTC by a vote of 38 to 10 voted to donate the money anyway. Obviously the Council was no reluctant supporter of the political cause.[14]

The FTC also collected funds to pay for lectures by Socialist legislators, who were underpaid by the state and had no independent incomes. Minor things could also be done, such as handling the tickets for the Social Democratic fair. Virtually every enterprise of the Socialists was underwritten by the FTC in some way. When the *Social Democratic Herald* was brought to Milwaukee as the English-language voice of the Socialist Party, the FTC adopted this, in addition to the Wisconsin *Vorwärts,* as its official paper. The Council loaned the *Herald* $600 in 1908, $500 in 1909, and at the beginning of 1910 owned 48 shares worth $240 in the Social Democratic Publishing Company. This financial support for the *Social Democratic Herald* was not, however, an unmixed blessing. In 1907, for example, the *Herald* had to turn down advertisements from Gimbels Department Store because it was on the "unfair list" of the Council. The executive board held that it was "not consistent for the official organ to print an advertising of the firm at this time."[15]

In 1909 the FTC joined with the Socialists in the formation of the People's Realty Company. The purpose of this company was to erect Brisbane Hall to house the offices of the Socialist Party, the publishing plant of the Socialists, and provide offices for the FTC and other unions. The prospectus of the company emphasized the advantage to the unions of a sympathetic landlord who would not evict them at some critical moment. The FTC had years before dropped the idea of building a labor temple "when it was seen that labor would have to put itself in bondage to the money lenders and become a victim of the rapacious law of profit and interest."[16] It now subscribed $200 to the undertaking and, when the building was ready, moved to the new headquarters. The willingness of the FTC to aid the Socialists financially was again demonstrated during the election of 1910. In that year, the nonpartisan papers claimed that if the Socialists were elected, the city's credit would be impaired and Milwaukee bonds could not be sold. The FTC replied by offering to take these bonds should the Socialists be unable to market them.

The Socialists attempted to repay the support of the FTC and the local unions as best they could. As already mentioned, the city convention of the Socialist Party in 1900 had resolved to "require all our members to join their respective trade unions where such exists; further . . . we recommend to all our party members to respect and patronize every existing union label." Victor Berger, himself, became a delegate to the FTC by becoming a member of the Newspaper Writers Local 9.

Of the 18 Socialists elected to the state legislature from Milwaukee during the period from 1904 to 1910, 6 were union officials, 10 union members, and the others probably union members if not officers. In 1908 Socialist aldermen refused to march in the parade celebrating the dedication of the auditorium because the parade was led by a nonunion band. Also of great importance was the fact that Socialist members of the state legislature and the city council were able to lend a sympathetic ear to the legislative demands of the trade unions.[17]

Opposition to the Alliance

The close cooperation between the Socialists and the leaders of the FTC did not mean that opposition to the Socialist-labor alliance had ended. During 1901, for example, Printing Pressmen's Local 7 threatened to withdraw from the FTC if more money was spent to aid the Socialist Party. A delegate from Coopers Local 30 protested the discussion of political questions in the meetings. In the same year a number of unions withdrew from the Wisconsin State Federation of Labor because they felt it had been absorbed by the Socialist Party. The FTC defended the policies of the state body on the grounds it had done nothing that was not provided for in the preamble and constitution.

One of the most persistent centers of opposition to the Socialist-labor alliance was in Typographical Local 23. In October, 1900, the FTC refused to endorse the request of the Typographical Local to use the label of the Allied Printing Trades, rather than that of the Socialistic German Typographia Local 10, on all matter printed in the English language. The FTC decided to permit the use of either label. The following year, the FTC asked Local 23 to remove their delegate, Fred W. Stearns, because he had used the name of the FTC and his newspaper, the *Union Signal* (a quasi-Populist-labor paper), to endorse the candidacy of a non-Socialist for county judge in Milwaukee County. Local 23 retaliated by notifying the FTC that unless it "discontinue[d] socialistic discussions" at its meetings, the Typographical Union would withdraw from the organization.[18]

At the same time it was reported that Local 23 was about to appoint a committee to get other unions to abolish Socialistic discussions in the FTC, requiring the Council to authorize its organization committee to devise ways and means "to offset such destructive work . . . ."[19] When in early 1902 the Typographical Union temporarily carried out its threat of withdrawing from the FTC, the Council seriously considered recognizing only the label of the German Typographia Union. As late as 1908 the delegate from the Typographical Union introduced a motion that the *Social Democratic Herald* no longer be the official paper of the Council; the motion was overwhelmingly rejected. In that same year, a prominent member of Local 23 was among a number of unionists who endorsed the slate headed by the arch-enemy of the Socialists, Dave Rose.[20]

Conflict with the AFL

At times the opposition to the cooperation between the Socialists and the FTC seemed to threaten the very existence of the Council. In 1902 anti-Socialists formed a Central Trade and Labor Union as a dual central labor body. When the executive board of the FTC learned of the plans, it expelled from its ranks those delegates who had participated in the formation of the new central body. Nels Andersen, business agent of the FTC, was dispatched to Washington, D.C., to confer with Samuel Gompers about the dual body. Gompers said the new central would not be recognized. According to Andersen:

Mr. Gompers said he was not opposed to Socialism as a political system for the emancipation of the workers from wage slavery and believed the time would come when it would be necessary for the workers to take it up, but he thought the time was not yet come to do this, that it opened the way for disruption and individual aspirations of leaders on the political field. The policy Mr. Gompers advised was to maintain a silent vote of labor so that the old parties would not know our strength and would thus grant labor laws out of fear. He agreed that old party politics was rotten, that all legislators deserved condemnation and said he wished labor could be led to turn them all out so that the next batch would be more afraid of the labor vote.[21]

Gompers' placating attitude soon gave way to one of bitter opposition to the Socialists throughout the nation. The first important break between the Milwaukee Socialists and the leadership of the American Federation of Labor began in July, 1902. In that month the FTC sent

letters to all subordinate central bodies of the AFL urging the formation of a National Municipal Labor League. The FTC declared:

Before we can hope to do much on a national scale, we must obtain the control of city and state governments. The proper course for the toilers is to use
their trade union strength . . . as the guiding spirit and rallying point for
their municipal campaigns. This being true, it is also important that these
city and town movements work along uniform lines and in full knowledge of
what each other is doing. . . . Only by such united action can we hope to
burst the fetters that bind us and establish the rights of man.22

The AFL soon declared its opposition and claimed the plan was "un-
wise and calculated to bring about a new federation of labor."

The opposition from the leaders of the AFL raised some doubts
within the FTC about their plan. Frederick Brockhausen urged the
FTC to go ahead, noting that Gompers had once said each central
body had local autonomy and was sovereign unto itself. He also pointed out that Wisconsin was behind in the field of labor legislation and
that such municipal conferences were needed to make advances.
Frank Weber, recently-elected business agent of the FTC, noted, however, that the charter of the city central in Pontiac, Illinois, had been
revoked for being "too radical." Weber advised caution and prudence,
claiming the AFL had had "spies in the city to see what the council
was up to." He pointed out that only 40 answers to the circular urging
the formation of a National Municipal Labor League had been received, and only 20 replies were really favorable.

Early in 1903, Weber felt compelled to confer with Gompers in Chicago to receive assurance that no new central charter would be granted
in Milwaukee. With this, the project died.

In the following years, the conflict between the FTC and the leadership of the AFL became more acute. Victor L. Berger, elected delegate
of the FTC to the convention of the AFL in late 1902 by a vote of 54
to 12, denounced the convention for refusing to go on record in favor
of national old-age insurance for workers. The affection of the Socialists for Gompers was not increased when in the convention of the
following year he denounced them with the words, "Economically, you
are unsound; socially, you are wrong; and industrially you are an im-
possibility."23

The *Social Democratic Herald* began to attack the "shameless betrayal of labor by its leaders" citing particularly the convention of the
International Association of Machinists in Milwaukee. The IAM endorsed Socialism and industrial unionism and was anti-Gompers, but
when the leaders went to the AFL convention, they voted just the
opposite. At the AFL convention of 1904, Berger was one of twenty-

four delegates who voted against the re-election of Gompers. He was the only one to object to Gompers' election being made unanimous—a move that caused an uproar at the convention requiring fully twenty minutes to quiet. In the convention of 1906 E. H. Basenberg, the FTC delegate introduced a resolution calling for partisan political action. The chairman of the convention ruled the question out of order. According to Basenberg, ". . . all respect for the subject matter before the meeting was lost sight of and it became only a matter of who could abuse the Social-Democratic Party and its members the most—and right here I want to say that President Gompers was no exception; in fact, it seemed as if his whole life and position depended upon his ability to belittle Comrade Berger and the Social-Democratic party."[24] When the delegate to the 1907 convention gave his report to the FTC, it was approved with the "exception of the delegate's voting for the election of Gompers."[25]

The opposition of the FTC to Gompers was even more emphatic in its rejection of his non-partisan political policies. The Council endorsed the statement of the Wisconsin State Federation of Labor that Gompers' political policy was one of "throwing the labor vote to capitalist candidates in the hope of getting labor legislation out of them . . . ." In 1906 the FTC decisively rejected the request of Gompers to back the candidacy of Republican W. J. Cary, a trade-union member, for congressman from Milwaukee. The FTC claimed Cary's union membership did "not make him any less a servant of the capitalist party."[26]

The Milwaukee Idea

Despite the differences between Gompers and the Socialists in the Milwaukee trade-union ranks, any thoughts of seceding from the American Federation of Labor were promptly squelched. When in early 1905 a secret meeting was called to form a new national organization of labor unions, Berger, one of the few invited, refused to attend the meeting in Chicago. Through the columns of the *Social Democratic Herald,* Berger cautioned the Milwaukee Socialists and trade unionists against joining the new Industrial Workers of the World. "For us blindly to begin a fight with the American Federation of Labor at this time," wrote Berger, "would be a crime against the trades unions and a fatal error in . . . Socialist propaganda."[27]

The FTC itself was less opposed to the IWW than Berger. In June, 1905, the FTC by a vote of 26 to 39 defeated a motion to endorse a letter from the State Federation opposing the attempt to form a rival national body. Berger appreciated the damage the IWW could do to the Milwaukee party's policy toward the AFL. He persuaded the rest-less FTC to decline to send a delegate to the founding convention in Chicago and instead endorse the State Federation's opposition stand. Berger himself did not even bother to reply to an invitation to attend the formal launching of the IWW on June 27.

A few days after the founding convention of the IWW, Eugene Debs, who supported the IWW, met Berger in Racine, Wisconsin, and pre-dicted the IWW would soon have an important following in Milwau-kee. Berger laughed at him. The next issue of the *Social Democratic Herald* charged that Debs and his colleagues were splitting the trade unions and advised them to return to the AFL and the Socialist Party. An angry exchange of letters between Debs and the Milwaukee So-cialist leaders followed. Debs indignantly inquired whether the *Herald* had become the champion of the AFL and its leadership. Frederic Heath, replying for the Milwaukee Socialists, maintained the success of the Socialists in capturing the labor movement in Milwaukee could be repeated elsewhere. He urged Debs to disassociate himself from the IWW.

The determined opposition of the Socialist leaders in Milwaukee ended for all practical purposes any chance the IWW had for success in Milwaukee. Individual machinists, cigar makers, brewery workers, tailors, and leather workers did join the IWW; but the craft unions of the city took alarm and, backed by the Socialists, reduced the IWW contingent to a mere handful.

Without the support of the trade unions of Milwaukee, the So-cialists were leaders without a constituency. Only through a close al-liance with the labor movement could the Socialists achieve political success. In achieving this alliance, the Socialists had the initial advan-tage of the German background of the skilled laborers in the city, but this alone was not enough to bring victory at the polls or win the support of the trade unions who were chiefly interested in economic gains.

Perceptively, Berger modified the militant tones of the earlier So-cialists to appeal to the conservative elements among the citizens of the community and within the ranks of the trade unions. Declarations like: "We do not care . . . whether our Socialism be Marxian or other-wise, as long as we change the present system and emancipate all the people and especially the proletariat," indicated Berger's pragmatic policy. Berger recognized that the Socialists could not expect a radical transformation of the trade-union movement. As he wrote in the *Social Democratic Herald* on December 6, after the 1902 convention of the American Federation of Labor:

No matter how various and manifold are the tasks of the trade unions, the aim of bettering the wage and work conditions immediately will be in the foreground. Their political helpfulness should not be over-estimated by a party which ought and must work for the future. Trades unions as such recognized the competitive system. They stand upon the same economic basis as the capitalists.

The trades unions as such are at the present time the greatest conservative force in the country, just as the trusts are the greatest revolutionary force.

Berger was careful to distinguish what to him was a two-fold task of the labor movement, the political and the economic. To Berger, the "Milwaukee idea" was not to have either movement dominate the other, but to have a "personal union of the workers . . . [by] having the same persons take an active interest in both the trade-union and the political labor movement . . . . Then we find the same men, with the same thoughts, aims and ideals working in the economic and political field, thus forming a giant army moving on two roads for the abolition of the capitalist system."[28]

In the field of economic action, Berger did not urge militant strikes against the employers, but rather used his influence to promote integrity within the labor movement in its relations with the employers. "The trade-union men, who are socialists," he wrote, "are not willing to fight on every slight pretext. There is no danger of Social-Democrats going to strike simply for the fun of it . . . . One will find that the leaders, the spokesmen in the Milwaukee trade-unions, are not hotheads, if they occasionally do use strong language. When it comes down to actual work they will weigh long and act conservatively . . . . The Social-Democrat wants to get as much as possible and at the same time knowing the capitalist system, he knows that he cannot go too far . . . ."[29]

While the Milwaukee unionists adopted the radical language of the Socialist movement, their emphasis was upon the conservative aims of winning wage increases, improving working conditions, and securing favorable labor legislation within the framework of capitalism. The Socialist movement was important to them, not because of its ultimate objective of replacing capitalism with the Socialist commonwealth, but because it provided a unifying ideology through which they could channel their drives and ambitions. To the trade unionists of the city, Socialism was no utopian folly, but a practical idea. The city administration, in which the workers had no voice, was corrupt. Employers were becoming militantly anti-union, using the weapon of the injunction to crush the demands of the workers. Labor legislation in the state was below the meager standards of other states in the nation. What better proof could there be to the workers that government was allied with the employers against the workers? What better answer could there be than the political program of the conservative Milwaukee Socialists?

Caught up in the Progressive revolt then sweeping the nation, labor's alliance with Socialism would soon bear fruit.

CHAPTER VIII

The Progressive Movement

THE origins of the Progressive movement in the United States are diverse. In part the movement stemmed from the long tradition of agrarian discontent—the Greenback, Granger, and Populist movements. Reaction to the trust movement, to the Morgans and the Rockefellers, contributed its share. The Social Gospel movement led by Washington Gladden and Walter Rauschenbusch lent a religious fervor to the protest.

The "muckrakers" provided documentation for the protestations of the Progressives. Ida Tarbell's articles on the Standard Oil Company, Lincoln Steffens' indictment of city government, the "muckrake" magazines, like *McClure's, Everybody's,* and *Hampton's,* were part of the chorus demanding reform. Middle-class women, enlisted through the General Federation of Women's Clubs, became actively interested in factory and general working conditions.

On the national scene, Theodore Roosevelt was the embodiment of the Progressive movement, though his denunciations of the "malefactors of great wealth" were not always matched by his political programs. But the most successful Progressive of all was Robert M. La Follette. Capitalizing on discontent, La Follette was able to defeat the conservative or stalwart forces within the Republican Party and capture the governor's chair in Wisconsin.

La Follette served as governor from 1901 to 1906, going on then to the United States Senate and national prominence. The governorship was filled by the Progressive Republicans James O. Davidson (1906-11) and Francis McGovern (1911-15). Not averse to the use of experts, the Progressives established the Wisconsin Reference Library, under the brilliant direction of Charles McCarthy, to perform necessary research and to draft bills for the legislature. Experts and consultants were drawn from many areas, particularly from the faculty of the University of Wisconsin.

The progressive regime of 1901 to 1915 reached its pinnacle in the legislative session of 1911. With majorities in both houses, the Progressive Republicans, aided by fourteen Socialists and a few Democrats, were able to pass an impressive array of programs.

Despite the successful cooperation between the Progressive Republicans and the Socialists, the differences between them should not be overlooked. The Progressives' power resided among the farmers in the rural areas; the Socialists were urban based, with labor unions their source of power. The Progressives were nationalistic and despite the varied ethnic groups—especially Scandinavians—attracted to their banner, nativistic. The Socialists were at least nominally internationalist and received their strongest support from more-recent immigrant groups. Cooperation was possible because the Socialists were primarily interested in labor legislation, which generally did not affect farmers, and were willing to support the other programs of the Progressives.[1]

Each group had its own, willful leader. It would be rather difficult to expect Victor L. Berger to accept Robert M. La Follette as leader, or La Follette to accept Berger. Oscar Ameringer reported "there never had been any love lost between Victor and old Bob, whom he [Berger] regarded as a scrapping but rather superficial statesman . . . ."[2] Finally, there were basic ideological differences between the two groups. The Progressives accepted capitalism but wanted to reform it. The Socialists wanted to abolish capitalism but were willing to accept reform.

They were not completely divergent groups, but rather the left and right wings of the Progressive revolt. They showed a mutual interest in reform, although for different reasons. This mutual interest bore fruit in the 1911 legislative session in the passage of an income-tax and a conservation program, the creation of a highway commission, and the enactment of the most comprehensive program of labor legislation in the history of Wisconsin.[3]

The Progressive Labor Laws

Workmen's Compensation

One of the first of the Progressive labor laws passed was the Workmen's Compensation Act of 1911. Prior to that act, there had been a few modifications of employers' liability under the law. In 1909 bills were proposed to modify the employers' liability defenses in manufacturing. These proposals were displaced by consideration of an entirely different approach to the problem, workmen's compensation. Under workmen's compensation, negligence is not an issue, and the employer must pay benefits for almost all injuries incidental to the employment he provides. The scale of benefits is fixed beforehand, and the settlement of claims is largely taken out of the courts.

Trade unionists were the first groups to propose workmen's-compensation laws in Wisconsin. In 1903 Frank Weber and Frederick Brockhausen of the State Federation of Labor began to plan for a system which would supplant employers' liability. At the 1904 convention of the State Federation, this issue was discussed and a recommendation for workmen's compensation was made part of the State Federation's legislative program. Charles McCarthy of the Legislative Reference Library drafted a bill along lines favored by the State Federation. Brockhausen, one of the first two Socialists in the state legislature, introduced it into the Assembly of 1905. The bill was defeated, as were attempts in 1907 and 1909.

In 1908 the Milwaukee Merchants and Manufacturers Association met to discuss the system. Following the practice of similar groups of the period, the association, in 1910, sent its secretary to England and Germany to study their systems of compensation. This increased attention to the plan induced the 1909 state legislature to form an interim committee to study the proposals and draft a bill to be presented to the 1911 legislature. The committee held hearings throughout the state and completed its work in December, 1910. The Milwaukee employers were represented at the hearings by the Merchants and Manufacturers Association, organized labor by the Wisconsin State Federation of Labor. In no city other than Milwaukee were the employers as interested, well informed, or cooperative.

There were differences between the unions and the employers, but the State Federation of Labor, convinced that the bill would not pass if both farmers and employers opposed it, decided to compromise. In the campaigns of 1910, all three major parties, Socialist, Republican, and Democratic, committed themselves to a workmen's-compensation law. Governor McGovern in his message to the legislature emphasized the importance of passing a law at that time. Both labor and management backed the law, but unexpected opposition to the bill came from farmer members of the legislature. However, an amended bill passed the legislature and was signed by the governor on May 3, 1911. The law provided for an Industrial Accident Board to administer the law, but when the legislature later created the Industrial Commission, the work of administering the act was shifted to the Commission. Subsequent amendments to the law strengthened its application and increased the awards for injuries to employees under the law.[4]

Safety Legislation

Another signal legislative victory of 1911 was the passage of the safety or Industrial Commission law. The law substituted for the detailed safety legislation of the past the duty of employers to provide a safe place of employment; it gave the Industrial Commission the power to fix reasonable standards of what constituted safe employment. Hence, statutory safety legislation was replaced almost entirely by orders of the state Industrial Commission.[5]

Women's Hours Legislation

Legislation regulating the hours of work for women was also enacted in 1911. The Wisconsin Consumers League was the first organization which sponsored such legislation. Professor John R. Commons of the University of Wisconsin and the Socialists were also interested in securing legislation. All but one of the women's hours bills introduced in 1905, 1907, and 1909 were sponsored by the Socialists. The State Federation of Labor approved the action of its Socialist members in supporting the movement, but its endorsement was less enthusiastic than that granted the bill for workmen's compensation. By 1910 the liberal group, composed of University of Wisconsin people and members of the Consumers League, was strengthened by the addition of groups of Milwaukee social and religious leaders.

In the election of 1910, the Republican and the Socialist platforms included promises of a law regulating hours of women workers. Despite vigorous opposition by the Milwaukee Merchants and Manufacturers Association, the law, as finally passed, provided a ten-hour day and a forty-eight-hour week for night work. The law was to be enforced by the Industrial Commission, and in 1913 the Commission was given power to issue orders regulating the work of women.[6]

Child-Labor Legislation

In 1911 the Progressives also revised the child labor law. The law of that year, drafted by Professor John R. Commons with the help of Alexander Fleischer, prohibited the employment of children under fourteen except during school vacations. During vacations, children over twelve with permits were allowed to work in a limited number of occupations. Permits were also required of all children between fourteen and sixteen, and the number of occupations open to them was limited. The law, enforced by the Industrial Commission, also limited the number of hours children could work.[7]

Minimum-Wage Legislation

A more controversial piece of legislation within the ranks of the trade unions was the passage of a minimum-wage law. The National Consumers League took the lead in a nationwide movement for a minimum wage. In 1909 the league held its annual meeting in Milwaukee, giving special attention to the question of a minimum-wage law for Wisconsin. Proponents of the law consisted chiefly of members of the Wisconsin Consumers League and a group of University of Wisconsin people led by John R. Commons. The Wisconsin minimum-wage bill of 1911 was the first before any legislature in the United States. The bill failed to pass, but the Progressive Republican Party included the minimum-wage plank in its 1912 platform. In 1913 a bill was introduced which differed from the 1911 bill in that it excluded men.

By 1913 minimum wages for women had gained the support of the Milwaukee Federation of Churches, but the Wisconsin State Federation of Labor did not favor a minimum-wage law at the time. Frank Weber contended that trade unionism would be more lasting protection for women than laws and expressed fear that employers would regard the minimum as a maximum wage. The Merchants and Manufacturers Association was the chief opponent of the bill, but it was passed without much opposition. Some of the Socialists in the legislature supported the bill, but those who were trade-union leaders as well as Socialists followed the union point of view. The State Federation later changed its position and when the law was attacked in the 1920's and 1930's, the Federation was one of the most active supporters of the law.[8]

Laws Affecting Unions

More pertinent to trade unions themselves was the law of 1911 governing advertising for labor during a strike. For a number of years, Wisconsin trade-union leaders had actively sought such a law. The law of 1911 made it illegal to persuade anyone to change employment by making false representations concerning the job, including false statements on wages and conditions of employment and failure to state the existence of a strike on the job.

The act creating the Industrial Commission in 1911 also abolished the old State Board of Arbitration and Conciliation. The Commission was authorized to use any of its deputies as mediators in labor disputes and to appoint temporary boards for voluntary arbitration. No chief mediator was ever employed because the legislature failed to appropriate funds. The Commission itself did act as mediator to effect settlements in a few strikes, but the work of mediation was incidental in the life of the Commission.

These significant improvements in labor legislation were by no means the achievement solely of the Milwaukee Socialist trade unionists. Without the Progressive Republicans and the cooperation of the employers, Wisconsin labor legislation would probably not have been materially ahead of other states. Moreover, the intellectual guidance for the actual drafting of the legislation came more often from the ranks of the University of Wisconsin, especially from John R. Commons, than from the Socialist intellectuals. However, the importance of the Socialist influence in the state legislature is not to be underestimated. Nor should the contribution of the trade unions, which popularized and supported the laws, be minimized. Whatever political coalitions might have been necessary in the state legislature to pass the laws, political support of the Socialists by the trade unions seemed to have brought highly satisfactory results.[9]

The Victory of Socialism

In Milwaukee, the patient wooing of the trade unions, the emphasis upon immediate reform in the administration of the city government, and the unexcelled political machine built up by the Socialists bore fruit in 1910. The Socialist vote in mayoralty campaigns rose from an unimpressive 2,500 in 1898 and 1900 to 8,500 in 1902. Two years later Victor L. Berger polled 15,000 votes. In 1908 Emil Seidel, the Socialist candidate came in second, losing to the Democrat, Dave Rose, by only 3,000 votes. The next election brought electrifying results. In a three-way race, Seidel received a plurality of the votes, becoming the first Socialist mayor of a major American city. That fall Berger became the first Socialist elected to the United States Congress.

The victories of Seidel and Berger were landmarks for Socialists throughout the nation. Though Seidel was defeated for re-election in 1912 by a coalition candidate—a coalition joined by the Progressive Republicans—his two year rule provided the first clearly pro-labor administration in Milwaukee's history.

The Socialist city administration supported labor's demand to use the Allied Printing Trades Council label on all city printing. The city ordinance to compel safety and sanitation in factories was strictly enforced. Police were granted two days off a month, and the wages of common laborers working on the library and museum were raised. The city attempted to eliminate contract work and employ workers directly in order to enforce union standards.[10]

During the Garment Workers' strike of 1911, Mayor Seidel warned the police chief, known for his anti-labor views and severe methods, not to go beyond the law in keeping order. Daniel Hoan, the city attorney, refused to prosecute a picket for calling a strikebreaker a scab. Mayor Seidel finally stepped in and gained a settlement through arbitration. The strong support of the Garment Workers Union alienated the Board of Directors of the Merchants and Manufacturers Association. The Association resolved that it "condemn all public expressions designed to incite class hatred and to destroy respect for law and order; that we demand the punishment of those who threaten the safety of their fellowmen and who wantonly destroy property; that we pledge ourselves to employ every honorable means to secure obedience to the law and secure that peace and good will which is so vital to the community's material and social progress and welfare."[11]

The Socialist city administration also used its influence indirectly to help the unionists. In one case, the administration used a Milwaukee paving contract as a lever to persuade a Chicago firm to permit union organization in its operations. Pleased with the performance of Seidel's administration, the Milwaukee trade unions continued their financial and moral support of the Socialist cause.

This first Socialist administration also aided in the formation of the Milwaukee Citizens Committee on Unemployment. In the spring of 1911 there was considerable unemployment in the city. Consequently on August 14, 1911, the Common Council passed a resolution creating the Citizens Committee composed of representatives of the Common Council, the County Board of Supervisors, the Merchants and Manufacturers Association, and the Federated Trades Council. The purpose of the committee was "to study the unemployed problem and to submit a plan to provide funds and a scientific method to dispense them to the unemployed of the city during the coming winter." As one of its principal activities, the Committee conducted a free employment office. During its first three months, the office placed 1,443 persons, while the office of the Industrial Commission placed only 800. Appropriations for the Industrial Commission office in Milwaukee were inadequate, and, therefore, it asked for support. The Common Council agreed to contribute $3,000 and the County Board of Supervisors $2,000. The Citizens Committee on Unemployment then became an advisory body to the Commission on matters in the Milwaukee area.[12]

At the end of 1912, unions could look back with satisfaction at the accomplishments in the legislative and political areas. The Progressive labor laws in Wisconsin and the victories of Seidel and Berger in Milwaukee were substantial rewards. The Progressive revolt was at its zenith. Even on the national level, the presidential contest of that year was really between two Progressives, Wilson and Roosevelt, with the conservative Taft running third, and Eugene Debs gathering 900,000 votes on the Socialist ticket.

These great advances were not duplicated by the unions within their own ranks.

CHAPTER IX

Stagnation

WHEN the Socialists gained control of the FTC at the end of 1899, there were 70 locals with 20,000 members affiliated with the Council. In the four years that followed, about 35 locals and 3,000 more members were added to the Council's ranks. To accomplish this, the organization committee of the FTC had worked diligently, but by 1901 it had become apparent that a full-time business agent was necessary to carry on the work. Therefore, in that year Nels Andersen was elected first business agent of the FTC and permanent rooms were rented to carry on the work. The permanent office was to serve as a center for organization work, register unemployed unionists for other jobs, and provide a meeting place for the various sections of the FTC. It was estimated that the gross cost of the business agent and office would be only $1,113, half of it paid by the affiliated locals.

Organizing

The excellent progress made in the first four years of the Twentieth Century was not repeated in the following decade. Organizational work was impeded by language problems, concern over political action, time spent on "union welfarism," conflicts between the Building Trades Council and the Federated Trades Council, and, most important, the militant anti-union policies of the employers. Working together, these factors left the FTC with fewer members in 1913 than it had in 1904.[1]

The Polish Workers

The overwhelmingly-German membership and character of the FTC made organizational work difficult, particularly with the important block of Polish workers. In 1905 the FTC gave permission to the organization committee to appropriate $5 a month to aid in its work among Polish workers and empowered the committee to hire a Polish unionist, John Barkowski, to help in the work. Two years later, each delegate to the Council was asked to get Polish-speaking members in his local to help organize the Polish population. In the same year, the Wisconsin State Federation of Labor passed a resolution noting the rapid rise of the Polish population and the need for introducing unionism to them. The Federation endorsed the Polish daily newspaper *Dziennik Ludowy*, which contained labor and general news of Wisconsin and Milwaukee, as the best means of "educating" the workers. Despite these few efforts, the Polish population generally remained outside the ranks of the trade unions. Partially this was because the skilled workers of the city were more often Germans and "Yankees" than Poles, and partially, though there is no direct proof, the lack of success among the predominantly-Catholic Poles may have been caused by the conflicts between the Catholic Church and the Socialists.[2]

Union Welfarism

Another factor accounting for the poor organizing record of the FTC was the time spent in union-welfare activities. However commendable these activities may have been, they became a substitute for economic organization. Because of inadequate state laws, the FTC constitution of 1901 created a standing committee on local sanitary conditions. The purpose of the committee was to "examine into the conditions affecting the health and well-being of the workers in the shops, manufactories, stores and other work places in the city." The concept behind the creation of the committee also induced the FTC to back such projects as a traveling tuberculosis exhibit from the city of Boston. The Council also advocated that public buildings, such as the five-cent theaters, be properly ventilated. Other unions in the city also planned various welfare projects for their members. In 1905 two Milwaukee locals of the Brotherhood of Electrical Workers made plans to purchase a large house to serve as a home and hospital for sick and disabled members, as well as headquarters for the locals. Two years later Bakers Local 205 planned to establish an "out of work" fund to provide unemployment benefits during the winter "dull" season.

In the same year, Hod Carriers Local 1 filed articles of incorporation in Madison to provide mutual support in case of sickness, death, or injury. During the depression of 1908, the Machinists' unions gave a vaudeville show at the Shubert Theater for the benefit of unemployed members, and the FTC backed a move by the Musicians to have the city give free public concerts. The FTC also urged the Common Council to provide work for the unemployed on public works and to issue $500,000 worth of emergency bonds to build schools and bridges.

In an attempt to eliminate the "middleman," the FTC endorsed the proposal of the Society of Equity to form a partnership between the farmers and labor to provide food for workers at low prices. The proposed corporation was to be called the Milwaukee Equity Producers and Consumers Exchange. Only union members and members of the American Society of Equity were to be permitted to join. The advance expenses of the Equity Exchange were borne by the FTC, and committees were sent out to promote the idea among the local unions. However, the Exchange never began to operate. Two years after the project was initiated, the money was returned to the subscribers.[3]

The Building Trades Council

The Milwaukee Building Trades Council had been independent of the FTC since 1895. The disunity in the local labor movement further impeded economic organization. In November 1900 the FTC appointed a committee to confer with the Building Trades Council to devise ways to amalgamate the two bodies. Both councils agreed they would be better off if they did merge, but the Building Trades Council refused to surrender its charter from the National Building Trades Council (a body dual to the AFL) and enter the FTC as separate unions. The representatives of the Building Trades Council suggested that the FTC constitution be changed to allow the Building Trades Council to enter as a constituent group. In the middle of July, 1901, the FTC did adopt a recommendation of the organizing committee that all building-material-men's unions belonging to the Building Trades Council be recognized as constituting the Building Material Trades Section of the FTC, but within two months the plan was abandoned. Another attempt at amalgamation was tried the following year, but again the Building Trades Council insisted it be allowed to retain its charter and also use the union cards of the National Building Trades Council rather than the Federated Trades Council.

Conflicts between the bodies continued, and in 1905 the FTC set up its own Building Trades Section. The Building Trades Council was actually not a stable body itself. On October 4, 1905, Frank Weber and the president of the FTC's Building Trades Section reported the creation of a "new Building Trades council" and said it was "the history of the labor movement in Milwaukee that it sailed under a clear sky until just before a city election, when certain elements became active for mischief and sought to cause trouble for political reasons." The disagreements over jurisdiction, political action, and trade autonomy between the two councils came to a temporary halt in 1907 when the Building Trades Council became a part of the FTC. Subsequently, the Building Trades Council received a charter from the Building Trades Department of the AFL. The strength added to the FTC by the addition of the Building Trades Council was offset by the Panic of 1907 which temporarily cut union membership in half.[4]

The factors mentioned above may have contributed to the stagnation of the labor movement from 1904 until 1913, but together they were not as important as the determined opposition of the employers, fortified by the powerful legal instrument of the injunction.

Employer Opposition

Although Milwaukee, with an extensive German population and a growing alliance between the labor and the Socialist movements, presented a unique picture on the labor scene, employer attitudes and policies of the period did not differ markedly from those of other employers of the times. It does not seem probable that even the German employers differed fundamentally in their attitudes towards their workmen. The German brewers may have shown a greater amount of paternalism toward their workers than did other employers, but E. P. Allis' and Stowell's activities indicated that "Yankee" employers could also be paternalistic. Shortly after the turn of the century, Allis-Chalmers Company and Bucyrus Erie were among the leaders in working out welfare programs in Milwaukee, but few companies in the city exhibited any "advanced" stage of labor-management relations. Further, while a few employers were interested in or adherents of Socialism—such as Val Blatz in the Nineteenth Century—it would be impossible to conclude that their interest in Socialism had any significant effect upon the total labor-relations scene in Milwaukee.

The gradual "Americanization" of the immigrant workers also seemed to have little influence on employers' attitudes toward trade unionism. At the time the Americanization process was going on, there was a concomitant increase in the concern of employers with welfare programs, safety movements, and union drives, but it would be difficult to claim one was the cause of the other; nor did the then influential National Civic Federation have much significance in Milwaukee. While a number of the participants in the National Civic Federation, such as John R. Commons, were close to Milwaukee employers, and while some of the ideas of the National Civic Federation were reflected in the Milwaukee branch of the National Metal Trades Association, there is no evidence of speakers from the Federation appearing in Milwaukee. Rather, the typical attitude of Milwaukee employers toward trade unions ranged from one of grudging toleration to that of outright hostility.

Milwaukee Foundrymen's Association

One of the important rallying points of the anti-union forces was the National Founders Association. Its Milwaukee branch, the Milwaukee Foundrymen's Association, grew to include the most important industrial concerns in the city—Allis-Chalmers, William Bayley and Sons, the Bucyrus Company, Filer and Stowell, the Falk Company, Greenslade Foundry, Gilson Manufacturing Company, Hoffman Manufacturing Company, Johnson Service, Lindeman and Hoverson, Milwaukee Stove and Foundry Company, Northwestern Malleable Iron Company, National Electric Company, Nortmann-Duffke Foundry, Pawling and Harnischfeger, Fred M. Prescott Steam Pump Company, R. J. Schwab and Sons, George H. Smith Steel Casting Company, Sheriff's Manufacturing Company, Stowell Manufacturing and Foundry Company, Vilter Manufacturing Company, and the Western Malleable and Grey Iron Manufacturing Company.

The National Founders Association was organized in 1898 to settle labor disputes on the national level and to provide assistance to members who suffered strikes because of the union's refusal to accept the decisions of the Association. Although the Association was prepared for industrial war, the International Molders Union took the opportunity offered by the formation of an employers' association to ask for a national agreement. Consummated in 1899, the agreement provided machinery for settling disputes but no guiding principles.[5]

In Milwaukee, the first strike under this new agreement occurred in September 1899. Molders employed at Filer and Stowell's foundry struck because the company objected to a clause in the agreement providing for a shop committee. The company refused to compromise until it heard from the National Founders Association; the union was also unwilling to compromise. On September 30 molders at the Greenslade Foundry struck over essentially the same issue. The dispute was finally ended by eliminating the clause calling for intervention of the Molders Union in the settlement of grievances but granting the important concession of minimum wages for various types of workers.

Relations between the Milwaukee Foundrymen's Association and the union remained relatively cordial until the strike of the coremakers in June, 1902. At that time, the coremakers struck ten companies affiliated with the Association demanding a five per cent increase in wages and establishment of a minimum wage of $2.65 for a ten-hour day. The Milwaukee Foundrymen's Association refused the demand and announced that they would thereafter run an open shop. After this, relations between the companies and the union steadily deteriorated until, in November, 1904, the National Founders Association brought an end to all relations with the union.[6]

Metal Trades and Founders Bureau

The National Founders Association combined its efforts in Milwaukee with a branch of the National Metal Trades Association to establish a Metal Trades and Founders Bureau. According to the *Social Democratic Herald,* the Bureau provided strikebreaking detectives and maintained a blacklist. With headquarters in the Hathaway Building and a full-time secretary, William J. Fairbairn, the Bureau circulated blanks among the member companies to get information on each employee's efficiency, disposition, habits and union affiliation. Attempts were also made to get hold of the membership rosters of local unions. One small merchant offered a seven-per-cent discount on goods purchased by union men under a coupon system, a percentage to go to the union treasury. It was charged that the purpose of the discount system was to get a list of union members for the use of the Metal Trades and Founders Bureau.

The various elements of the employers' open-shop drive were welded together under the leadership of the president of the National Association of Manufacturers, David M. Parry. Led in Milwaukee by Thomas J. Neacy, manager of the Filer and Stowell plant, the followers of Parry—dubbed by the Milwaukee unionists as the "Parry-sites"—bitterly assailed the tactics of organized labor and urged employers to make sacrifices for an effective fight against unionism. This group organized Citizens Alliances to propagate their views and carry on the fight against trade unions.

Private detectives also began to be used extensively for the first time in Milwaukee. In March 1903 Frank Weber reported that employers of the city "had arranged with certain detective agencies to gather all the information possible on the doings and actions of the unions . . . ."[7] The Corporations Auxiliary Company of Cleveland, Ohio, sent a letter to the Cutler-Hammer Manufacturing Company of Milwaukee noting a representative of their company would be in Milwaukee in early 1904. Corporations Auxiliary Company pointed out:

Wherever our system has been in operation for a reasonable length of time, considering the purpose to be accomplished, the result has been that union membership has not increased if our clients wished otherwise. In many cases local union charters have been returned without publicity and a number of local unions have been disbanded.[8]

The detective agency also claimed they would help to eliminate "agitators" and aid in an educational campaign to "resist the spread of socialistic theories." The use of detectives in labor relations became so common that John I. Beggs, manager of the Milwaukee Electric Railway and Light Company, frankly admitted: "We have plain clothes men constantly about listening to the gossip of our men . . . ." According to Beggs, the use of detectives was "not so much for the purpose of ferreting out strikes as to hear what gossip is floating about." However, unionists claimed the main impediment to unionization of the company's employees was the fear of losing their job because of company spies.[9]

The School of Trades

What seemed in the unionists' eyes like another threat to their existence came on January 2, 1906, when the Milwaukee Merchants and Manufacturers Association opened its School of Trades. The Merchants and Manufacturers Association had been formed on May 18, 1894, when the Merchants Association and the Manufacturers Club consolidated. Since at the time manufacturing was largely concentrated in Milwaukee, it was this organization that lobbied on labor legislation until its functions were taken over by the Wisconsin Manufacturers Association in 1915. From the date of its inception, the Milwaukee Merchants and Manufacturers Association had a legislative committee to follow developments at the state capitol, but at first it was more interested in civic projects than labor. However in 1904 and 1905, Frederick W. Sivyer, of the Northwestern Malleable Iron Company, was president of the Association, and in 1905 A. J. Lindeman was chairman of the legislative committee. These men were prominent metal manufacturers, and because of conflicts with unions in their industries, they were acutely aware of the "labor problem." Strikes in Milwaukee metal trades and the growing interest of liberal groups in protective legislation for working women and children directed the attention of the Association from its former concern with civic projects to labor problems and labor legislation.

The first real achievement of the Association was the formation of the School of Trades, designed to provide industry, especially the metal trades, with skilled workers. At the suggestion of Sivyer, the Merchants and Manufacturers Association appointed a committee to gather data regarding trade schools in America and abroad. In the fall of 1905 part of the original premises of the Pawling and Harnischfeger Company were rented. On January 2, 1906, the school was opened to 60 young men. In the beginning, instructions were given only in patternmaking and plumbing, but in September the machinist trade was added.

The FTC denounced the plan as part of the schemes of the National Association of Manufacturers and charged that the School of Trades was in reality a "school for strike breakers." However, the financial burden of subsidizing the school became oppressive to the Association. At its request, legislation was passed in 1907 which permitted inclusion of the school in the Milwaukee public-school system. With control shifted from the Association to the Milwaukee School Board and the training period extended from six months to two years, the fears of the unionists that it would be used to supply strikebreakers was ended.[10]

The Injunction

Whatever threat the unionists might have felt from the Milwaukee School of Trades, or the private detectives, or the Citizens Alliance, or the Metal Trades and Founders Bureau, it was not to be compared with the real damage inflicted by the use of the injunction. Prior to the turn of the century, there was no instance of the use of an injunction in Wisconsin. However, at the end of May, 1901, the machinists went on strike against Vilter, Filer and Stowell, E. P. Allis, Doelger and Kirsten, and Nordberg Manufacturing companies. All but Nordberg belonged to the National Metal Trades Association. As part of a nation-wide strike of the International Association of Machinists, the Milwaukee members demanded a nine-hour day, a wage increase, one apprentice for every five machinists and one for the shop, and a definition of the duties of a machinist. Each company objected to certain proposals and claimed the National Metal Trades Association had a contract with the international union; hence, the issues should be arbitrated. In fact, the strike was part of a nationwide break in relations between the international union and the Metal Trades Association that would result in open warfare between the two until the 1930's.

An injunction was issued against the striking machinists. Since they were unschooled in their legal rights and unfamiliar with the labor injunction, the unionists regarded it as an incontestable order of the court and obeyed it without question. As a result, eight weeks after the beginning of the strike, the men returned to work on the company's terms. The strike had been broken by the injunction and the concerted action of the employers.

After this time, the injunction became a more common weapon in strikes, although the original fear it struck tended to disappear as union members gained more experience. During the 1906 strike of the molders injunctions of unusually broad character were issued. In May,

1,200 molders in Milwaukee struck for shorter hours and an increase in pay. Most of the companies involved were associated with the Milwaukee Metal Trades and Founders Bureau which imported strikebreakers, some from as far away as Providence, Rhode Island. The Bureau issued notices that the companies were running with one-third the usual number of men and that wage increases had been offered. The *Social Democratic Herald* claimed the companies had less than one-sixth the usual force and said the men were "mostly incompetent at that."

The Common Council soon entered the fray, and with only two dissenting votes adopted a resolution, introduced by the Socialists, sympathizing with the strikers and condemning the strikebreakers. The resolution was passed before galleries packed with workingmen, evidently prearranged. In June attorneys for the Milwaukee Foundrymen's Association served papers on 35 members of the union, proposing to examine them under the discovery statute in hope of finding something on which to base a suit for conspiracy to injure the business of the foundrymen.[11]

A number of injunctions against the striking Molders Unions were soon issued. Two of these were appealed to higher courts. Both cases illustrated the breadth of prohibitions which injunctions were covering at this time. One, issued to the Vilter Manufacturing Company, was appealed to the Wisconsin Supreme Court. The Supreme Court described the injunction issued by the lower court in the following words:

The injunction restrained the defendants, among other things, from interfering in any way with the plaintiff's business or property, from compelling, or attempting to compel, by threats, intimidation, fraud, persuasion, or violence, any of the plaintiff's employees from leaving its employ, from congregating about the plaintiff's shop or picketing or guarding the streets for such purpose, from assaulting employees, or going to their homes to intimidate or coerce them, from persuading or inducing any person to join said conspiracy, and from doing any act tending or intended to compel the plaintiff against its will or the will of its officers to operate its factory or employ or discharge any workmen in any manner or upon terms prescribed by any association or union, or to refrain against its will or the will of its officers from operating its factory in any lawful manner.[12]

The second major injunction, even broader in scope, was issued on behalf of the Allis-Chalmers Company. At the end of June, Federal Judge Joseph V. Quarles issued a temporary injunction against the Iron Molders Union and its members restraining them from interfering with the business of the Allis-Chalmers Company and forbidding members of the union from frequenting the streets or visiting the homes of the non-striking molders in order to peacefully persuade them to quit work. The FTC promptly adopted a resolution condemning this as an abridgement of free speech and called upon the Wisconsin State Federation of Labor to prepare a complaint setting forth reasons why Judge Quarles should be removed from office by the President of the United States. The *Social Democratic Herald* on September 15, 1906, acidly noted: "The Allis-Chalmers Company is still pursuing the striking Molders with injunctions. This injunction business is getting to be such an old story that a striker who hasn't been served with his daily 'injunct' does not feel quite right."

Despite the outcries, Judge Quarles granted a permanent injunction in September which prohibited, among other things, "any interference with the plaintiff's business, peaceful persuasion to induce its employees to stop work, and all picketing." At the hearings on the petition for a permanent injunction, Allis-Chalmers had presented 50 affidavits to show strikers' violence, but the union countered with 300 affidavits of citizens and storekeepers in the vicinity of the company's plant contending that the strikers were well behaved and law-abiding.

Under this broad injunction, eight members of Molders Local 125 were found guilty of contempt of court. Six of them were sentenced to terms in county jail ranging from 15 to 40 days. Subsequently the injunction was appealed to the Circuit Court of Appeals at Chicago. Two years after it was originally issued, the injunction was modified to allow peaceful picketing, peaceful persuasion and to permit workingmen to boycott plants used for strikebreaking purposes.

The partial victory in the injunction case did not mean a successful conclusion of the strike. The FTC raised over $2,400 in support of the striking molders, but the actions of strikebreakers and private detectives ultimately spelled failure in the strike. By August 1907, 53 strikebreakers had been brought to court on various charges, 36 for carrying concealed weapons; all but two were convicted. An investigation into the relations between the Allis-Chalmers Company and the Burr-Herr detective agency brought a certified statement from the comptroller of the company that Allis-Chalmers had, in less than one year, spent $21,745.92 for services of the agency. The union had retaliated by employing the tactics of the detective agency. It planted an agent, William O'Conner, in the ranks of the detectives. O'Conner subsequently testified that he had been offered $10 a head by the detective agency to beat up strikers. The combination of the Milwaukee Metal Trades and Founders Bureau, strikebreakers, private detectives and injunctions proved too much for the Molders Union. The strike, for all practical purposes, was lost.[13]

Attempts to pass effective legislation restricting the use of injunctions did not succeed until 1919, and in the meantime the Milwaukee labor movement faced a new threat with the formation of the first comprehensive company union by the Milwaukee Electric Railway and Transport Company.

Company Union

In late 1911 and early 1912, the FTC again attempted to organize the employees of the Transport Company. The FTC charged that the company sent eight supervisors to "shadow" a meeting of a committee of Streetcar Men's Division 578 and discharged all its men who had attended. The company also refused to accept advertisements of the FTC announcing meetings on the grounds that space in the streetcars was already overcrowded. The employees struck for an improvement in working conditions and offered to arbitrate the issues, suggesting to the company four acceptable plans of arbitration. The company refused, contending arbitration meant recognition of the union. The strike failed but brought an investigation by the industrial Commission into working conditions in the company. As a result of the strike and the investigation, the Employees Mutual Benefit Association was formed.

All permanent employees of the company were eligible for membership in the Benefit Association after a probationary period of 60 days. About 80 per cent of the employees eventually joined. The Employee Mutual Benefits Association developed a health program to reduce absenteeism, a life insurance system, a welfare department to counsel the workers, a building and loan association, a loan fund, and a bonus system to reward those who minimized damage to company property. This comprehensive program was run by the board of directors of the Benefit Association which had 11 employer and 13 employee representatives. The president and secretary of the Association were appointed by the directors of the Milwaukee Electric Railway and Transport Company.

In early 1919 the Benefit Association proved a convenient vehicle for the company to crush a new attempt to organize the workers and to demand a rate increase from the Railway Commission. In May 1918 the unions again attempted to organize the workers. Shortly thereafter the Benefit Association demanded a 15 cent wage increase. The company refused the demand of the Benefit Association, but at the behest of the Association of Commerce, the increase in wages was temporarily granted on January 1 in the belief the Railway Commission would grant an increase in streetcar fares. Should the commission fail to grant the increase, it was agreed that the company and the Benefit Association would share the losses of the company. After the wage increase was granted, a number of the members of the Amalgamated Association of Street and Electric Railway Employees, the union which was attempting to organize the workers, were discharged on the presumed grounds of pocketing fares or failing to collect them, but more probably because of their union activities and passivity (though not opposition) to the wage "demands" of the Benefit Association.

An investigation of the affair by the state legislature brought a report which found that: (1) "the association . . . in fact leaves the ultimate control [of its affairs] to the company," since the company had the power to discharge the officers, and (2) by "assumed benevolence" the company had obtained undue influence in the Association, "making it possible to unite the members with the company against the public interest."[14]

The stagnation of unions in Milwaukee had been brought about by many factors, including perhaps the time and zeal union leaders spent on political activities. On the other hand, the failure of the labor movement to grow appreciably after 1904 in Milwaukee or nationally, may have been the reason so much attention was given to politics and labor legislation. Here at least were fields that offered results. But all this was to change. War was coming.

CHAPTER X

The Strains of War

THE trade-union movement had been relatively quiet during the economic doldrums prior to 1916. But in that year there began a revival in activities that raised union membership in Milwaukee from the 20,000 claimed in 1913 to 35,000 in 1920. This increase almost paralleled the doubling of AFL membership nationally. The outbreak of war in Europe in 1914 had spurred prosperity in the United States. The Wilson administration had brought the passage of the Clayton Act in 1914, which the unions hoped would prevent the federal courts from issuing injunctions in labor disputes. When the United States entered World War I on April 6, 1917, labor found that its demands were sympathetically heard by the administration. Labor's right to organize was incorporated into the rules of the War Labor Board, and labor was represented on the National Council of Defense, the Emergency Construction Board, the Fuel Administration Board, the Food Administration Board, and the War Industries Board. Thus, with a growing shortage of labor, legislation which was presumably helpful, and a voice on important boards controlling the war effort, unions faced a new opportunity for expansion.

Policy Towards War

While the wartime period provided excellent organizing opportunities for the trade-union movement, it also produced the first strain in the relations between the Socialists and the trade unions. Prior to the entrance of the United States into the war, there was but little difference between the attitudes of the Socialists and the Milwaukee labor movement toward the "European conflict." Immediately after the momentous days of late July and early August, 1914, the FTC unanimously adopted a resolution condemning "the actions of the rulers of certain European countries in plunging that continent into a state of war,"[1] and on August 17 the Trades Council voted to participate in the anti-war meeting held by the Socialist Party.

The following year at its twenty-third Convention (July 1915) the Wisconsin State Federation of Labor adopted a manifesto on the war which read: "The State Federation of Wisconsin is not opposed to reasonable measures of national defense, but we do point out that the acquisition of homes and decent conditions by the workers is of far greater importance as a means of preservation than is the construction of battleships or other implements of war. Armies may be beaten, navies destroyed, but a nation that will give justice to its toilers can never be crushed."[2]

When in June of 1916 the Wisconsin Branch of the National Security League invited the FTC to participate in a conference on a proposed preparedness parade, the FTC replied:

... we desire to say organized labor ... is not opposed to National Preparedness. It has no desire to see the American union destroyed, or placed at the mercy of any invader, because of the unwillingness of its citizens to defend their homes; but it is opposed to preparedness that has in view only the strengthening of the capitalist class.

This is a preparedness which in Colorado produce[d] the infamous Ludlow massacre, and in West Virginia, the military despotism that deprives citizens of rights upon which their institution must rest if they are to endure. ...

The great capitalists who are now so fearful that the United States may meet with disaster by invasion, have never shown the slightest pride in race or love of country, save as they could turn it to their profit. The Pacific coast today would be an oriental colony as surely as the sugar plantations of Hawaii, if the American working class had not stood for race purity and American civilization.

.   .   .   .

We must decline your invitation to participate in a preparedness parade or mass meeting. . . . You, as the employers of labor and as representatives of the employing class, may promote American preparedness, by considering the demands of organized labor and assist in creating the improved conditions of employment, which are found where union wages and hours of labor prevail.[3]

At the end of the same year, the FTC rejected overtures of the Milwaukee branch of the War Relief Committee to aid war victims of European countries. The Council expressed its sympathy with the victims but, noting the increase in "degenerative diseases in the United States," claimed the "capitalist class is responsible for Europe's emaciated as well as for America's hungering people." The FTC also demanded that Congress end exportation of American food and "instruments of murder to Europe's God of War."[4]

The United States broke off diplomatic relations with Germany on February 2, 1917. Five days later the Council declared that: " . . . we are for peace and against taking away our food to feed the soldiers of Europe—that we protest against any declaration of war against the central powers or any other powers, and that we protest against the murderous and inhuman agitation of the capitalist press for war . . . ."[5]

In the following months, the position of the FTC became more critical. On April 6 the United States declared war on Germany. Shortly thereafter a special convention of the Socialist Party, meeting in St. Louis, adopted a majority report denouncing America's entry into the war as a criminal act and declaring the war an outgrowth of the commercial and financial rivalries of capitalism. The war itself, conscription, and censorship were to be fought by the Socialists. The first reaction of the Federated Trades Council was to adopt a manifesto declaring that "whether in peace or in war the organized labor movement seeks to make all else subordinate to human welfare and human opportunity, and therefore undertakes to protect the wealth producers . . . against the exorbitant greed of special interests . . . ." "Our country," it went on to say, "whether justifiable or unjustifiable, has been drawn into the maelstrom of the European war"; therefore, the Council demanded that certain essential minimums of safety, sanitation, hours, wages, and social welfare must be maintained to "promote the success of our country in war as in peace . . . ."[6]

In the early stages of the war, the FTC tended to follow the lead of the Socialist Party, although it never declared specific opposition to the war. In June 1917 the Council appointed a committee to work with the Socialist Party; they hoped to petition Congress for a referendum on the conscription act. In August the Council voted to affiliate with the pacifist People's Council despite the vigorous opposition of some locals, such as Typographical Local 23.

However, as the war progressed, the unions, benefiting from the excellent organizing opportunities, were driven from the anti-war position of the Socialists by the inclusion of the labor movement in the County Council of Defense and the outspoken pro-war attitude of the national leadership of the American Federation of Labor. Labor leaders of both the Wisconsin State Federation of Labor and the FTC were appointed to the Councils of Defense and given a voice in determining the status of labor during the war. Fred Brockhausen was on the State Council of Defense, and E. H. Kiefer, A. J. Melms, Frank B. Metcalfe, and Frank Weber were on the County Council; all were labor leaders, Socialists, and past or present public officials.

At first the FTC was reluctant to support Samuel Gompers' American Alliance for Labor and Democracy. A committee elected to form a local branch of the Alliance reported the Alliance had been organized in opposition to the People's Council and its purpose was to mobilize labor behind the war. On December 19 the committee reported:

We find this is an organization composed of individuals over which the Federated Trades Council and its affiliated unions have no control. Although the work of the alliance has met with the half-hearted approval of the great majority of delegates to the recent AFL convention, it is not mandatory or compulsory for any central body or local to affiliate.

The report concluded that the FTC "to our best knowledge at no time acted in opposition to the government," and this organization might "bring dissension and strife within the rank and file of organized labor." By a vote of 65 to 5, the FTC refused to affiliate with the Alliance.[7]

The Split With Socialism

However, the pressure of public opinion, the declarations of the national leaders of the AFL, and the more-conservative attitude of labor leaders like Frank Weber soon changed the position of the FTC. In early February, 1918, the FTC, at the instigation of the American Alliance for Labor and Democracy, arranged a "patriotic mass meeting" with Mayor Daniel W. Hoan as principal speaker. Later in the year the FTC complied with the request of the AFL to make the slogan for Labor Day: "Win the War for Freedom," and in October the executive board of the Council recommended that the FTC "to prove its fidelity, loyalty and patriotism to our government purchase $200 of Liberty Bonds . . . ."[8]

This evolving pro-war attitude of the FTC evoked the criticism of anti-war Socialists, such as Victor L. Berger. On February 2, 1918, Berger wrote to Senator Robert M. La Follette about the local union movement, attributing its policies to Gompers' influence. "The walking delegates, business agents, etc., for some reason or other," he wrote, "trail more or less behind Gompers. In other words, these petty officials try to be 'diplomats' and 'statesmen' . . . . The fact that these fellows depend on favors from Gompers at times will account for their behavior."[9] On May 6 Berger wrote a letter to the secretary of the Industrial Workers of the World saying: "I am beginning to believe that the IWW (or some labor organization that will succeed it but that will inherit its matchless spirit) is destined to take the place of the American Federation of Labor in our country and fulfill the mission in which the American Federation of Labor has failed."[10]

The anti-war stand of Berger, carried on through the columns of the Socialist Milwaukee *Leader,* resulted in the indictment of Berger and four other Socialists on charges of violating the Espionage Act. The *Leader* was banned from the mails. Algie M. Simons, a pro-war Socialist who had bolted the party to become Director of the Bureau of Literature of the Wisconsin Loyalty Legion during the war, charged that the Socialists had not played fair with the trade unionists in Milwaukee. Simons charged that union wages in Milwaukee were lower than in other cities and that the *Leader* had deliberately played down news of union strikes. "The professional politicians and office seekers who have fastened themselves upon the labor and Socialist movement of this town," wrote Simons, "have refused to endanger their own precious political jobs in order to help organized labor."

A more influential member of the party, Winfield Gaylord, who had supported the minority pro-war report of the St. Louis' convention of the Socialist Party, became a leader in the Loyalty Legion and a field agent for Gompers' American Alliance for Labor and Democracy and the Committee on Public Information's Division of Labor Publications. Gaylord also supplied the federal government with Socialist documents and letters which he thought proved the party treasonable.[11]

The Unpopularity of War

Despite the disrepute of the Socialist Party in the eyes of the public during the war and despite the (belatedly) pro-war stand of the FTC, the First World War was not popular within the Council. In October, 1917, the FTC appointed a committee to confer with the management of the Milwaukee *Leader* after it was banned from the mails. The committee reported simply that the paper had lost its mailing privileges because of its anti-war stand. The following month the Trades Council adopted a resolution asking unionists to patronize those advertisers who had retained their ads in the *Leader*. In January, 1918, with but one dissenting vote, the Council asked Senator La Follette, who had opposed the war, to address the trade unions in Milwaukee. A similar request to invite Theodore Roosevelt, who favored the war, received only one vote. On November 20, immediately following the Armistice of November 11, 1918, the FTC voted to sever all connections with the County Council of Defense, supposedly because the County Council had printed literature without the union label.[12]

The dislike of the war was caused partly by the fear that the anti-German, anti-radical hysteria of the war and postwar years would be turned against the union movement. (Carl Haessler, a member of the

Newspaper Writers Union and a former delegate to the FTC, was sent to Alcatraz for his political activities during the war.) There was also animosity among German union members towards the anti-German, pro-British sentiments of the time. For example, in August, 1917, William Coleman of Painters Local 781 introduced a resolution at the FTC meeting calling upon Congress to find out whether Lord Northcliffe (Alfred Harmsworth) had purchased a number of daily papers in the United States in order to shape American public opinion—a common story of the times. During the municipal elections of 1918, the Socialist campaign sheet noted that Samuel Gompers, James Duncan, and Frank Morrison, all leaders of the AFL, were British born, and said: "It is hard to understand why these former British subjects should have an exclusive monopoly for loyalty and Americanism, unless the United States is really considered an English province, especially since Americans of Germanic Blood and descent form in every way as valuable and intelligent and as loyal a part of the newly forming American nation than they do, to say the least."13

Postwar Militancy

The end of the war found the labor movement stronger than it had ever been before. The continuation of the war-sponsored prosperity into the postwar era made possible a new, more militant attempt to organize workers. Revulsion against the war and wartime hysteria brought a more militant political program.

In Politics

In Milwaukee, as in the nation, the labor movement shifted to the left. In 1919 and 1920 the FTC adopted resolutions condemning the House of Representatives for refusing to seat Victor L. Berger after he had been elected. Both during and after the war the FTC opposed legal measures to suppress "radicalism" and "disloyalty." In February, 1919, the Council adopted a resolution, presented by Newspaper Writers Local 9, calling for amnesty for all political prisoners and conscientious objectors. The Council also adopted a resolution calling upon Milwaukee labor to join a nationwide strike unless Thomas Mooney, who had been convicted on specious evidence of throwing a bomb during a preparedness parade in San Francisco in 1916, was given a new trial. Only a poor return of votes in a poll of the local unions prevented a general strike on July 4, 1919. The same year, the FTC endorsed and sent a delegate to the Freedom Convention in Chicago. The Convention was working to secure the release of prisoners like Mooney and Eugene Debs, the latter imprisoned under the Espionage

Act for a speech he had made in Canton, Ohio.

In February of the following year the FTC appointed a committee to work with the Socialist Party to arrange a demonstration to "protest against any further infringements or curtailments of the liberties and freedom of the American people." In 1920 the Wisconsin Trades Union Liberty League, founded in 1915 to "devise ways and means to combat local, county option, national, or state prohibition," changed its principal objective to carrying out

the real intention of the Bill of Rights as declared in the Constitution of the United States and the Declaration of Rights stated so clearly in the Constitution of the state of Wisconsin, which is the essence of true Democracy and real Americanism. To fight for personal liberty and the economic welfare of the people and to support all persons, organizations and the press in the exercise of the privileges as guaranteed in Article I of the Bill of Rights. . . .[14]

Eager for some new outlet, the FTC sent Louis J. Green to Chicago in November, 1919, to attend the founding convention of the National Labor Party. However, the Council failed to endorse the organization because Gompers removed the leaders of city centrals who were active in the movement and because the Socialists denounced the movement as dualistic and urged its followers to back the Socialist Party instead. The FTC also refused to comply with the request of the League to Enforce Peace to adopt resolutions approving "Wilson's" League of Nations.

The militancy of the era received a boost from the Bolshevik revolution in Russia in November, 1917. In late 1918 the FTC adopted a resolution demanding the immediate cessation of hostilities in Russia and rapid demobilization of American troops. In January, 1920, the Council endorsed a report signed by William Coleman and Herman Tucker reporting that: "The working class of Russia has established a new form of government, in every sense of, for and by the people, and destined to become the guiding star for the workers of other capitalist ridden countries." The report recommended that the FTC consider the "Socialist Soviet Republic of Russia as the beginning of the liberation of the toiling masses from the injustices of the capitalist system and . . . protest against the obstacles placed in their way." The report also urged that the United States establish diplomatic relations with the Soviet Union and withdraw all troops from the country and that the unions affiliated with the FTC purchase Soviet literature to distribute to their members "in order that the rank and file of organized labor will not have to rely upon a corporation owned, controlled, and prostituted press for enlightenment upon this subject."[15]

One member of the group, John Geerlings of Typographical Local 23, refused to sign the report, arguing that the present form of government in the United States was satisfactory and that the Council should not endorse the Soviet form of government until there was more information available. Geerlings' objections were swept aside, and in December of the same year, the FTC appointed a committee of five to work with the American Labor Alliance for Trade Relations with Russia. This endorsement of the Soviet form of government, while rash, did not constitute an endorsement of American Communists. Indeed, the small group of Communists organized in 1919 included only a few former Socialists in Milwaukee and no important Milwaukee trade unionist of the time.[16]

The postwar radicalism of the FTC was not brought about by any new ideological convictions. Rather, the labor movement was reflecting the reaction against the war that swept the entire community. In the mayoralty campaign of 1920, Socialist Mayor, Daniel Hoan, increased his popular majority over that of 1916. In the fall presidential elections, Eugene V. Debs, still in prison, received almost 43,000 votes in Milwaukee county. This represented an even higher percentage of the total vote than the peak year of 1912.

In Organization

The militancy of the years during and following the war also reflected itself in the field of union organization. As early as June, 1917, the FTC discussed the advisability of starting a movement to organize the unorganized workers in Milwaukee. However, it was not until early 1918 that the Labor Forward Movement, as it was called, got underway. In March the FTC appropriated $500 for the Movement, and organization began in earnest. The Movement distributed hundreds of thousands of flyers and had representatives of the various international unions speak to unorganized workers. Open meetings were held in every section of the city. The favorable labor market created by the war, the attitude of the federal government on labor policy, and the vigorous organizing work resulted in the unionization of 2,100 workers by October. The secretary of the Movement, Louis J. Green, was able to report in October that nine new unions had been organized: Meat Cutters and Butchers, Furriers, Tannery Workers, Flat Janitors, Auto Truck Drivers and Teamsters, Molders (in railway shops), Ship Carpenters, Street Railway Employees, and Maintenance of Way Employees. Many of the existing unions increased their membership.

A campaign was started in the steel mills just prior to the outbreak of the influenza epidemic which called a halt to all public meetings in the city. With the end of the war (and the epidemic) the work of organizing the steel workers began in earnest. In August a conference of 24 national iron and steel trade unions met in Chicago. The conference adopted a program of cooperative action and created a National Committee for the Organization of the Iron and Steel Industry. Louis Green was appointed local secretary for the organizational campaign in Milwaukee, and the FTC elected William Coleman as part-time assistant business manager to work with the Movement.

It was hoped that the work of organization would be made easier when the Wisconsin state legislature passed laws restricting the use of injunctions and private detectives in labor disputes. For many years the Wisconsin State Federation of Labor had been working to secure such legislation. Its efforts were finally rewarded in 1919 when the state legislature passed a law limiting the use of the injunction. Despite the vulnerability of the state law, it was used to advantage by Wisconsin labor, especially in the first years after its enactment. The same legislature had also passed a bill requiring police and fire commission approval of license applications of detective agencies.

With the belief that the new labor legislation would in some measure curb the use of injunctions and private detectives, and capitalizing on the favorable economic conditions and the militancy of the era, the FTC and the County Central Committee of the Socialist Party formed a Strikers Aid Committee to provide help to strikers, primarily in the Cudahy packing houses, the Wisconsin Motor Company and the Illinois Steel Company. The original union representatives were Frank Weber, William Coleman and Maud McCreery, and the representatives of the Socialist Party were S. H. Franklin, George Hampel, Casimir Kowalski and Emil Seidel.

The Committee took a census of the strike situation. Rations of staples were either given to the strikers or sold at low prices. Legal aid, handled primarily by Joseph Padway, was provided in all cases growing out of the strikes. The Committee also provided medical aid, headed by Dr. S. H. Franklin. A nurse, or "strike mother," was appointed to care for the wives and children of the strikers. If any striker was threatened with eviction because he was unable to pay his rent, the Committee asked the owner to donate the rent to the strike or to give the tenant additional time to pay the rent. If all else failed, the Committee paid the rent. A number of strikers had subscribed for war bonds but had paid for only part of them when the strike began. The company refused to pay the money back or allow the strikers to get the money or bonds until the pledge had been paid in full. Therefore, the treasurer of the Strikers Aid Committee arranged for a bank loan to purchase the bonds. All told, the Committee spent about $3,500 in aiding the strikers.

In December, 1919, Frank Weber reported that 28 new unions had been organized during the past year and that there had been major gains in membership in existing unions. This was the greatest increase in the number of local unions and in membership in Milwaukee since 1903.

Despite the elaborate preparations for the strike and the excellent record of achievement in the years 1918 through most of 1920, the trade unions did not continue to improve but declined. The legal safeguards granted to trade unions proved ineffective. In June, 1920, the Wisconsin Supreme Court ruled that a strike for a closed shop at the A. J. Monday plant in Milwaukee had nothing to do with wages or conditions of employment. Therefore, the strikers were not protected by the Anti-Injunction Act of 1919. Despite the vehement protests of state labor leaders, the decision stood, putting a serious limitation on the law.[17]

In the case of the law to regulate private detective agencies, the Wisconsin Supreme Court upheld the licensing power as a constitutional delegation of power. However, despite the efforts of the FTC to use the law to keep detective agencies from operating in Milwaukee, many of the agencies failed to comply with its provisions. When the Fire and Police Commission of Milwaukee held hearings in September, 1919, three of the eight agencies summoned refused to appear. In a letter to the Commission, these agencies contended that the sheriff, the undersheriff, and several members of the Commission who were Socialists had declared before passage of the law that the agencies would not be licensed. Therefore, the agencies contended, they would not receive a fair hearing. Of those agencies which had been most active in opposing the law (Pinkerton, Burns, Russell, and Corporations Auxiliary), only the Corporations Auxiliary received a license. Most of its licensed offices did not engage in industrial espionage.

Though there were few licensed detective agencies in the city, there was evidence that the agencies continued to do industrial work for employers. An investigation by the Industrial Commission in October, 1920, made clear that the Russell agency was using labor spies as effectively as before the law was passed. Russell admitted that he held several unions cards and could get his men into key positions in almost any union in Milwaukee.

A second factor halting the continued expansion of the unions was lack of cooperation among the various trade unions during the postwar strike wave. The campaign to organize the iron and steel industry nationally had been successful in its initial phase. Its ultimate defeat was in no small part caused by the wrangling of the "cooperating" international unions. The same situation occurred in other cases. Machinists Local 66, for example, charged that during a strike at the Power Mining Machine Company of Cudahy the Molders Union had conspired with the company to break the Machinists' strike.[18]

Finally, the militancy of the time alienated public opinion. The creation of the Communist Party in 1919 convinced some the nation was in danger. A strike that paralyzed Seattle, Washington, in the same year caused the mayor of Seattle to denounce the strikers as Bolsheviks and revolutionaries. The denunciation was quickly circulated throughout the nation. A strike of policemen in Boston in September, 1919, brought an outbreak of rowdyism in that city. The public was not simply alarmed but became almost hysterical. Capping this was a strike of almost 400,000 men in steel and the beginning of long and violent struggles in the bituminous coal industry. A "Red Scare" enveloped the nation. Affecting the Socialists least, it drove the Communist Party underground and virtually destroyed what was left of the IWW. Though not directed at orthodox trade unions, it convinced many that unions were at least suspect.

Thus, the inadequacy of legal protection, the lack of cooperation between unions, and the alienation of public opinion coupled with a sharp, though brief, recession in 1921 brought an end to the advances of labor. A new era of stagnation and decline began. "Normalcy" had arrived.

A Decade of Deterioration

THE depression brought an increase in the rate of unemployment from 2.3 per cent in 1919 to 11.9 per cent in 1921. Average hourly earnings in manufacturing, which had been 55.5 cents in 1920, fell to 51.5 cents in 1921 and 48.7 cents in 1922. A number of unions in Milwaukee, such as the Sheet Metal, Brewery, and Railroad Workers, started strikes in the years 1921 to 1923 in an attempt to resist wage cuts; they were unsuccessful. The Federated Trades Council urged local and federal government to launch a public-works program, but the suggestion was not followed, and in 1923 the depression ended and the rate of unemployment in the nation fell to 3.2 per cent. Throughout the remainder of the Twenties, money-wage rates slowly rose while prices remained relatively stable.

Normally the prosperous times would have been the signal for renewed attempts to organize workers and a resumption of the growth of trade unionism. Organizational drives were started in 1923, 1924, and 1925 but with very discouraging results. During all of 1924 and half of 1925 the FTC failed to appoint a general organizer, partially because of lack of funds but primarily because of the failure of unionism to attract the unorganized workers. From 1923 through 1933 there were but 40 strikes in Milwaukee, and in 1927 the Bureau of Labor Statistics recorded none. Similarly, trade-union membership in the city declined from the high of 35,000 in 1920 to only 20,000 in 1932. In other words, trade-union membership in Milwaukee in 1932 was no greater than it had been at the turn of the century. The advantages obtained from years of work had been completely wiped out.[1]

The disappointing results of these years prompted Frank Weber to write in 1927: "After being an active member of the organized labor movement for three score years, I am becoming somewhat discontented with the members of organized labor for their POLICY OF IN-DIF-

FERENCE and DO-NOTHING SPIRIT that is at present prevailing among the members of the organized labor movement." Two years later, Weber wrote to his long-time Socialist friend, William Coleman: "The Labor movement is going through a crucial period, as it is being mislead by the glitter of the age . . . and does not see how the links for the chain that will bind to a most degraded servitude condition are being forged."[2]

The American Plan

The decline of the labor movement was caused in part, as Weber said, by the "glitter of the age." But the resumption of the open-shop movement by employers materially aided the decline of the unions. Just as the growth of unions between 1899 and 1904 brought a counterattack by employers so too the phenomenal growth of unions during and after the war brought a new assault by employers. Just as before, employers centered their campaign around the principle that every American had the right to accept employment under conditions he felt were satisfactory without interference by a union. The campaign for the open shop was fought in virtually every state in the nation; in the Middle West the campaign was probably more virulent than elsewhere. In January, 1921, a conference of 22 state manufacturers' associations meeting in Chicago officially adopted the name "American Plan" for the campaign.

In March, 1919, Frank Weber predicted that "Big Business would henceforth withdraw its open opposition to the Trades Union Movement, having commenced to inaugurate so-called Independent Councils . . . ." The first move in the attempt to replace the unions in Milwaukee with independent councils, or company unions, was the elimination of the advantages unions had gained during the war. Consequently, in the next few years, a number of unions were engaged in strikes to prevent the adoption of the open-shop policy. Often employers coupled a demand for "deflating wartime wages" with the demand for the open shop. On March 26, 1920, about 40 of the leading mason contractors of Milwaukee adopted, with but one dissenting vote, a resolution in favor of the open-shop policy. Other employers in the building trades followed suit. By early 1922 the secretary of the Milwaukee Master Carpenters Association was able to report that the carpenters, who had never organized more than 50 per cent of the workers, had only 10 per cent organized.

The heart of the open-shop campaign in Milwaukee was centered about the Milwaukee Employers Council. During the strike of the Auto, Aircraft, and Vehicle Workers Union at the A. J. Monday plant in 1919, a number of open-shop employers had joined with the company to defeat the demand of the union for a closed shop. These employers decided to continue their cooperation, and as a result the Milwaukee Employers Council was organized. By July 1921 the Employers Council included 28 industrial groups, representing a total of 602 plants and about 60,000 workers in the city, more than half of Milwaukee's total industrial strength. The Employers Council defined the open shop to mean "the employment of workmen as individuals, regardless of their affiliation or non-affiliation with a labor union, and no employment contracts with labor unions." The council retained an attorney, Leon B. Lamfrom, to handle the employers' side of most strike cases in the state. The Employers Council also maintained membership in the League for Industrial Rights (formerly named the American Anti-Boycott Association) which fought the demands of the unions before the courts and gave advice to its members on the latest developments in personnel work and "industrial democracy."

Beginning in January, 1924, the Council also published a monthly bulletin, *Freedom in Employment*. One edition of the bulletin contained general information critical of unionism and was distributed to interested persons throughout the state; a supplement, dealing only with the activities of the organization was sent to members only. Early in its organization the Council also conducted an "information exchange" which supplied details about active unions and their members. Later, the Council maintained an open-shop directory to encourage its members to patronize only open-shop manufacturers.[3]

The Milwaukee Employers Council's conception of the open shop did not mean simply a shop where union and non-union members were equally accepted. An important requirement was the refusal of any contract with a closed shop. In the words of the Milwaukee Employers Council: "Please understand that when you contract with closed shops in *any industry,* or buy from them, you are more an opponent of the Open Shop than organized labor itself, *because you undermine the sincerity of the movement.*"[4] The requirements of the Employers Council were quite high. In December, 1930, the Council blacklisted a sheet metal contractor for allegedly being an opponent of the open shop. As a consequence, the contractor lost business and asked the Employers Council to retract its statement. The contractor claimed he employed both union and non-union men, had no agreement with the union, and did not comply with the union wage scale. The Employers Council refused to retract their statement, because "by more important tests he is still unable to qualify." The Council noted that at times he accepted contracts requiring the exclusive use of union men and the payment of union wages, he secured his men from the union, and, worst of all, he was on the union "fair list" of contractors.

It soon became apparent to the unions that the tactics of the Milwaukee Employers Council were quite successful. The unions attempted to meet the threat by promoting union-label products, by calling upon union members to demand the union card of fellow workers, and by asking the American Federation of Labor and the Building Trades Department to carry on a vigorous organizing campaign in Milwaukee. However, all of these efforts proved ineffective, and trade-union membership continued to decline while company unions grew.[5]

The Appeal to Legislation

The rebuff on the economic front turned the emphasis of the FTC to legislative activity, causing the Milwaukee Employers Council to change its method of attack on unions. In Milwaukee, the Socialist administration awarded city building and printing contracts only to unionized firms. Hence, the Employers Council attempted to reduce the influence of unions in the city government. Its greatest victory came when Herman A. Wagner, president of the Employers Council, asked the courts to restrain the city council from paying bills for public printing unless the contracts had been awarded to the lowest competitive bidder. The Wisconsin Supreme Court concurred with Wagner's contention. The real objective of the suit was to end union printing, although this was not mentioned in the decision.

On the state level, the Milwaukee Employers Council began to send representatives to oppose many of labor's bills and to introduce a number of its own in the legislature, particularly regarding labor disputes. However, the Council did not meet with much success because: (1) it represented a comparatively small group of actively-open-shop employers in Milwaukee, (2) there were few big strikes in Wisconsin during the twenties to make labor-disputes legislation important to employers outside of Milwaukee, and (3) the Wisconsin Manufacturers Association, formed in 1910, but not active until 1915, had already taken the position as the accredited representative of employers in the state.

The Wisconsin Manufacturers Association took the position that labor legislation not greatly in advance of other states was desirable but any law imposing additional burdens on Wisconsin manufacturers was undesirable. The more conciliatory attitude of the Wisconsin Manufacturers Association and the relative weakness of the Milwaukee Employers Council in the state legislature helped the unions.

Moreover, the progressive Republicans regained control of the governorship under John J. Blaine (1921-27).[6]

Limitation of Injunctions

As was previously noted, the 1919 state law restricting the issuance of the injunction was seriously weakened in the A. J. Monday case. However, in 1923 an amendment to the law made the restriction on injunctions applicable to picketing "growing out of any dispute whatsoever concerning employment." The law also provided that a temporary restraining order could not be issued without 48-hours' notice to the party against whom it was to be issued. Another act passed in 1923 provided for trial by jury in any case arising from a violation of an injunction. An attempt was made to question the constitutionality of the jury trial law in a case which arose from a long strike in Milwaukee.

Since 1916 the David Adler Clothing Company had had intermittent disputes with the Amalgamated Clothing Workers local union. On the death of the senior partner, a complete break with the Amalgamated local began. In April, 1928, the company announced the adoption of an open shop and ordered its employees to sign yellow-dog contracts. About 800 employees were locked out by the company. During the ensuing struggle, Socialists, such as Victor Berger, Daniel Hoan, George Gauer, Hauser, and Norman Thomas provided moral support to the workers. An injunction was issued against the union; when one of the strikers violated the injunction by throwing paint he was tried for contempt of court. A jury trial was granted, but the jury disagreed and did not return a verdict. The guilt of the defendant was obvious, and the judge protested the outcome of the case. He questioned the constitutionality of the jury trial law and referred the question to the Wisconsin Supreme Court. The higher court refused to take jurisdiction since the lower court had not made a decision. Meanwhile the Supreme Court dissolved the injunction on the grounds that the parties did not come into court with "clean hands." The contempt proceedings died with the closing of the injunction case, and no further action was taken. This left the constitutionality of the jury trial law in doubt, since a judge in the lower court had questioned it, but the higher court had expressed no definite opinion.

To strengthen the jury trial law, the Wisconsin State Federation of Labor introduced a new bill into the 1929 legislature. The bill passed, but, largely through the efforts of the Milwaukee Employers Council, was vetoed by Governor Walter Kohler, Sr. Success was finally achieved in 1931 when the progressive Republicans, led by Governor

Philip La Follette, passed the desired law.

On the federal level the labor movement was less successful. The immunity from injunctions labor believed it had gained through the Clayton Act was steadily whittled away in a series of decisions by the United States Supreme Court.[7]

Fraudulent Advertising

In 1922 a decision of the Wisconsin Supreme Court seriously limited the effectiveness of the 1911 law requiring companies to mention the existence of a strike in their ads for additional help. In a case growing out of a dispute at the West Allis Foundry Company, the Court, in essence, ruled that the employer could determine whether or not a strike was still in effect. Immediately after the decision, the Wisconsin Federation of Labor, supported by the Socialists and Governor Blaine, was able to get the legislature to pass a bill taking the decision out of the hands of employers. The Milwaukee Employers Council attempted to have the law repealed but was unsuccessful.[8]

Regulation of Detective Agencies

An attempt was made by the detective agencies in 1921 to take the issuance of licenses out of the hands of the Fire and Police Commission and instead have them issued by the Secretary of State with the approval of five citizens. Organized labor and the Socialists vigorously fought the bill, but it passed. Assemblyman Polakowski, a Socialist from Milwaukee, took the bill to Governor Blaine who vetoed it. However, the law passed in 1919 regulating detective agencies had been less effective than the unions had hoped. In 1925 organized labor was successful in getting a law which required agencies, and also individual private detectives, to get a license.

Almost immediately the Pinkerton and Corporation Auxiliary agencies in Milwaukee tried to get the federal courts to declare the law unconstitutional, but the United States Supreme Court upheld the law in 1927. The agencies did almost nothing to comply with the law. Of those engaged in industrial espionage, only the Russell agency had a license, obtained in Whitefish Bay after Milwaukee refused to grant one. In 1927 the Corporation Auxiliary agency applied for an injunction from the circuit court on the grounds that its employees were not private detectives but "welfare workers, efficiency engineers, and educational experts" whose job was to "harmonize industrial conditions," secrecy being essential to their business. The judge refused the injunction, holding that the names used by the agencies did not conceal the fact that they were private detectives.

The law was effective primarily because the Milwaukee Fire and Police Commission followed the policy of refusing approval of license applications of agencies engaged in industrial espionage. Several agencies abandoned their Milwaukee offices; others, like the Pinkerton agency, obtained licenses by dropping their industrial work. The Russell agency kept its Whitefish Bay office, but did little industrial work after 1928.[9]

Other Legislation

Labor was also victorious in having the yellow-dog contract declared unenforceable in the courts. Support of rural legislators was gained by including contracts directed against farmers' cooperatives. The bill passed the legislature in 1929, anticipating by three years the Norris-LaGuardia Act.

During the 1920's wage and hour laws were improved, a number of laws licensing trades were passed (significant as an indication of the breakdown of the protection which unions formerly provided) and the state minimum wage law was changed to meet the objections of the United States Supreme Court. On the whole, the 1920's were fruitful years in the abundance of favorable labor legislation passed. But whatever potential impact the flood of legislation might have had in opening doors for the expansion of trade unionism, in fact, the trade unions were incapable of taking advantage of their opportunities. Attention drifted from organization to cooperation and labor education.[10]

Labor Education

In 1920 the Federated Trades Council became interested in the Milwaukee Consumers Cooperative Association. The cooperative was organized in conjunction with the American Society of Equity along the lines of the Rochdale plan. In the beginning it was hoped that the cooperative would handle commodities purchased in car lots and delivered from a central point to the purchasers, thereby materially reducing the cost of the products. Interest in the venture grew, and in 1921 the first store was opened on Nineteenth Street and Fond du Lac Avenue. The FTC soon endorsed the proposal, and other stores were opened.

In 1921 the FTC also purchased stock in the city-sponsored Garden-Homes project, primarily as an endorsement of the first public, low-cost, cooperative housing project in the United States. Only because the Milwaukee Socialists had started the Commonwealth Mutual Savings Bank in 1912 did the trade unions of the city fail to become deeply involved in union banking, an interest common among unionists in the 1920's. Much more important was the growing interest in workers' education—the only real achievement of the unions in an otherwise bleak decade.

As early as 1888 the trade unions in Milwaukee had organized a Workingmen's Reading Club with contributions of money, books, and papers from citizens of the city. Lectures were given by public officials and religious leaders, but nothing permanent resulted from this attempt to "elevate the minds" of the working people. The Workingmen's Reading Club was purely a manifestation of the "uplift" mentality of the time. In 1890 the FTC had discussed the advisability of arranging for a series of debates on economic and political questions, but the Council failed to create any educational program which would analyze current events. In the following years, the idea of workers' education languished while attention was diverted to other problems. In 1908 the FTC urged members of organized labor to take advantage of correspondence courses offered by the University of Wisconsin, and in 1909 the Painters Union established a reading room for the benefit of painters who were out of work because of cold weather.

At the 1905 convention of the Wisconsin State Federation of Labor, Victor Berger, chairman of the Committee on Education, presented a resolution recommending that "suitable lectures be arranged in meeting halls or lodge rooms from time to time." This and another resolution calling upon the labor press to give periodic reviews on books of interest to workers were adopted, but nothing concrete was done. At the 1914 convention of the State Federation another resolution was adopted urging central labor bodies and individual unions to organize classes for the study of labor problems and have their members take suitable courses offered by the University Extension Division; again nothing was done. The convention of 1920 brought a recommendation from the Special Committee on Education that labor provide instruction for its membership.[11]

Finally, in December, 1921, the Executive Board of the FTC recommended the adoption of a plan sent out by the State Federation to establish a labor college. On January 4, 1922, the Council formally endorsed the proposition and elected nine trustees—Brown, William Coleman, Jacob Friedrick, James P. Sheehan, Metcalfe, Edward H. Kiefer, John J. Handley, Schaefer and Henry Ohl—to inaugurate the program. The program called for a ten-weeks' course with instruction in the history of the labor movement, economics, and English. A budget of $400 was proposed to cover expenses. This money was to be raised through a moderate tuition fee and contributions from the unions. The Board of Trustees of the labor college sent out a letter to the affiliated unions outlining the plan.

Realizing the need for training facilities through which men and women in the ranks of organized labor may gain a better knowledge and insight into the problems confronting labor so that they may be able to work more effectively in the cause of labor, the Milwaukee Federated Trades Council has undertaken the establishment of the Milwaukee Workers' College.

It is our ultimate aim to train economists, statisticians, organizers, and speakers from our own ranks, with our own point of view, who are fully capable of representing our own interests. As the school grows and develops other courses will be added, such as Statistics, Parliamentary Practice, and Psychology. Special lectures will also be given by persons prominent in the labor and educational fields.

The Milwaukee Workers College had an auspicious beginning. Meeting in the civil-service rooms of the City Hall, the first three classes of the College had an average enrollment of 95 and an average attendance of 35. The following year, the College began to receive valuable assistance from the Milwaukee Public Library. Miriam Tompkins and Catherine Hitt of the library worked to make the facilities more useful to the unions. The library compiled a list of trade books useful to the Workers College and made available rooms where classes could be held—the first public library in the country to take great interest in workers' education.

The workers'-education movement in Wisconsin outside of Milwaukee started slowly, but largely through the efforts of Henry Ohl, Jr., the movement grew, and by the winter of 1927-1928 there were some 17 classes in a dozen industrial centers of the state. However, 1928 was the high point of the movement, and only Milwaukee maintained its college without a break in the years following 1922. This may be attributed to the presence of the Wisconsin State Federation of Labor leaders in the city, the larger financial resources of the FTC, the wide choice of capable teachers available, and the large membership which could be induced to attend.

Even with these advantages, the Workers College in Milwaukee during the years 1922 to 1936 rarely offered more than two classes, and often there was but one class in session at any given time. The results were disappointing, but, as Ernest Schwarztrauber wrote:

. . . a great deal had in fact been accomplished. Through experimentation on its own, labor had learned what its handicaps were and what a stupendous task was ahead of it. And while it was carrying on this intra-labor experimentation, its attention was also drawn to the possibilities opened up by two other ventures in the field of workers' education, ventures initiated and financed in those very areas to which its fundamental philosophy had been turning its attention. These were the state-financed University Summer School for Workers and the federally financed workers' education project of the depression era of the 1930's.

The University of Wisconsin's School for Workers had its beginnings in the Summer School for Women Workers initiated by the
University YWCA in Madison. This Summer School started on a bad
footing in 1924, but in 1925 a planning committee of University faculty members, YWCA leaders, and upper-class University-of-Wisconsin
students worked for the first official Summer-School-for-Women-Work-
ers' session. In the beginning, the Summer School was supported by
employers, women's clubs, and some miscellaneous groups and individuals. Organized labor slowly began to take interest in the project, and
from 1925 to 1937 union enrollment rose from 10 to 97 per cent. Similarly, from 1925 to 1936 non-labor financial support dropped from 100
to 63 per cent, and by 1949 labor support and labor union enrollment
was nearly 100 per cent. In 1928 the School became coeducational
when two men were able to attend the sessions with the aid of two
$100 scholarships offered by the FTC. However, whatever benefit was
derived from the workers' education movement in the long run, the
trade unions themselves continued to decrease in membership during
the 1920's. This decrease served to undermine the Socialist Party in
Milwaukee, ultimately resulting in a reorientation of the ideology of
the Federated Trades Council.[12]

The Recess of Politics

As mentioned in the last chapter, the postwar radicalism of the
FTC had, among other things, brought an endorsement of the Soviet
form of government. Following this, there was a brief period of friendly toleration for the Communists in America. In 1921 the FTC voted
to permit the Workmen's Circle of the city to send letters to FTC-
affiliated unions appealing for financial aid for a hospital in the Soviet
Union. The same year the FTC joined with the Socialist Party to arrange a meeting—poorly attended—for William Z. Foster, the Communist leader, to speak on the labor movement and the Russian fam-
ine. A local branch of Foster's Trade Union Educational League was
also formed. Unconscious of the objective of the TUEL to capture the
labor movement for the Communist Party, the FTC gave it some support. However, the outspoken opposition of the leadership of the
American Federation of Labor, combined with the hostility of the
right-wing Socialists represented by Victor L. Berger, changed the
attitude of the FTC. By 1930 the growing opposition of the Council
was expressed in the appointment of a committee to investigate the
activities of the "Communists and anti-AFL" organizations.

The primary allegiance of the Milwaukee labor movement remained with the Socialist Party—a very conservative Socialist Party.

While there had been strains during the First World War, the breach was healed in the postwar years. The FTC continued to give financial aid to the labor-Socialist members of legislative bodies. The unions also continued to benefit from the Socialist city administration.

The policy in Milwaukee was as follows: immediately after a strike was called, the chief of police would invite the strike committee into his office where he would receive a pledge of no violence, and a promise of aid in ferreting out any violators. The strike committee would also agree to cooperate with the department in the protection of property and to limit the number of pickets to avoid interference with traffic. In turn, the chief would offer his cooperation in guaranteeing their right to picket and offer to send the police to protect pickets if necessary. Even in the year-and-a-half-long struggle between the Amalgamated Clothing Workers and the Adler Clothing Company, no arrests were made on the picket line. According to Mayor Hoan, the only disorders worth mentioning were caused by private detectives. (He evidently forgot the paint-throwing incident.) "The police," wrote Hoan, "cooperated in running these culprits out of the city and from then on no further disorders occurred."

The trade unions also continued to support the Socialist Milwaukee *Leader*. When the mailing privileges of that newspaper were restored in 1920, it became apparent that the paper would have to be refinanced; 72 Milwaukee unions subscribed to its stock. After Victor Berger's death in 1929, the *Leader* required a second refinancing, and again the labor unions came to the rescue. A new organization was chartered, Publishers Inc., and the unions subscribed to its stock. The Brewery Workers took $16,000 worth of stock, the Carpenters, $2,500, the Bricklayers, $1,500, and the Hosiery Workers, Plasterers, Amalgamated Clothing Workers of Milwaukee and the Amalgamated of Chicago each invested $1,000. The FTC itself, as of 1929, owned $200 worth of mortgage bonds and nearly $1,000 worth of stock.[13]

The relationship between the Socialists and the trade-union movement was not, however, as close as may have been suggested. Quite noticeably in the years following the war, the FTC tended to be politically conservative and to shy away from third-party activity. Increasingly the Council refused to endorse any political party or person. Typical was the response of the executive board of the FTC to a request of the Amalgamated Meat Cutters and Butcher Workmen's Local 409 to endorse one of its members as a candidate for alderman from the sixteenth ward.

Your Board holds that if organized labor desires to remain a militant body of workers in the many economic battles . . . then the Federated Trades Council

... cannot afford to recommend or endorse any political party or any person ... for, the organized labor movement must never surrender its rights in the economic struggle, that is, the right to criticize, to oppose and to demand, which right it would abrogate if it would recommend and endorse ... for it would then become ... directly responsible for the acts and deeds of the political party and those persons it recommended....

Your executive board is in no way opposed to political action by the organized workers, but it also realizes that organized labor can only succeed in the political field when the members of organized labor have been sufficiently educated to understand that there is a working class struggle and that it is the duty of every member of organized labor to support ... the political party that demands for the worker the full value of his or her labor.[14]

The "no politics" policy was illusory. The Socialist Party, it would be argued, was still the only party that demanded for the worker the "full value of his . . . labor." But there was a real cooling of trade-union ardor for political action. When in March 1921 the Socialist Party asked the aid of the unions in getting out the vote in the coming judicial and school board elections, the members were merely told to "take note." In previous years, this request would have resulted in the immediate appointment of a committee to canvass all the affiliated unions and probably brought about a mass meeting.

It is interesting to note that in 1924 the FTC did not pass any resolution officially backing the candidacy of Robert M. La Follette for president. Here was a man who was known as a "friend of labor," who had been endorsed by the American Federation of Labor, the Wisconsin State Federation of Labor, and the Socialist Party. Yet the FTC passed no resolutions, appointed no committees, held no mass meetings. The files of the Council show but one mimeographed letter sent to affiliated unions urging them to vote for La Follette and Wheeler. It was not that La Follette was disliked by labor for, when he died, he was eulogized by the FTC in these words: "The members of the organized labor movement in the state recognize . . . the fundamental truth that Senator Robert M. La Follette spent his life in doing good and ever defending what he believed to be the true guide for social justice." Rather, the inactivity of the Council was the result of its growing disenchantment with third party politics.[15] There were a number of reasons for the declining influence of the Socialist Party in trade-union circles.

1. The growth of Socialism in America, as in Milwaukee, had been encouraging, but in 1912 the party had reached its peak. The labor unions wanted more political victories and consequently looked for a broader base for political action. On March 7, 1920, the Wisconsin State Federation of Labor sponsored a Conference of Liberal Or-

ganizations of Wisconsin. Present were six members of the Socialist Party representing the State Federation and three, the Party proper. There were also delegates of the three railway brotherhoods, the Society of Equity, the Nonpartisan League, and the Committee of 48, a group of intellectual liberals headed by Arthur J. Sweet. The group rejected the idea of capturing the Republican party or asking candidates of any party to support their platform and decided instead to create a new vehicle which would name candidates wherever the Socialists were not strong.

At the 1921 convention of the State Federation, the delegates went on record favoring a Farmer-Labor Party and asked the approval of unions in the state. A number of labor groups, like the FTC, rejected the proposal, indicating they still wanted to work with the Socialist Party. As a result of the vote by the affiliated unions, the State Federation decided against immediately launching a new political party. The Executive Board of the State Federation did, however, send representatives to the Conference for Progressive Political Action, which served as the political vehicle for La Follette's presidential campaign in 1924.

The Wisconsin State Federation enthusiastically entered into the La Follette campaign, and by the end of the 1920's, there was again serious discussion about a political movement that would not be exclusively Socialist. While nothing concrete was done to form a Farmer-Labor Party until the 1930's, the discussions of the 1920's indicated dissatisfaction with the performance of the Socialists. Further, when the Socialists did enter various alliances, such as the 1924 La Follette campaign, it proved disastrous to its membership, already much reduced after World War I.

2. The trade unions were no longer completely dependent upon the Socialists for legislative work. In 1915 the State Federation of Labor employed its own lobbyist in Madison. Also, it had become apparent that almost all of the legislative victories on the state scene depended on the cooperation of the progressive Republicans.

3. There was mutual dissatisfaction over the necessity for a candidate to be acceptable to both the Socialists and the trade unionists. For example, in 1930 Meta Berger was not endorsed by the Socialists to succeed her late husband in Congress because she had used non-union labor to build her son-in-law's home in Ozaukee County. Although the Building Trades Council denied it had used its influence to prevent her nomination, the nomination went to county supervisor James P. Sheehan, an active union member. Various local unions were also disappointed when their members failed to receive the endorsement of the FTC because they were not Socialists.

4. The Building Trades Council in 1928 endorsed its own slate of candidates for Common Council in the spring and for the Senate and Assembly in the fall. It believed that by endorsing Democrats and Republicans as well as Socialists, it could strengthen its political bargaining position.

5. In the 1920's, the Socialists lost certain important symbols. The death of Eugene V. Debs, beloved by Socialist trade unionists, was followed by the death of Victor L. Berger who had been so important in forging the Socialist-labor alliance.[16]

6. Some labor leaders came to believe that the Socialists were not particularly interested in trade unionism but were only interested in furthering their own political fortunes. In 1931 J. J. Handley of the State Federation wrote:

> When the re-organization [of the Milwaukee *Leader* in 1929] took place we expected the labor unions would receive more direct information concerning our economic organizations, but the policy has fallen into the same old rut. The political party is the one and only thing considered.
>
> The Wisconsin Federation of Labor presented a large number of labor measures to the legislature. Many of them were given to Socialist members to introduce, but in each instance when a measure was introduced, or when it was heard before a committee, or action taken by the legislature, if any views at all were given they were given as Socialist measures, sometimes mentioning that the measure was supported by the Federation of Labor.
>
> . . . The fact is the paper is a socialist publication and does not intend to further the interest of the economic organization if there is an opportunity to promote the political end.
>
> . . . I trust the labor members on the Board of Directors will consider this matter, and if no marked change can be made steps should be taken by the Wisconsin Federation of Labor to issue its own publication, if only a weekly bulletin.[17]

In the face of the many things working against the Socialist-labor alliance, it is a wonder the alliance was not ended in the 1920's. Working against an immediate severance of the historic relationship were principally three factors: (1) The Socialists had been in the past, and were presently, aiding in the passage of favorable labor legislation through collaboration in the state legislature with the progressive Republicans. (2) The continued personal popularity of Mayor Daniel Hoan kept the Socialists in control of the mayor's office where some aid and comfort could be given the unions. (3) The FTC was still led by faithful Socialists like Frank Weber. Despite his relatively conservative views, which at times antagonized more progressive Socialists, Weber was personally loyal to the party. But as time went on, there would be fewer labor leaders who would denounce capitalism as "the sum of all villainies, the father of all crimes, the mother of all abominations, the devil's best friend, and God's worst enemy." Few indeed would be the number of labor leaders who cried out: "No nobler cause [Socialism] has ever called to action and no greater victory has stood within such an easy reach of those who battle for a nobler, higher and grander civilization of the human family."[18]

Declining trade-union membership robbed the Socialist movement of its dependable support; the increasing acculturation of the Milwaukee labor movement to the American scene lessened the attractiveness of Socialism itself; the conflicts of the past decade had loosened the bonds between the two movements. In the next decade the remaining bulwarks of the alliance would be removed, and the New Deal would deliver the *coup de grace*. The Socialist Party of Milwaukee was dying.

The Milwaukee labor movement had invested heavily in the Socialist Party, primarily in terms of time and effort. Now the returns on their investment—political victory by the Socialists—seemed near an end. The alliance had given rise to the story that the Socialists had "put the trade-union movement out of commission in Milwaukee." No easy answer could be given to the charge. If the energies channeled into political action had been translated into organizing activities, the Milwaukee labor movement might have had a larger membership and internal conflicts might have been minimized. However, such an answer is purely conjectural, for the emotional basis for action would have been removed. Further, the trade unions of Milwaukee had gained a friendly city administration and favorable legislation from both city and state, the latter partially due to the work of the Socialists.[19]

However, at the end of the 1920's the situation was not particularly encouraging, and in 1929 the prosperity of the age came to an end.

CHAPTER XII

Unions in the Great Depression

T HE stock-market crash in October, 1929, was but a herald of things to come. In the next three years, stock prices fell to one-third their former level while the business failure rate rose from 104 in 1929 to 154 per 10,000 in 1932. By 1933 employment had dropped by nine million to less than thirty-eight million, and the number of unemployed persons had increased by more than eleven million to twelve million; the rate of unemployment was an unprecedented 25 per cent. Wages and prices plummeted as national output fell by one-fourth.

Business and labor leaders and public officials were equally despondent. They neither understood the causes of the greatest economic calamity in the history of the nation nor were they able to offer any way out.

The national leadership of the AFL declared it favored jobs, not a dole, but failed to indicate how jobs could be created. In Milwaukee unions were less opposed to direct government action. The Federated Trades Council appealed to local government to issue vouchers for lodging and meals to unemployed workers, and fought attempts by the city to cut the wages of its workers. The FTC declared "it is the province, duty and in the power of the national government . . . to give immediate and adequate relief." The Council demanded that the federal government pay the veterans' bonus and issue $10 billion in "emergency currency" to finance public works.

But the situation continued to deteriorate. Wages of many workers were cut, and a number of affiliated locals found it impossible to pay their dues to the FTC because of financial distress. Between 1929 and 1933 the number of employed wage workers in Milwaukee dropped by over 50,000. It became apparent that Milwaukee was harder hit by the depression than most industrial communities. The outlook seemed bleak.

On June 15, 1932, the FTC heard an address by an instructor in economics at Milwaukee State Teachers College on "Are We Drifting Toward Revolution?" The minutes of the meeting summarized the address as follows:

> He analyzed the conditions which brought about revolutions in the past and showed that the same conditions of poverty and oppression on the one hand and concentration of wealth and extravagant luxury on the other are existing today. He urged the appointment of committees by labor to study the present situation and to work out plans for the workers taking over industries and establishments necessary for the production of the necessaries of life.

The Council passed a motion to investigate the proposal and report back at a future meeting. No report was ever made, but the transient interest in the idea was indicative of the dispirited attitude of the Council.[1]

The already-depleted membership of the AFL fell from three million in 1929 to slightly over two million in 1933. The Milwaukee labor movement declined proportionately. There was little to cheer labor. It did not realize it was on the eve of its greatest advance.

Relief for the Unemployed

The large number of unemployed finally brought action by government. On the local level, the Socialist Party appeared to be in a position to act. In the election of 1932 the Socialists captured three of the four major city offices and almost gained a clear majority in the Common Council. However, when the Socialists sought to implement their program of a shorter work week to stimulate employment, the nonpartisans defeated the measure.

On the state level, Wisconsin started a program of eliminating grade crossings in 1931 to provide employment for 75,000. The state Emergency Relief Act of 1932 provided that public-relief agencies should attempt to give the opportunity to work to those in need of relief. From the beginning of the depression to November, 1933, work relief in Wisconsin was under local control with the Industrial Commission drawing only broad outlines for local plans. In November 1933 the federal government started its Civil Works Administration which provided new employment opportunities. All local relief in Wisconsin was either stopped or absorbed by the CWA. On April 1, 1934, the Wisconsin Emergency Relief Administration was organized to act as the state agency for the Federal Emergency Relief Administration.

The local, state, and federal relief programs did not meet with the unqualified support of the unions. Wages on work programs were set to equal prevailing rates in the community. Unions complained that these wages were generally lower than union rates. In most of the larger cities of the state strikes disturbed the programs, and discontented groups of unemployed workers sometimes used mass demonstrations to focus attention on their plight. When long-range relief programs were instituted, particularly the Works Project Administration, unions in Milwaukee renewed charges that wages were too low, that unskilled were replacing skilled workers, and that relief workers were used to do the work of regular city and county employees.[2]

Another approach to the problem was unemployment-compensation legislation, although it was obvious that this could not cope with the large numbers of unemployed. Most influential in securing final passage of a bill were persons from the University of Wisconsin, religious and public groups, and the Wisconsin State Federation of Labor. The State Federation led the movement to gain endorsement of unemployment insurance by the American Federation of Labor. The long struggle, begun in 1921, ended with the signing of an unemployment-compensation bill by Governor Philip La Follette on January 29, 1932. But the unemployment-insurance law, the first passed in the nation, and the various relief projects neither ended the depression nor provided the incentive for increased organizational work by the unions.[3]

Legislation Affecting Unions

One achievement that, to some extent, helped unions in the state was the passage of a unified labor code. The Wisconsin State Federation of Labor had listed a unified code as one of the important labor measures it planned to introduce in the 1931 state legislature. Primarily a codification of existing legislation, the bill provided additional limitations to temporary restraining orders and gave further legal protection to strikes and boycotts. The bill was introduced into the Senate in 1931 by Senator T. N. Duncan, a Socialist. Despite opposition from the Milwaukee Employers Council, it was passed, becoming the first unified labor code in the United States.

Even more important was legislation on the federal level. The Norris-LaGuardia Act of 1932 severely limited the use of injunctions in labor disputes and made the yellow-dog contract unenforceable as a matter of public policy. The law also recognized the right of workers to organize and bargain collectively, but employers frequently evaded the law by forcing employees to join company unions.

The situation changed, however, after the election of 1932. Franklin Roosevelt's "New Deal" represented no coherent economic philosophy, but it was willing to experiment. The first New Deal measure directly affecting unions was the National Industrial Recovery Act passed in June, 1933. The act was intended to aid business by allowing industry to write codes of fair competition. The codes, however, had to contain safeguards for labor. Section 7(a) required that every code include recognition of the workers' right to organize unions free of employer domination and to engage in collective bargaining. This legislation was less significant for its specific safeguards for labor unions, which were almost impossible to enforce, than for the interest in organization that it stirred among the workers.[4]

The Revival of Unions

On August 18, 1933, the Milwaukee *Sentinel* reported:

An intensive effort to unionize all laborers in Milwaukee under provision of the National [Industrial] Recovery Act, giving them the right to organize as they wish without interference from employers, has brought about 5,000 into labor unions here in the last few weeks. . . .

. . . .

Union meetings are being held here nightly and labor is invading industries which always have closed the door to unions, with considerable success, the labor leaders say. Application for memberships in the various unions are pouring into headquarters in Brisbane Hall so rapidly that officials find themselves swamped, [J. J.] Handley [secretary of the Wisconsin State Federation of Labor] asserted.

The increased activity of the labor unions was reflected in the strike statistics. In 1933 there were but six strikes in Milwaukee; in 1934 the number increased to 42. In 1934 there were 13,980 workers involved in strikes whereas in 1933 there had been only 482.

The Street Railway Strike

The outstanding strike of 1934 involved the Milwaukee Electric Railway and Light Company. The conflict started when the company refused to comply with an order of the NRA's National Labor Relations Board. The Board found the company guilty of discrimination and directed it to reinstate thirteen discharged employees. Subsequent investigations by the United States Senate's Civil Liberties subcommittee disclosed that during 1934 the company paid $39,000 to the Bergoff Detective Agency for strikebreaking activities. The strike started on June 26 with only a handful of union men, but rapidly spread until transportation in the city was paralyzed and the power plant temporarily shut down. The city's population, overwhelmingly sympathetic to the strikers, swarmed out to the carbarns in different parts of the city. There were riots at the carbarns resulting in broken windows and damaged equipment. The company felt it necessary to place wire on the streetcars to protect the windows.[5]

President Sylvester B. Way of the company wrote to Mayor Hoan saying the city would be held liable for all damage to the company's property. On June 28, Hoan replied:

I now notify you and through you, the most powerful trust the world has ever known, which you represent, that you alone are solely responsible for the riots that have so far blotched the good name of this city. . . . Your attitude toward your employees, our people, our city, our Federal Government is more arrogant than that of any ruler in the world. Not since the days of King George III of England has any such ruler successfully defied our nation. . . . It was your company that sponsored the company union called the E.M.B.A. [Employees Mutual Benefit Association]. Now in the face of a Federal Government request to negotiate settlement of the strike an alleged contract with this company union is paraded as an obstacle you cannot break. Is it possible that you really think the people of Milwaukee are so dumb as to believe you cannot now induce this organization to comply with an honest and sincere request of the President's representative in the face of the crisis you have brought on? . . . I further notify you that the caging of your street cars with fence wire is in fact acting as an open invitation to violence and their operation is provocative of unlawful assemblage and should cease forthwith.[6]

The strike came to an abrupt end on the evening of June 29. That night, a young man went inside the fence of the company's Lakeside power plant during the course of a demonstration. He intended to smash a window with an iron bar. Allegedly, an employee of the plant turned a water hose in his direction. The grounds had been charged with live wires, resulting in his electrocution. There was no violence by the crowd, but the incident helped to congeal sentiment against the company. Following this, the company for the first time met with the union leaders and agreed to recognize the union and rehire the discharged workers as well as all strikers. Thus ended the historic attempt to organize the company, an attempt which had begun more than 40 years before.

Although the street-railway strike was the most notable victory of 1934, strikes elsewhere brought unionism to many new industries. The year ended with a strike of clerks at the Boston Store, the first big department-store strike in the nation. Federal labor unions began to be used extensively to organize workers on an industrial rather than a craft basis. Newly-formed company unions, rather than keeping out regular unions, sometimes served to inspire interest in trade unionism among the employees. Now under the leadership of Herman Seide, the Federated Trades Council was able to view the results of 1934 with great satisfaction.

In 1935 the United States Supreme Court declared the National

Industrial Recovery Act unconstitutional, but the labor provisions of Section 7(a) were maintained and broadened by the passage of the National Labor Relations (or Wagner) Act in the same year. The effect of the Wagner Act was not immediately felt in Milwaukee; 1935 brought a reduction in the number of strikes in the city, but it also saw the beginning of a strike at the Lindemann-Hoverson Manufacturing Company which lasted for seventeen months.[7]

The Boncel Ordinance

Lindemann-Hoverson refused to negotiate with its employees and continued to operate its stove works. Large crowds gathered at the plant, outbreaks of violence between pickets and police occurred, and hundreds of policemen were unable to prevent or control trouble. Threatened with the breakdown of local authority and faced with the possibility of intervention by the state militia and the declaration of martial law, the Common Council passed the Boncel Ordinance on September 30, 1935.

The Boncel Ordinance, citing the declaration of policy in the Wagner Act, empowered the mayor and the chief of police to act in certain labor disputes. If an employer refused to bargain collectively and his refusal brought a crowd of 200 persons around the plant on two successive days, then the mayor or the chief of police could order the plant closed within 24 hours. The mayor was authorized to appoint an advisory committee of employers, labor, and religious leaders. An employer who refused to close his plant could be fined or imprisoned.

The adoption of the ordinance had the immediate effect of causing the board of directors of Lindemann-Hoverson to close the plant voluntarily. Employers attacked the ordinance as an unconstitutional attempt to force them to accept collective bargaining. In the municipal election of 1936 the Socialists suffered severe losses, including the defeat of Frank Boncel, author of the ordinance, and the nonpartisan Common Council repealed the ordinance before it was ever used or tested in the courts.

The repeal of the Boncel Ordinance did not slow down the drive to expand the frontiers of trade unionism. In February, 1936, the American Newspaper Guild began a seven-month strike against the Hearst-owned *Wisconsin News*, peppered with a drive to get people to cancel their subscriptions to the paper and a boycott against all Hearst magazines and the company's radio station, WISN. The strike ended in September, the union winning wage increases, a reduction in hours, and recognition.[8]

Reaction of Employers

While many employers reluctantly accepted the expansion of unions, a number actively opposed it. During the early 1930's, some employers helped organize the Citizens Law and Order League to oppose the "lawlessness" of the unions. This prompted the FTC to create Labor's Committee for Justice to combat the activities of the Law and Order League.

Investigations by the La Follette Civil Liberties subcommittee in 1936 and 1937 indicated that Wisconsin legislation had not freed the state from industrial espionage. Corporations Auxiliary admitted that it had evaded the Wisconsin laws by correspondence training of detectives for certain Wisconsin plants, the spies reporting only to the plant management where they were employed. The Pinkerton Detective Agency also admitted that it had several unregistered agents in Wisconsin plants whom it had listed as "watchmen." As already noted, the Milwaukee Electric Railway and Light Company employed the services of the Bergoff Agency. The Milwaukee branch of the National Metal Trades Association, which in 1936 included 42 Milwaukee firms, regularly sent funds to the national office in Chicago. The national office hired the Pinkerton agency to send detectives to Wisconsin. While not all Milwaukee members of the Metal Trades Association used the service, the National Metal Trades Association did give the Lindemann-Hoverson company about $5,000 to use at its discretion. The wide publicity of the La Follette committee hearings led most companies to discontinue their use of labor spies.

A number of companies in the city also disregarded the provisions of the Wagner Act. During its long strike, the Lindemann-Hoverson company sent a letter to its employees saying, "Their [the unions'] lawyers know just as well as ours that the Wagner Law and the Boncel Ordinance are both illegal and void." Consequently it was an important victory for the unions when the United States Supreme Court unexpectedly upheld the constitutionality of the Wagner Act in 1937.

In the same year, 1937, Wisconsin passed a "baby Wagner Act." A labor-relations bill had been sponsored by the Wisconsin State Federation of Labor in the 1935 legislature, but was defeated by two votes in the Senate. The measure was brought up again in early 1937 after the sweeping victory of the Progressives in the preceding fall election. With the blessings of Governor Philip La Follette, the bill was passed and signed on April 14.[9]

Strategically, the Wisconsin Labor Relations Act had been passed at an inopportune time. The Milwaukee labor movement was in the midst of its civil war.

CHAPTER XIII

The Explosion of Unionism

THE reaction of unions to the catalyst of the New Deal was impressive. By 1935 the losses suffered in the first four years of the depression had been restored. However, the AFL still generally excluded the unskilled workers, and the mass production industries, which had become so important, were largely outside the pale of unionism. The AFL had made half-hearted attempts to organize workers in the auto, rubber, and steel industries, but the absence of a concerted, coordinated effort was compounded by the question of organizational structure.

Many argued that the craft unionism of the AFL was ill-suited to the task of organizing factory labor—industrial unionism was the answer. The AFL did have industrial unions in its ranks, such as the United Mine Workers and the Amalgamated Clothing Workers, and made some obeisance to industrial unionism by chartering federal labor unions to organize workers in new industries. However, the organization was dominated by craft-union leaders jealous of their jurisdiction. The 1934 convention of the AFL did vote to issue charters for unions in the mass-production industries and launch an organizational campaign in steel, but little came of it.

When the time came for the 1935 convention in Atlantic City, the proponents of industrial unionism were no longer in the mood for compromise. At the convention, the industrial-union advocates were led by John L. Lewis of the UMW, Philip Murray, vice president of the UMW, Sidney Hillman, Amalgamated Clothing Workers, David Dubinsky, International Ladies Garment Workers, and Charles Howard, Typographical Union. Pitted against them were William Green, president of the AFL since Gompers' death, "Big Bill" Hutchinson, Carpenters Union, Dan Tobin of the Teamsters Union, John P. Frey, head of the Metal Trades Department, and Matthew Woll of the Engravers Union.

The CIO

The convention ended with the industrial-union position defeated by a vote of 18,024 to 10,933. Unwilling to concede defeat, the officers of eight national unions met in November, 1935, to form the Committee for Industrial Organization. The purpose of the Committee was to organize workers into industrial unions within the framework of the AFL.

The leadership of the AFL, however, feared that the new organization would actively compete with established unions and in January, 1936, ordered the Committee to disband. The Committee refused and, consequently, the AFL Executive Council ordered the suspension of the unions unless they severed connections with the Committee by September, 1936. The suspended unions failed to appear before the 1936 convention, and the convention supported the suspension. The break was complete.

The suspended unions launched an aggressive organizing campaign, which the AFL challenged with a campaign of its own. The early success of the Committee for Industrial Organization assured its continued existence, and in 1938 it assumed its permanent name, the Congress of Industrial Organizations.[1]

The Wisconsin Plan

In Milwaukee the concept of industrial unionism was neither new nor frightening. For many years the Socialists had been calling for the organization of workers on industrial lines, and the FTC had many times endorsed the proposal. To allay the pending split in the labor movement, the Wisconsin State Federation of Labor at its convention in July, 1936, unanimously adopted the "Wisconsin Plan." The plan was actually devised at a session of the Committee on Adjustments which coordinated nine resolutions and the executive council's report. The Committee recognized that:

under the present status of our industrial system which presents complex and varied problems in different occupations and industries, no hard and fast rule seeking to establish one uniform organization set-up can adequately or effectively meet all the varied needs of workers in every line of work. . . . There are large and important industries in which craft unions have not been able to reach the masses of workers. It is unfortunate that at this time when labor should have harmony and unanimity of action in order to advance the organization of the workers this controversy has developed to the point where it threatens to cause a serious split in the ranks of labor.[2]

The compromise Wisconsin Plan proposed that: (1) all charges against organizations affiliated with the CIO be immediately dismissed and all plans for suspension or expulsion of the organization from the AFL be dropped, (2) the AFL should participate wholeheartedly with the CIO in a drive to organize the steel and rubber industries on an industrial basis so that the Wisconsin Plan and the industrial form of organization would have a fair chance to prove its efficiency, (3) the CIO should confine its drive to the steel and rubber industries until further action was taken by the AFL, and (4) the president of the AFL should within 60 days appoint a special committee of two representatives of international unions, two from federal labor unions, three from state federations, and three from city centrals to study all phases of the organization of the labor movement.

To demonstrate their own support for the idea of cooperation between industrial and craft unions, the Wisconsin State Federation elected to the executive board two staunch supporters of industrial unionism, Emil Costello and John Banachowicz. A week after the suspension of the industrial unions from the AFL by the national executive council, a provisional committee was formed at a meeting of 44 union leaders from all parts of Wisconsin to study the problem. They reaffirmed the decision of the State Federation's convention and urged careful consideration of the Wisconsin Plan at the coming national AFL convention.

The FTC also endorsed the Wisconsin Plan, and urged that the coming convention take no hasty action. At the national convention, the delegate of the FTC, J. F. Friedrick, spoke against the recommendation to support the previous expulsion action of the Executive Board of the AFL. However, the convention upheld the suspension, as well as rejecting a proposal of the FTC to give the industrial unions greater representation in the city centrals.[3]

Split In Milwaukee

In the city itself, the CIO began its organizing work in the summer of 1936, and the locals were accepted as members in the FTC. But in February, 1937, a controversy arose involving Federal Labor Union 20136 at the Allis-Chalmers Company that ultimately led to a split in the Milwaukee labor movement. Molders Local 125 and Electrical Workers Local 494 protested about the seating of delegates from the federal labor union because they had been former members of craft unions at the Allis-Chalmers plant. The protests were referred to the AFL.

Before the meeting of March 3 was called to order, General Secretary Herman Seide, coming in from the executive board meeting, noticed Harold Christoffel, president of the federal labor union at Allis-

Chalmers, and other delegates from the Allis-Chalmers group in the meeting hall. Seide told the delegates that they would not be seated until information on their status had been received from the AFL. Christoffel, however, told Seide that he would not leave. Seide again pointed out it would do no good to stay and would merely create a disturbance and again asked the Allis-Chalmers delegates to leave. Seide then left the group. Later, Seide noticed Biddle of Teachers Local 79 talking with the Christoffel group and asked him to use his influence to get the delegates to leave the meeting peacefully. This was just prior to the opening of the meeting, as the minutes relate:

... when the Secretary [Seide] noticed that Delegate William Biddle left the delegates of the Allis-Chalmers group, he requested them to leave the meeting hall. He was informed very snappishly that they were going to stay, whether he or anybody else liked it or not. After the president and the vice president were elected the meeting opened, and the secretary informed the president of what had occurred and pointed out that the constitution was being violated by these delegates. The chairman [Frank Klaesing] called on these delegates to leave the hall. Delegate Michelson moved that the delegates be permitted to remain.
    The chairman ruled the motion out of order.
    An appeal was taken from the decision of the chair. The chairman refused the appeal, stating that this was a question of the constitution and that the constitution could not be set aside by a motion on the floor. ...
    He again requested the delegates from the Allis-Chalmers group to leave the meeting hall. They refused. After three or four requests by the chairman ... [he] was finally compelled to have the sergeant-at-arms remove these delegates from the meeting hall.[4]

Between the FTC meetings of March 3 and March 17, two incidents occurred that assured the coming split in the labor movement. Federal Labor Union 20136 abandoned its AFL charter to become Local 248 of the CIO's United Auto Workers, and the CIO sympathizers sent a letter to a selected number of FTC delegates inviting them to attend a caucus on March 14.

When the meeting of the FTC opened on March 17, Herman Seide read a letter from the AFL charging that Local 75 of the United Auto Workers (from Seaman Body) had participated in meetings to aid officers of the AFL's federal labor union to secede. The AFL ordered the FTC to expel the delegates of Local 75. A motion was immediately made to file the letter, but the chairman of the meeting ruled the motion out of order because the letter was an order from the AFL. This provoked a long and furious debate on the Council's floor.

Charles Nickolaus, Brewery Workers Local 9, moved to send a protest to the AFL and appeal the order to unseat Local 75, but J. F.

Friedrick contended that even if the order were appealed, it would have to be carried out until the AFL reversed its position. During the course of the debate, Arthur Olsen of Steamfitters 601 stated the case for the older unions. Olsen declared the delegates must abide by the constitution rules of the AFL and the FTC if they wanted unity. He went on to point out that in the past the delegates from the craft unions had been "very tolerant" and had permitted certain actions on the Council floor because they wanted unity and because they realized that the delegates from the new unions were unacquainted with the rules of the FTC. "But now it appears," the minutes summarized his talk, "as though this new group was attempting to take over a movement that had been built in the past 50 years by men in the labor movement, and . . . he was not ready at this time to turn this movement over to the CIO or anybody else, because in doing so, he would be betraying the people that he represented . . . ."[5]

Henry Ohl, Jr., delegate from the Typographical Local 23 and president of the Wisconsin State Federation of Labor, then charged that "the CIO and communist followers was organizing a conspiracy to take over the legislative functions of the State Federation of Labor." Ohl claimd the group had sent out a call for a People's Conference for Social and Labor Legislation to unite labor, farm, and liberal organizations in a state-wide mass campaign. He charged that the conference was designed to break up the friendly relations between the State Federation and the farmers. During Ohl's talk, delegates from Auto Workers Local 75 and some of the CIO sympathizers booed and heckled until the chairman was compelled to rap for order and threaten to remove the delegates from the hall.

Peter T. Schoemann of Plumbers Local 75 then took the floor and criticized the delegates for booing Ohl. Schoemann then brought up the matter of the caucus and attacked the CIO group for attempting to divide the labor movement. Friedrick noted that in 1934 the FTC had conducted Sunday-morning meetings of officers and delegates to discuss matters of interest to the labor movement—meetings open to all and not a selected few. Filtzer of Technical Engineers Local 54 defended the caucus as being necessary "for the liberal groups to get together and formulate plans to carry out their ideas." Biddle denied that the caucus was a CIO meeting but admitted they had set up a slate of candidates for offices in the FTC.

In fact, not all persons attending the caucus eventually became members of the CIO, but the act of holding a caucus and the actions of Local 75 of the United Auto Workers in aiding the Allis-Chalmers federal labor union to become an affiliate of the Auto Workers alienated many of the older unions. Consequently, the motion to protest the order of the AFL to expel the delegates of Local 75 was defeated. The Auto-Worker delegates left the meeting, and on orders of the AFL, the FTC expelled the delegates from Allis-Chalmers and the Gasoline Filling Station Employees Local 18617. The meeting also voted to authorize the executive board of the FTC to hold an investigation of the caucus.

On March 24 the executive board held an investigation on the complaint that the caucus group had sent out its letters with the initials AFL360. The Office Workers Union contended that this was done to mislead people and constituted a fake union label. Harry Miller, president of Teachers Local 360, said that neither the union not its officers had authorized the use of its initials. Roth, who had signed the notice of the caucus meeting, said the work on the letters had been donated by Mrs. Gompers, a member of Teachers Local 360 and the International Ladies Garment Workers. The board then discussed the advisability and purpose of caucus meetings and the right of Roth to use the name of the FTC in connection with the meeting.

The executive board ruled that the use of the initials AFL360 was an attempt to mislead people and an infringement on the Office Workers' label, and that the use of the name of the FTC without authority was a violation of the FTC constitution. The board held there was nothing to forbid the holding of caucuses, but stated that "under present circumstances [it] is inimical to the best interests of the labor movement." The board simply warned the persons involved to avoid any further violations. At the April 7 meeting of the FTC, the council voted to accept the report of the board. Mickelson of the Newspaper Guild caustically moved to amend the motion to "send a copy of this statement to Congress and the Senate of the United States, the State Assembly and Senate, Common Council and County Board and inform them that it was illegal to hold caucuses." After another heated discussion, the amendment was defeated.

While the censure of the caucus had been made on the specious grounds of using the union label improperly, the action had served its purpose in revealing the atempt of the caucus to elect its own slate of officers to the FTC. At the election held April 21, the caucus candidates received about 165 votes compared with the 450 for the "regular" candidates.[6]

The Industrial Union Council

Having failed to capture it, or at least elect more "favorable" officers, the CIO unions withdrew from the FTC. On July 7, 1937, the officers of 62 CIO locals in Milwaukee county met at the Knights-of-Pythias hall to lay plans for a new city central. Among the unions represented were the Steel Workers, United Auto Workers, Hosiery, Ladies Garment Workers, Wood Workers, Filling Station Attendents, Gas Coke and By-products Workers, Meat Packers, Paper Makers, Newspaper Guild, and the Maritime. On August 11 the first meeting of the new city central, the Milwaukee County Industrial Union Council (IUC), was held. Harold Christoffel, the 25-year-old head of Local 248 of the United Auto Workers, was elected president. Upon accepting office, Christoffel said, "The AFL no longer can claim the right to speak for organized labor. Its leaders are turning the organization into company union channels and responsibility for a genuine labor movement now falls upon the CIO." Wyndham Mortimer, vice president of the United Auto Workers, who was present at the meeting, indirectly brought up a problem that was to plague the IUC for a long time by saying that anyone who "cried red at a labor organizer is either a dumb-bell or a company agent."

The developments in Milwaukee were repeated on the state level. After the CIO had persuaded the workers at Allis-Chalmers to withdraw from the AFL, Emil Costello was asked to resign from the executive board of the Wisconsin State Federation of Labor because of his CIO and Communist activities. Costello refused and, for the first time in the history of the State Federation, a trial of an executive-board member was ordered. He was accused of allowing his name to be used in connection with the call for the meeting of the People's Conference for Social and Labor Legislation. Costello charged this was an attack on the whole CIO and accused the executive board of "red-baiting and disrupting and dividing labor's ranks."

Although Costello did not attend the trial, he was found guilty on April 28 and expelled for "taking orders and following dictation of the Communist Party, fostering dual unionism, seeking to ridicule and discredit officers of both the American Federation of Labor and the Wisconsin Federation of Labor, and subordinating interest of the state federation to other labor organizations." Banachowicz, the other CIO advocate on the executive board, handed in his resignation following Costello's dismissal.

A week after Costello's expulsion, the CIO broke away completely from the State Federation and set up a temporary state CIO federation at a state-wide conference in Milwaukee on May 8. The one day convention was attended by 250 delegates, representing 56 unions and 64,-772 members. With Costello as president, the Wisconsin State Industrial Union Council, as it was called, made its first job the establishment of city centrals in the state, a move already completed in Milwaukee in July.

The split in the Milwaukee labor movement had been completed. In the eyes of the Milwaukee unionists loyal to the AFL, the CIO's claims to a superior form of organization and a more aggressive spirit were fictitious. The FTC had for many years been receptive to the concept of industrial unionism, and the increase in union membership in Milwaukee from 20,000 in 1932 to 60,000 in 1936 seemed adequate testimony to the new vigor of the Council. Moreover, the State Federation and the FTC believed their adoption of the "Wisconsin Plan" had quite sufficiently demonstrated their desire to ameliorate the differences between the AFL and the CIO. Finally, the AFL group was antagonized by, what seemed to them, the attempt of the CIO to take over unions they had worked to create, at Allis-Chalmers, for example. Consequently, many were ready to endorse the belief of Henry Ohl, Jr., that the CIO leaders were simply "political adventurers."

On the other hand, the CIO unions were convinced that the organizing vigor of the early 1930's was dying. While the FTC may have paid lip service to industrial unionism, the industrial unions believed it was in fact dominated by craft unions more interested in preserving their jurisdiction than organizing new workers. They charged that in the Allis-Chalmers case, the AFL had shown its hostility to industrial unionism when William Green ordered the Federal Labor Union to relinquish its craft workers to their particular locals and then directed Paul Smith to seize the books and funds of the union and if necessary suspend it for refusal to give up its craft workers.

In the last analysis, the situation was largely out of the hands of the local union movement, for they could not have long delayed the consequences of the split on the national level. However, the situation was not improved by the violent denunciations of the Wisconsin CIO unions by some like Henry Ohl, Jr., who charged them with "treachery, disruption, perfidy, and treason," or the counteraccusation by the CIO that "Henry Ohl has at last enthroned himself . . . among the labor mis-leaders of American history."[7]

Counterorganization

The split in the labor movement provoked vigorous organizing campaigns by both the IUC and the FTC. Often CIO and AFL unions competed for the right to organize workers. For example, unions from both groups demanded the right to negotiate with the owners of the Wrigley restaurant since each had members working there. The restaurant owners refused the demands of the CIO union since they could not tell which union had a majority of the workers. Consequently, CIO leaders on May 17 ordered a sit-down strike—one of the first in the state—to compel recognition. The owners then asked for an injunction to compel the strikers to vacate the premises. Judge Charles L. Aarons of the Milwaukee County Circuit Court overruled the objections of the union and issued an injunction. The strikers vacated the Wrigley restaurant before the court order was served. On June 1, in the first such election held by the state labor board, the workers voted 100 to 5 to affiliate with the CIO United Catering Workers rather than the AFL Waiters and Cooks Alliance. The AFL used similar tactics. On July 8, 40 members of Molders Local 125 started a one-day sit-down strike protesting the employment of CIO members when they were the recognized bargaining agent.

The competition between the two groups in many other cases led to a rapid increase in trade-union membership. The Wisconsin edition of the *CIO News* on March 26, 1938, was able to say with some justification:

Take a look at Wisconsin. If we had not had this "tragic split" at least 125,-000 men and women enrolled in CIO or AFL unions would still be unorganized. The 8,000 Allis-Chalmers workers would still be at the mercy of wrangling craft union leaders. Harley-Davidson, Fairbanks-Morse, Evinrude Motors, Milprint, Louis-Allis, Gisholt, Highway Trailer, Marathon Electric and more than 100 other industrial plants would today be open shop . . . strongholds, instead of organized in powerful, industrial unions.

At the same time, the vigorous drives had brought the unpopular sit-down strike, violence, mass picketing, and a proliferation of independent unions (not company dominated), formed in many cases by the tactlessness of AFL and CIO organizers. The large number of strikes often caused even supposedly friendly unions to work at cross purposes. Consequently, in late 1938 the FTC formed a Labor Disputes Committee to consider the cases of local unions who wanted aid from other unions in a strike. Its purpose was to avoid misunderstandings when other unions were involved. If a local declared a strike without applying to the Labor Disputes Committee, other unions were to be absolved from giving any support, other than moral.[8]

At the end of 1938, the Wisconsin Labor Relations Board described the situation by saying:

In Wisconsin the gains in union membership were relatively much greater than in the entire country. The unions affiliated with the Wisconsin State Federation of Labor more than doubled their membership during the year intervening between the conventions of 1936 and 1937; yet in the same year the Committee for Industrial Organization came into existence and gained tens of thousands of members in Wisconsin. Employers who had never dealt with unions suddenly found themselves confronted with labor organizations which embraced in their membership all or a large part of their employees. Many smaller organizations discovered that unionism is not merely a matter affecting the large industrial centers but industrial employees wherever they may work.

It was inevitable that at such a time there should be much friction between employers and employees. While the Wisconsin employers generally were willing and anxious to comply with all requirements of the national and state labor relations acts and prepared to give unionism a trial, there were naturally some employers who were uncompromisingly hostile to the policies embodied in these acts. There was misunderstanding of the requirements of the law, on the part of employees no less than on the part of employers, with resulting irritations and disputes. In many communities in which unionism had been previously unknown there was very general resistance to unionism, not only on the part of employers but in some cases by many of the employees and the general public as well.

Nor were all the difficulties due to employers. Some of the new unions made quite unreasonable demands. It is not surprising that working people who have long been unorganized should not at once act as responsibly as many of the older unions have long been doing; but, nevertheless, the lack of experience in collective bargaining on the part of the unions no less than on that of the employers, was a major factor in the disturbed industrial relations in 1937. The difficulties in this respect were enormously increased by the unfortunate split in the American labor movement which developed a few months before the Wisconsin law came into operation. This split developed many situations which were extremely exasperating both to the employers and the general public, and which did the cause of organized labor an incalculable amount of harm. In its report to its 1937 convention the executive committee of the American Federation of Labor listed Wisconsin and Minnesota as being the two states which constituted the real battleground between the AFL and the CIO.[9]

Public Reaction

Reaction was building up. In 1938 the unions committed the strategic error of organizing the employees of a cooperative creamery at Richland Center and sponsoring a strike at the spinach cannery at Franksville, Wisconsin, thus helping to alienate the already-alarmed farmers. In November, 1938, conservative Republicans helped elect Julius Heil, a Milwaukee industrialist, as governor. The stage was set for a major change in the state labor law.

The principal backer of the new legislation was the Wisconsin Council of Agriculture, formed in 1926. In 1938 its membership consisted of 35 organizations, mostly cooperatives, but also the Wisconsin State Grange and the Wisconsin Farm Bureau. The council had endorsed unemployment insurance in 1931 but was otherwise inactive in promoting or opposing labor legislation before 1938. At its 1938 convention, the Council of Agriculture adopted a ten-point program including equal rights for employers before the state labor board, the protection of individual property rights, the right of employers to ask for a representation election, security from violence and intimidation, and the obligation of unions to be held responsible for their acts.

In February, 1939, the Council of Agriculture hired a Milwaukee corporation lawyer, Walter H. Bender, to draft a labor relations bill which was introduced into the legislature by Assemblyman W. R. Peterson. Hearings on the bill indicated that farm support for the measure was based partly on dissatisfaction over farm prices and partly on the belief that labor leaders did not really represent their membership. Several dairy cooperatives, the Building Trades Employers Association, the Wisconsin Manufacturers Association and the state Chamber of Commerce backed the bill.

The Wisconsin Farmers Union, long friendly to labor, opposed the bill and denounced the leadership of the Council of Agriculture for having "sold them [its affiliates] down the river and joined hands with farmer-and-labor-hating racketeer-capitalists." Two consumer cooperatives and one marketing cooperative withdrew from the Council of Agriculture in protest against its sponsorship of the bill.[10]

Labor was, of course, also vigorously opposed to the changes in the law, but its efforts to prevent passage were weakened by the feud between the AFL and the CIO. On January 23 Meyer Adelman, secretary-treasurer of the IUC, wrote to Herman Seide asking for cooperation to fight any changes in the state labor act. In reply Seide agreed there should be no changes in the state law but contemptuously added:

We see no need for any conferences with other groups at this late date to work out any new or different program. In our estimation such conferences might just take time away from the main work and might dissipate rather than concentrate our efforts, for as we understand it your Milwaukee County Industrial Union Council and even your state CIO organization do not include quite an appreciable number of CIO organizations, and if we started conferences with your group, we might reasonably be expected to hold such conferences with all the other groups or factions.

Under these circumstances, may we suggest that if you are concerned about these attacks and want to do something, there is nothing to stop you and your other minority groups from supporting the program which the majority group, namely, the Wisconsin State Federation of Labor has already undertaken.[11]

Thus, the forces of labor divided, many farmers opposed to the tactics of the unions, employers clamoring for changes in the law, and conservative Republicans in control, the state legislature adopted the Wisconsin Employment Peace Act in 1939. A number of the changes in the state labor law anticipated provisions of the Taft-Hartley Act of

1947. The state labor board was required to hold secret-ballot elections to determine bargaining units and whether the workers wanted a union shop. Union dues could not be checked off unless the worker signed an authorization. A long list of unfair labor practices of unions was added, and unions were required to give each member a detailed financial report.

While the passage of the Wisconsin Employment Peace Act did not mean an end of union gains, it signaled a change to a more hostile social environment and underlined a weakness in labor's political efforts.

CHAPTER XIV

The End of the Alliance

MILWAUKEE labor unions in the early 1930's continued to cooperate with the Socialist Party, but were becoming increasingly restive and anxious for greater political success. Hence, the 1935 convention of the Wisconsin State Federation of Labor instructed its president, Henry Ohl, Jr., to invite representatives of labor, farmers, and liberal groups to a conference. Those answering the call for a meeting in Milwaukee on October 1 were, in addition to the State Federation of Labor, the railroad brotherhoods, the Farmers Equity Union, the Wisconsin Cooperative Milk Pool, the Wisconsin Farm Holiday Association, the Wisconsin Workers Alliance, the Socialist Party, the Progressive Party, and the Farmer-Labor Progressive League.

The Farmer-Labor Progressive Federation

The conference founded the Farmer-Labor Progressive Federation. One of the major purposes of the Progressive Federation was to end the rivalry between the Socialist and Progressive Parties in Milwaukee County. The Progressive Party, separated from the Republican Party since 1934, competed with the Socialists for votes in the county. This sometimes resulted in the election of conservative Democrats and Republicans to the state legislature. With the formation of the Progressive Federation, the Socialists no longer had a slate of state officers and a separate column on the ballot. In return, they were allowed to write the statement of principles of the Federation. However, Philip La Follette and some other Progressives did not join the Federation, supposedly because its declaration favoring "production for use" might be open to misinterpretation. To some extent, this lack of wholehearted support from the La Follettes, plus the continuing differences between the urban-Socialists and the rural-Progressives, helped to undermine the future effectiveness of the Federation.[1]

The FTC, however, enthusiastically backed the newly formed Farmer-Labor Progressive Federation and supported its candidates. Its attitude towards the Federation was expressed in an open letter published shortly before the November, 1936 elections.

The record clearly shows that of all the Milwaukee legislators only the Progressives and Socialists stood solidly for the interests of the workers and the common people. The most that can be said for the Republican and Democratic legislators is that the best of them were none too good and most of them were positively rotten as far as labor and social legislation was concerned.

. . . .

It was this gross betrayal of the interests of the workers by the Democrats and Republicans which impelled the Wisconsin State Federation of Labor to take the initiative in organizing the Farmer-Labor Progressive Federation in the hope that through it we could unite the strength of workers, farmers, small business men, professional people and all liberal and progressive forces.

The Farmer-Labor Progressive Federation is now functioning in many parts of the state. It is particularly active in Milwaukee County where in the recent primary election it was successful in nominating all of its three candidates for the state senate and 18 out of 20 assemblymen. In addition it was to win the nomination of all but one county candidate, both Congressional Candidates, and two of the candidates on the state ticket.

Since all of them are candidates on the Progressive Party ticket, the simplest way to ensure their election is to vote the straight Progressive Party ticket for State County officials.[2]

This new interest in the Farmer-Labor Progressive Federation materially lessened the interest of the FTC in the Socialist Party. In 1936 the FTC adopted a new constitution which dropped all the Socialistic verbiage and all the distinctly Socialist planks, other than a call for the public ownership of public utilties. Almost symbolically, the FTC on July 1, 1936, voted 71 to 61 to move to the Metropolitan Block from Brisbane Hall, which also housed the Socialist Party. Quite differently from times gone by, in 1937 the FTC declined to participate in the Socialist-sponsored May-Day meeting, and in 1938 rejected the request of the Socialist Party to enclose a letter with the FTC's minutes to sponsor a "Frank Weber Day" at the state Socialist picnic in August. The FTC argued that it would "establish a precedent that would open the door to all other political parties that might sponsor some labor man at a picnic . . . ."

The leaders of the national Socialist Party also committed a blunder as far as Milwaukee was concerned. At a special national convention held in Chicago in March, 1937, the party endorsed the CIO, criticized the AFL, and directed party members to form "Socialist Leagues" within unions—a tactic of the Communist Party. Henry Ohl, Jr., and J. J. Handley immediately resigned from the party after learning of the Chicago endorsement of the CIO. The Milwaukee Socialists then asked the national party to exempt Wisconsin from the party's union program, a right they eventually received, but great harm had already been done to the party by the national action.

Another factor working against the Socialists in Milwaukee was the pressure brought to bear on local labor leaders by national leaders. For example, Leo Krzycki, an active Polish Socialist in Milwaukee, told Norman Thomas that his connection with Sidney Hillman, through the Amalgamated Clothing Workers, made it necessary for him to resign from the Socialist Party and support the candidacy of Roosevelt, although he personally wished the Socialists success.

The Socialists lost another contact with the unions in June, 1938, when the Milwaukee *Leader* slipped out of their control. The paper was unable to get $85,000 from the unions which it needed to carry on. Three newsmen from the Hearst morning paper took over, and under new ownership and management, but with approximately the same staff as before, the *New Milwaukee Leader* made its appearance as a liberal-labor paper. In June, 1939, the local AFL unions bought out what was left of the paper. The FTC furnished $11,000 and about 200 other unions were expected to raise $150,000 to run the paper. Even this general newspaper, which offered some support to the Socialists, was disbanded in 1942, and the FTC began to publish its own newspaper, the *A. F. of L. Milwaukee Labor Press*.

Within the Farmer-Labor Progressive Federation, a number of problems arose. First, the Wisconsin Industrial Union Council demanded that the CIO unions be admitted as a group, rather than have the CIO members enter the Progressive Federation as individuals. The proposal was vigorously opposed by the AFL unions, and the Progressive Federation, recognizing it as a move toward Communist control, rejected the request by a narrow margin. Rebuffed by the Progressive Federation, the CIO unions of the state denounced the Federation saying: "Instead of being a genuine expression of the liberal and progressive forces in Wisconsin, it was in fact little more than a caucus of right-wing Socialists, completely controlled by the same AFL leaders who have unscrupulously sabotaged the CIO throughout the state, since its beginning." However, the CIO finally did urge individual affiliation upon its members. Another problem was the instability of the Progressive Federation. Farmers' and trade unions had found common cause in protesting the depression, but with the aggressive organizing campaigns of labor, the farmers took alarm and the depression-born friendship was impaired. Further, as prosperity returned with the war, the differences between the rural mentality of the farmers and the urban outlook of the Milwaukee unionists became more apparent.[3]

The End of the Socialist Party

A crucial decision was reached by the Socialist Party of Milwaukee in November, 1941. They decided to abandon both the Farmer-Labor Progressive Federation and the Progressive Party and return to the ballot in 1942 in the Socialist column. All members of the party were given the choice of declaring their loyalty to the party by December 1 or being dropped. Many took the opportunity to break with the party, including J. F. Friedrick, the party's last major link with the trade unions. During a discussion of the endorsement of Congressman Wasielewski in 1942, Friedrick gave what might be considered the funeral oration for the Socialist Party of Milwaukee.

> For many years I was a member of the Socialist party . . . I am no longer a member of that party, not because I have changed my ideas about the principles of Socialism, but because I am convinced that these principles can never be put into effect through the political action of a small group. They will be put into effect only if those who stand for them will be able to get part of such a program adopted by a major political party. In this respect the Roosevelt administration has done perhaps more than any other previous administration. The development of the T. V. A. project certainly brought into being the largest government owned, government operated, and government controlled public utility service in this Nation. During all of the time that the Socialist party was active and strong in Milwaukee, we were never able to bring about public ownership of public utilities.

> . . . .

> If we want to be realistic and see facts as they are we must recognize that the contest in the fourth congressional district lies between . . . Wasielewski and the . . . Republican . . . John C. Shaefer. One of the previous speakers has intimated that this need not be the choice as there are other candidates in the field and he urged support of the Socialist candidate, Robert Buech. Surely no one who uses common sense and reason can believe that there is any chance for the election of the Socialist candidate in view of the fact that during the height of the power of the Socialist party in Milwaukee County, that party was never able to elect a Congressman from the fourth congressional district. Surely it will not be able to do so now.[4]

Preceded by the defeat of Mayor Hoan in 1940, this sealed the fate of the Socialist Party. It was no longer able to get its once-dependable support from the trade unions. The Socialist Party of Milwaukee was dead as an effective political force. Only its empty shell lingered on.

The Socialist Party had crumbled and the Progressive Party disbanded in 1946, re-entering the Republican Party with generally disastrous results. In 1940 labor had created its own vehicle for political action, the United Labor Committee of Wisconsin, composed of representatives of AFL, CIO, and railroad unions. The end of the depression had meant an end to third-party politics.

Attention shifted. As the effects of the new world war began to be felt in America, the country became concerned with the problem of defense mobilization. This concern emphasized the issue of Communists in the Milwaukee labor movement.

CHAPTER XV

The Rise of Communism

DURING the Twenties, the Communists made little appreciable headway in the labor movement. From 1920 to 1928 they followed the dictates of Lenin's *Left Wing Communism: An Infantile Disorder,* which urged them to infiltrate existing unions. In response, the Communists created the Trade Union Educational League, headed by William Z. Foster. Although making some gains in such unions as the Machinists, Ladies Garment Workers, and United Mine Workers, the TUEL met vigorous opposition by union leaders which soon made apparent the futility of "boring from within." Hence, on direction of the Fourth Congress of the Red International in Moscow, the Communists abandoned the TUEL in 1928 and set up the Trade Union Unity League to organize dual unions. Communist unions were established in a number of industries, but again they made no spectacular gains.

Their greatest opportunity arrived with the Great Depression. Capitalism, though it did not collapse, lost the glamour it had acquired in the Twenties. Radical movements of every variety flourished. The Technocrats, the Townsend Plan, Huey Long, Father Coughlin, and the EPIC plan were all children of the depression. The Communists hoped to become its master.

The mounting number of unemployed workers presented the first tempting target for the Communists. Men were enlisted into the Communist-controlled Unemployed Councils. In the spring of 1930, demonstrations broke out in New York, Detroit, Los Angeles, Chicago, Seattle, Boston, and Milwaukee. "These parades [of the unemployed]," wrote an official of the State Federation of Labor in 1930, " . . . are led by a small group of communists and it is natural that the unemployed who are standing around in large numbers fall in line in any kind of a parade that may be organized."[1]

In the very early Thirties, labor leaders in Milwaukee usually ignored the Communists because "their stock in trade is to get the trade unionists, public officials, etc., attacking them for the purpose of attracting attention and spreading their propaganda." However, as the Communists grew stronger the unions became increasingly irritated by their charges that the labor movement was assisting the employers to reduce wages and lower the living standards of laboring men in Milwaukee. Hence, anything connected with Communism became anathema to the Milwaukee labor movement.

The Communists themselves in the early 1930's stood outside the labor movement and were severely critical of developments inside. They denounced the Wisconsin State Federation of Labor for backing the "fake" and "rotten" unemployment-compensation law, condemned the alleged suppression of federal labor unions, and berated the State Federation for its implicit backing of the Progressive Party, which they termed "capitalistic politics." About all the Communists had to offer the workers was an encouragement to purchase insurance through the International Workers Order and to take courses in the Milwaukee Workers School which offered "training for the class struggle."

In January 1935 the Central Committee of the American Communist Party decided to reverse its previous policy and, as it had in the early Twenties, to attempt to work within existing unions. In Milwaukee the first few attempts to "bore from within" were unsuccessful, partly because the union leaders were conscious of the aims and policies of the Communist Party and often knew who the members were, and partly because of poor leadership among the Communists themselves. The latter problem was solved on March 3, 1935. Eugene Dennis took over the position of district organizer of the Communist Party from Morris Childs.

Dennis, reared in the Pacific Northwest, joined the party in 1926. Trained at the Lenin School in Moscow, he worked for the Comintern in China. Arriving back in the United States in the mid-Thirties, he became state secretary of the Wisconsin organization. His effective work in Wisconsin later attracted the attention of Earl Browder, causing Browder to move Dennis into the national office.[2]

In the May 1, 1935, issue of the Communist newspaper, the *Wisconsin Voice of Labor,* Dennis issued a call to his fellow Communists.

. . . we Communists must redouble and extend our day to day work in the trade unions and factories. We must intensify and broaden our efforts to become the most active builders and defenders of the trade unions. We must overcome the strong remnants of "opposition" work in the trade union field and energetically transform the existing rank and file groups in the unions into broad rank and file mass movements. Party recruiting and building, above all in the key shops, must be tackled with real Bolshevik enthusiasm and persistence to establish the base of our Party more solidly in the auto, metal, machine, and transportation industries.

Boring from Within

Through patient work, the Communists gained the support of various people, such as Meta Berger, Josephine Nordstrand (later active in the Wisconsin Conference for Social Legislation), Frank Ingram, county organizer for the Workers Alliance, and, an important addition, Harold Christoffel.

Christoffel first appeared on the union scene as a member of the bargaining committee of the Allis-Chalmers Works Council, a union set up by the company to meet the requirements of Section 7(a) of the National Industrial Recovery Act. When in 1934 a group of AFL craft unions, including the International Brotherhood of Electrical Workers, the Firemen and Oilers, the Machinists, the Boilermakers, and the Molders, began to have bargaining relations with the company, Christoffel was on the bargaining committee of the Electrical Workers. A more important aspect of Christoffel's career began with his connection with Federal Labor Union 20136. In December, 1935, the federal labor union received a charter from the AFL, but the charter group of 10 employees grew to only 39 in the next 9 months. However, beginning in October, 1936, there was a wholesale desertion of the craft unions, and by January 1937 the federal labor union had over 2,000 members.

While the rapid increase in membership in the federal labor union was caused partially by the ineffectiveness of the craft unions at Allis-Chalmers, the important reason was vigorous organizing work by the Communists. Christoffel had joined the party. While the craft unions and the federal labor union had in the past relied primarily on inside organizers, the Communist Party in mid-1936 sent fellow travelers to Allis-Chalmers to facilitate the growth of the federal labor union. The promise of this effective aid had evidently been one of the major reasons why Christoffel was persuaded to join the Communist Party.

By early 1937 it was apparent to the CIO unionists, Communist and non-Communist alike, that it would be impossible to stay within the AFL. As was previously noted, the split in the Milwaukee labor movement occurred after the Allis-Chalmers federal labor union decided to leave the AFL and join the United Auto Workers as Local 248. With the split on the state level and a previous split on the national level, the CIO unions were now independent of the AFL. The new labor movement badly needed vigorous organizers—and who worked harder than the Communists?—and had relatively few leaders acquainted with the past problems of the labor movement, thus eliminating potential obstacles to the work of the Communists.

Local 248 continued to grow after the split in the labor movement. On May 28, 1937, the local signed a contract with the Allis-Chalmers Company which recognized the union on a non-exclusive basis. On January 4 of the following year, the union, by a vote of 6,086 to 1,645, won sole bargaining rights in an election conducted by the National Labor Relations Board. In general the Communists had reason to look back on 1937 with satisfaction. They had gained control of a number of CIO locals, the Milwaukee County Industrial Union Council, and the Wisconsin Industrial Union Council.[3]

Factionalism

From the beginning, however, the CIO in Wisconsin was faced with factional disputes. A number of local unions, particularly the locals of the UAW and the Amalgamated Clothing Workers, refused to affiliate with the state CIO. Before the temporary state CIO council was set up in May, George B. Kiebler, president of the UAW District Council, charged Emil Costello with usurping authority. Both the Kiebler and the Costello group had conducted individual organizing campaigns, Kiebler following the advice of Homer Martin, national president of the UAW, and Costello receiving his instructions from Van A. Bittner, regional director of the Steel Workers.

When the national convention of the UAW met in Milwaukee in 1937, it adopted a resolution encouraging state CIO central bodies and giving material aid in their formation. However, the Kiebler faction refused to recognize either the Milwaukee county or the Wisconsin central bodies. While a few of the larger locals, such as 248 and 75 (Seaman Body), affiliated, many of the smaller UAW locals refused to join. Kiebler broke with Costello, he claimed, because of Costello's Communist sympathies. The District Council of the UAW also decided to set up a sub-council in Milwaukee County, which the IUC leaders denounced as "an attempt to duplicate and eventually supplant" their own organization. A definite split was expected at the September, 1937 convention of the state CIO, but at the last moment the Kiebler-UAW opposition decided not to present an opposition slate.

Kiebler also irritated the Costello-Christoffel faction with his omnivorous organizing campaigns that brought tavern keepers, hotel and restaurant workers, junkyard workers, building trades workers, and leather workers into the UAW and under his control. Matters were kept fairly well under control until early 1938. At that time Homer Martin, a former Baptist minister, under the guidance of Lovestonite advisors (a factional group headed by Jay Lovestone which had been expelled from the Communist Party), decided to purge the UAW of his opposition which included the "orthodox" Communists.

On June 15 Martin suspended four vice presidents of the UAW and the secretary-treasurer, George Addes. Some UAW locals in Milwaukee consequently decided not to pay their per-capita tax to the international as a protest against the suspension. At a meeting of the UAW District Council in Kenosha, F. J. Michel, district representative of the international, warned that defiant locals and officers, which included Local 248, would face drastic punishment if they did not pay. The threat came true when Martin deposed Christoffel and the other officers of Local 248 and appointed Kiebler as administrator of the local.

On July 16 the Kiebler group, under directions from Homer Martin, invaded the headquarters of Local 248 and appointed a new set of officers for the local. The move was not completely successful because the local, in anticipation of action from Martin, had removed $20,000 from its bank deposits and placed its property in trust. Kiebler and his set of officers were subsequently kept out of the union offices by the "Flying Squadron," a group of strong-arm men from the Christoffel faction who guarded the offices 24 hours a day. The Christoffel group also demanded that District Attorney Herbert J. Steffes prosecute Kiebler and others who had participated in the raid on charges of unlawful assemblage and rioting.

The IUC expelled members who had participated in the raid, and the District Council of the UAW retaliated by expelling the Christoffel group. The Kiebler group attempted to get an injunction against interference by the officers of Local 248, and brought suit to force the Allis-Chalmers Company to recognize the administratorship. In turn, the attorneys for Local 248 asked the court to grant a permanent injunction barring the Kiebler group from maintaining a rival office, retaining property of the union, or interfering with the conduct of business. During the various hearings, Larry S. Davidow, chief council for the International UAW charged, quite truthfully, that Local 248 was controlled by Communists headed by Christoffel. Christoffel charged in turn that: "The real president [of the UAW] is Jay Lovestone, head of the Independent Communist League of America, and those who make the policies are Lovestone's followers."

Throughout the affair, the company continued to deal with the Christoffel group, refused to recognize the administratorship, and fought the suit to compel it to recognize the Kiebler group. In August the court ruled that Kiebler should be restrained from acting until there was a judicial ruling on his claim of authority and that the company should temporarily continue to recognize the old officers of the local. In October a compromise was worked out by national CIO leaders which reinstated the Christoffel leadership, but continued the administratorship under a new man, John Murphy of Bay City, Michigan. In the following days, meetings of Local 248 became so violent that the new administrator suspended all meetings for 90 days.

The Christoffel leadership clung to its control over the membership, moving ruthlessly to eliminate all dissenters. All persons but one who had served as officers under Kiebler's administratorship were expelled from the union. The imminent threat to Christoffel ended when Homer Martin walked out of the CIO and the International UAW elected a new president, R. J. Thomas. In the following years, the Communist leadership of Local 248 used violence, short strikes, and coercion, to which the company, through its policy of neutrality in union internal affairs, acquiesced, in order to eliminate opposition within the union.[4]

Opposition to Communist control of the state and county CIO centrals was similarly squashed. For instance, Fred Wolter, president of United Electrical Workers Local 1111 (Allen-Bradley Company) wrote a letter to the Milwaukee *News-Sentinel* saying, "The communistic element, which is [this was written during the administratorship] being ousted from leadership and control in the Allis-Chalmers Local, is also in control of the State and County CIO and this is the main reason, why the majority of the CIO Unions in the State refuse to affiliate." As a consequence he was charged with "conduct unbecoming to a union man and a delegate" of the IUC, attempting to mold public opinion against the IUC, working to injure the CIO with J. F. Friedrick, J. J. Handley, and Henry Ohl, Jr. through their mutual connections in the Socialist Party, and other minor charges. A trial committee was set up by the IUC which found Wolter not guilty on all charges but that of conduct unbecoming a CIO member. As a result Wolter was reprimanded by the IUC.[5]

The Defense Mobilization Period

While the feuds within the CIO had produced some notable explosions, it was not until 1941 that the effects of Communist leadership in Local 248 became widely known. On August 24, 1939, the Soviet Union and Nazi Germany had signed a ten-year non-aggression pact. The American Communists soon changed their line from one of opposition to fascism to attacks upon America's "reactionary war-makers." According to the later testimony of the not-always-reliable Louis Budenz, Christoffel, Sigmund Eisenscher, Fred Blair, Ned Sparks, Eugene Dennis, and Budenz met in the home of Meta Berger in the fall of 1940. (She was not present, but Dennis had a key to the house.) Dennis reviewed the war situation and emphasized that a strike must be called at the Allis-Chalmers Company to impede the defense mobilization effort. Christoffel said the friction with AFL members in the plant made possible a move that would halt production. Dennis gave the order but no definite time was set; Christoffel agreed to carry out the assignment.

An incident that occurred at the close of the midnight shift on December 18, 1940, provided the emotional fireworks that signaled a coming strike. At that time, Nicholas Imp and Michael Bohacheff, two former members of Local 248, were surrounded in their car by a group of unionists who attempted to get them to rejoin the local and pay back fines and dues. Imp and Bohacheff suddenly started the car and a union member standing in front of it narrowly escaped injury. The Wisconsin *CIO News* of December 30, 1940, featured the affair under the headline: "Frank Korb Saved from Death as 'Auto Plot' Effort Fails." Christoffel demanded that Max Babb, president of Allis-Chalmers, live up to a previous promise to dismiss opponents of the union and fire Imp and Bohacheff. After meeting with a federal mediator, the company agreed to lay off Imp and Bohacheff and six members of Local 248 involved in the affair.

The incident had occurred during the negotiations for a new contract. While the company had acceded to this demand of the union, it refused to grant any form of union security. Hence on January 19, 1941, the union held a strike vote but failed to get a majority as required by Wisconsin law. On January 22 the union held a second strike vote at its offices located 150 feet from the company's premises. This time a majority voted for a strike, and the strike began.

At the time the strike vote was being taken, the company made a careful count of the total number of persons entering the polling place. The count indicated that not more than 4,547 had entered the union offices, meaning that at least 2,200 less than the announced total of 6,759 had voted. Document experts, John F. Tyrrell and Clark Sellers, examined the strike ballots which had been impounded by the Wisconsin Employment Relations Board. The experts found there had been gross fraud, at least 2,200 ballots being falsely marked. The Wisconsin Employment Relations Board later reported: "Examination of the fraudulent ballots showed that they had been marked on a mass production basis, the imprint of the pencil showing through the ballots which had been marked onto the next two or three ballots."

Since the strike held up the completion of critical defense material, Secretary of Navy, Frank Knox and Office of Production Management Director, William S. Knudsen issued a call to the employees to return to work while the company and the union continued to negotiate. On March 28 a back-to-work movement began as a result of the appeal. Consequently on April 1 several hundred pickets invaded the plant, all windows in the area were broken with rocks, and three union members were subsequently convicted and sentenced to the House of Correction. The company closed the plant and made no attempt to re-open it during the remainder of the strike. The strike ended two days before the Wisconsin Employment Relations Board had scheduled a board-supervised strike-authorization ballot. The settlement was negotiated under pressure from the Defense Mediation Board.[6]

The following year the Committee on Naval Affairs of the House of Representatives issued a report on the strike which said:

It has been estimated that the strike delayed the completion and outfitting of destroyers, submarines, minesweepers, transports, net tenders, repair ships, and fleet tugs for periods ranging up to 6 months. The effects of the delay caused by the strike in the delivery of vital machinery and equipment are still being felt—and will be for some time to come.[7]

The storm of protest raised by the strike brought opposition to the Communist leadership of Local 248 in the local's election of officers. The Christoffel group managed to retain control of the union by suspending from all union privileges, including voting, all workers who had responded to the back-to-work appeal of Knox and Knudsen. Even this was evidently not enough, for the leadership of the union postponed the election a number of times and finally, almost without warning, held the elections on July 9 and 10. Although only 2,000 persons voted in the union election, Christoffel was re-elected by the relatively narrow margin of 200 votes over his opponent, Leon Venne. On July 13 the Local held an election for delegates to the international convention of the UAW. The credentials committee claimed that in this election the polls were open only 30 minutes and the highest vote cast for any delegate was 221 out of a claimed membership of 4,000. At the convention Walter Reuther denounced the local as being "dominated by political racketeers of Communist stripe" and described the election of delegates as "the worst kind of strong-arm political racketeering."

The threat of further strikes to impede the defense effort was ended on June 22, 1941. Nazi Germany invaded the Soviet Union. The Communists in Milwaukee, as elsewhere, ceased their former denunciations of the "reactionary war policy" of the administration and began to call for "all-out aid" for the enemies of fascism.[8]

CHAPTER XVI

Purge

The war years saw a continuation of the struggle between the Allis-Chalmers Company and Local 248, the union now overusing the grievance machinery rather than calling strikes. However, the Communists generally worked to aid the war effort since the interests of the Soviet Union were involved.

With the end of the war, relations between the United States and the Soviet Union became increasingly strained. The Communists again had no doubts as to the correct foreign policy for the nation. On March 6, 1946, the Communist-controlled IUC adopted a statement on domestic and foreign policy which was sent to President Truman and Secretary of State Byrnes. The statement charged there was "a direct connection between the lynch law of Tennessee and the police terror in Philadelphia . . . and the Big Stick foreign policy which our government is now carrying on . . . ." The incidents indicated, the statement read, that the "Truman Administration is subordinating itself completely to the wishes of the big trusts to establish reaction and even fascism here in order to wage war for conquest of the world." Turning to Winston Churchill's then recent "iron curtain" speech at Fulton, Missouri, the statement went on: "We are not fooled by Churchill's words about the menace of Communism any more than we were fooled by Hitler's words about a 'crusade against Bolshevism.' "[1]

Leaders of a number of CIO unions in the city became increasingly irritated by the policy pronouncements of the IUC and the articles published in the state CIO newspaper. Local 1114 of the United Steelworkers adopted a resolution in July 1946 which read:

WHEREAS, the facts have established that the Wisconsin State CIO News has gone far afield in matters of foreign 'ISMS' in its attempt to inoculate the rank and file members with ideologies that are Un-American and which are contrary to the desires and beliefs of the vast majority of CIO members, and

WHEREAS, such conduct on the part of the Wisconsin State CIO News has, and still continues, to cause labor much embarrassment and loss of prestige . . . .

RESOLVED, [the Milwaukee county and Wisconsin state centrals should give a] full and complete statement of the future Editorial Policy of the Wisconsin State CIO News and whether it will discontinue publication of news not directly related to the betterment and ideals of American Labor . . .[2]

CIO unionists were further troubled when Edmund Bobrowicz, who was officially backed by the CIO centrals and the local CIO's Political Action Committee, defeated incumbent Congressman Wasielewski in the Democratic primary on August 13. Shortly afterward Robert E. Tehan, Sr., leader of the Democratic Party in the state, repudiated Bobrowicz as a Communist. Wasielewski ran as an independent candidate officially backed by the Democratic Party. Bobrowicz, a representative of the Communist-dominated International Fur and Leather Workers Union, denied he was a Communist or that Communism was an issue in the campaign. Charging that the Democratic Party was "succumbing to the blackmail of the Republican Party" by using "red-baiting", the CIO-PAC decided to continue its support of Bobrowicz. (The split in the ranks of the Democrats resulted in the election of Republican John Brophy, a former union member and Socialist.)[3]

Revolt in the IUC

The course of events convinced the right-wing in the CIO that there must be a determined effort to rid the movement of Communists and fellow travelers. In the past the problem of counteracting the Communists in the IUC was impossible for two reasons. First, at the meetings of the city central the leadership had permitted visitors and unaccredited delegates to remain at the meeting. This had resulted in tremendous confusion, and often it had been impossible to tell who had really won on crucial votes. Second, many locals had refused to affiliate with the IUC or had withdrawn because of the Communist leadership. Therefore, it was imperative to get these unions to join the city central so that the Communists could be fought from within the IUC.

In 1946 the right-wing CIO leaders in Milwaukee began to lay plans for a revolt from within the IUC. At the September 18 meeting of the Council, amendments to the constitution were introduced calling for: (1) a change in the basis of representation to allow a greater voice for the small locals, (2) the end of all limitations to the number of representatives on the executive board from each CIO international union, and (3) a rule that no Nazi, Communist, or Ku Klux Klan member be allowed to hold office in the Council. The proposed amendments were defeated. To carry out the move to unseat the Communists it was necessary to call a special meeting of the IUC so that the delegates from re-affiliated and new locals could be seated in time to vote at the regular election of officers on October 16.

The Communists still controlled the executive board of the IUC and the secretary-treasurer's post, but had made a mistake in late 1945 by electing William Momblow as president of the Council. On October 7 Momblow was presented with a petition, signed by delegates representing 13 affiliated locals, requesting him to call a special meeting not later than October 13 so that the delegates from the re-affiliated and new unions could be legally seated and become eligible to participate in the coming election of officers. On October 8 Momblow showed the petition to Linus Lindberg, secretary-treasurer of the IUC, and Hy Cohen, executive secretary of the executive board, and asked them to send out notices to all delegates to attend a special meeting on October 11. The two secretaries, both of whom were fellow travelers, agreed that they could get the notices in the mail before six o'clock that afternoon so that the constitutional requirement of a 48-hour notice would be met. The notices were never sent.

On October 10 Momblow asked Lindberg for a mailing list of all delegates so that he could send out notices of a special meeting, but Lindberg refused to give him the list. Therefore, Momblow sent postcard notices in the mail to all affiliated locals and also had a notice of the meeting published in the press. The Communist-controlled executive board, on the same day, countered with a letter to the right-wing revolt leaders claiming the action of calling a meeting was a direct violation of the constitution of the IUC. The board threatened to expel the persons involved. In the state *CIO News* on October 11, 1946, the executive board charged that the move was designed to "split the labor movement and to stab in the back the strikes now in progress and being conducted by the CIO."

When the special meeting was called to order on October 13, Momblow related what had happened, and a motion to concur in his actions was adopted. A motion was then made and carried that all standing rules which would conflict with any motion passed at the meeting be suspended. The meeting then seated delegates from eight locals: Locals 409, 100, and 575 of the United Auto Workers, Local 1559 and 1398 of the United Steelworkers, Local 50 of the United Packinghouse Workers, Local 9 of the Brewery Workers, and Branch 16 of the American Federation of Hosiery Workers. This move brought 77 new delegates into the IUC, the largest block, 54, from the Brewery

Workers. Finally, a motion was adopted to interpret the constitution of the Council to mean that delegates of any local in good standing on Sepember 1, 1946, be placed on the official voting list. If a local paid its per capita tax for the month of September within the time allowed by the constitution, it would be considered in good standing as of September 1, 1946. This last motion cleared away any other technicalities that might have impeded the revolt.

At the regular meeting of October 16, the now dominant right wing voted down the various points-of-order of the Communist bloc and moved to proceed with the election despite warnings from Linus Lindberg that he would submit the whole question of the changed voting lists to the national CIO. Alfred Marriott, the clerk of the IUC's election commission, asked Lindberg for a list of the names of the delegates so that they could proceed with the election; Lindberg refused to hand over the list. Therefore, Momblow authorized the election commission to use its own discretion in deciding who would be permitted to vote.[4]

The commission decided to allow those delegates to vote who had a delegate card. Those not holding cards were permitted to vote if they were positively identified. Marriott later reported:

The election was conducted in the meeting hall. The polls were closed about 12:30 A.M. The Commission received no cooperation whatsoever from the officers of the Council in preparing for this election, nor during the election, and we were continuously jostled around by so-called appointed challengers who continuously made insulting remarks and on two occasions alleged that men were voting twice which is absolutely false and groundless.[5]

Since the meeting hall had to be vacated at one o'clock in the morning, the election commission vainly attempted to get a hotel room in which to count the ballots. They then decided to take the ballot box to the county Safety Building and place it in the care of the Milwaukee Police Department until they could get a room. During this time the members of the commission were followed by several cars of the left wing. The opposition group suggested that the ballot box be taken to the headquarters of Communist-controlled Local 248. The offer was refused. Arriving at police headquarters, the lieutenant in charge cooperated by getting the commission a room in the Republican Hotel.

Upon entering the hotel room—this was about two in the morning—an argument was raised by the opposition forces about who should be admitted to the room. The election commission allowed only the candidates and duly appointed challengers into the room. The rest of the mob stayed in the corridor. The counting of the ballots was occasionally interrupted by some who, like Philip Smith, field representative of the United Electrical Workers, called the commission members "stooges of the Manufacturers' Association and red-baiters." Strenuous objections were raised when the commission began to count the ballots cast by the delegates seated at the "illegal" meeting of October 13. At about three in the morning, a police officer entered the room and sat down; he was later joined by a second officer who ordered persons unauthorized to be in the room and those in the corridor to leave the building to conform with the city fire laws. It was not until 8:50 A.M. that the counting of the approximately 370 ballots was completed.

The ballot box was sealed and signed. Linus Lindberg, who was present, wanted to take the box to the IUC office. The commission, however, escorted by three police officers, took the ballot box and placed it in the safe-deposit vaults of a branch of the First Wisconsin National Bank. A rental card was signed by all members of the election commission with the understanding that the box could not be removed by less than three members of the commission. The election results brought victory—at least temporarily—for the right-wing slate. Arthur Conn, candidate for president on the right-wing slate, received 183 votes plus 53 which were challenged against 125 votes plus 2 challenged for his opponent, Roy Speth. Other candidates on the right-wing slate won by similar margins.[6]

The Communists were not to surrender so easily. They charged that the special meeting of October 13 was illegal and that the delegates seated did not meet the requirements of the constitution. Complaints about the election were filed with Philip Murray, president of the national CIO. Murray sent Allan S. Haywood, CIO Vice President and Director of Organization, and John Brophy, CIO Director of Industrial Union Councils, to Milwaukee to confer with the factions. The preliminary findings of Haywood and Brophy were that "We have found no evidence to support certain charges that the successful candidates in the election are the tools of unscrupulous, anti-labor forces connected with employers or reactionary political organizations . . . . Our remaining concern with the election relates primarily to questions of procedure . . . ."

Haywood and Brophy decided that the installation of new officers should be deferred until a final decision on the matter could be made. Rather than hold over the old officers, they appointed a temporary administrator, Peter Markunas, to assume the functions of the officers and the executive board until new officers were finally certified. All books, records, funds, and properties of the IUC were turned over to

Markunas to be investigated. The Haywood-Brophy report also noted:

It has been charged that the Council has exceeded its proper sphere of activity in dealing with questions on foreign and national issues on which the CIO has not declared itself, that delegates have been sent at Council expenses to meetings of organizations which the CIO has not endorsed, and that contributions have been made by the Council to such organizations. We hereby direct that any such practices be discontinued pending final decision, and in the event further investigation indicates that they have in fact occurred in the past, we shall make our order in this respect permanent.[7]

On November 22 a final report was issued. Haywood and Brophy ruled that the special meeting of October 13 had been properly called and the seating of delegates at that meeting was legal and valid. The Haywood-Brophy report also found that the election was fairly conducted and there was "no material irregularity, and certainly no fraud or dishonesty." They ruled that Local 9 of the Brewery Workers had been entitled to vote because the Brewery Workers International Union had only recently affiliated with the national CIO. While certain other locals might have been illegally allowed to vote, the ruling which permitted them to vote had been made in "good faith." However, because of the objections, a new election was ordered for December 4, 1946. It was further ordered, in a move obviously calculated to insure victory by the right-wing group, that all locals in good standing whose affiliation was accepted by the delegate body of the IUC in regular or special meetings or whose delegates were seated in any such meeting up to and including the special meeting of October 13 would be allowed to vote in the new election.

An audit of the books of the IUC revealed there had been "a decrease in the net worth of the Council of $488.87 for the period [from January 1, 1946, to October 31, 1946], not considering unpaid invoices of the amount of $347.25, on hand at the date of the audit." The examination of the books also indicated a "regrettable looseness in the handling of the petty cash account. Substantial sums were cleared through this account without any adequate record."

The accountant also submitted an audit of the "Civil Memorial Fund" collected to make a down payment on a labor temple. On January 10, 1945, the delegate body of the IUC had authorized the appointment of a committee to raise funds for the purpose. A total of $7,230.50 had been raised from advertisements published in a year book. Commissions and expenses of $3,092.33 were paid leaving a profit of $4,138.17. After that, the IUC was unable to purchase the property it had been considering at the anticipated price. The project was abandoned, but the minutes of the Council revealed that no report was ever made to the IUC on the developments. Thereafter, funds were paid out for airline transportation, to the Wisconsin Industrial Union Council, and to the *Wisconsin CIO News,* leaving a cash balance of only $63.17. At the time of the audit, the IUC held no notes or security for the repayment of the advances to the state Council or to the newspaper. The administrator, Markunas, took steps to recover the money from the transportation deposits and secure notes for the loans to the state Council and the newspaper. (Later, a proposed law suit against the former officers of the IUC to recover the funds was dropped on orders of the national CIO. The former officers had no assets, and it was believed the suit would only lead to more conflicts.)

The investigation also brought out that over a number of years the IUC had made substantial contributions to a large number of organizations which had not been endorsed by the national CIO, including such Communist-front organizations as the Wisconsin Conference on Social Legislation, the International Labor Defense, the Milwaukee Council of American-Soviet Friendship, the National Negro Congress, and the Civil Rights Congress. Delegates had often been sent to the meetings of these organizations at the expense of the IUC. Finally, the report found that in the past: "The Council has also taken stands and made statements, through messages of greeting, and otherwise, in respect to international and national events and policies on which the CIO has not declared itself in any way. This practice has been so frequent as to result in serious cleavages within the Council and to interfere with the discharge of the serious responsibilities of the CIO in local affairs."

The election held on December 4 again resulted in victory of the right-wing slate and ended the period of Communist control of the Milwaukee County Industrial Union Council. The revolt in Milwaukee was followed by the ousting of Communist leaders on the state level in 1947. Attention then turned to the strike of Local 248 at the Allis-Chalmers Company which had begun earlier in 1946.[8]

Purge at Allis-Chalmers

In October, 1945, the War Labor Board announced its loss of wartime powers to issue directives. The Allis-Chalmers Company then asked Local 248 to enter negotiations for a new contract. Negotiations continued until February, 1946, when the Union announced a tentative strike date of March 4. The chief issues unsettled were: (1) the refusal of management to retain a maintenance-of-membership clause which, under directions from the War Labor Board, had been in the contract since 1943, (2) a demand of management to change the grievance procedure and umpire system in order to restrict the activity of the union's stewards and committeemen, and (3) wages. Negotiations, which had been resumed under the Federal Conciliation Service on March 11, were broken off on April 23. Six days later the union held a strike vote, under somewhat-dubious conditions, and the strike began.

On April 30 mass picketing began at the company gates, and the management sent a telegram to the governor advising him of picket-line violence and stating that the police force of the city of West Allis was inadequate to cope with the situation. "All of this," read the telegram, "means that an incipient state of anarchy exists." The union in turn charged this was a "plot" by the company to "secure an injunction, or get the Governor to send in the troops and mow down the picket lines." On May 1 pickets entered the company office building and threw out two executive officers. Again the company wired the governor.

Ten days later, the president of Local 248 (now Robert Buse; Christoffel had been drafted into the Army) told the transport company to discontinue four scheduled streetcar routes serving the company's plant and West Allis. The company immediately filed a complaint with the Wisconsin Employment Relations Board charging Local 248 with illegal picketing. Pending a decision by the Board, the company instructed all office and shop employees, except those needed for vital maintenance work, to remain at home until further notice and broke off negotiations with the union. On May 31 the Wisconsin Employment Relations Board handed down an order that Local 248 should "cease and desist from mass picketing and from interfering with anyone entering or leaving the plant, and from demanding any type of identification from workers or others seeking to enter the plant." Upon issuance of the Board's order, the union abandoned mass picketing and negotiations were resumed on June 3.

A new element entered the picture. On May 27 Secretary of Labor Lewis B. Schwellenbach informed a company representative that there might be a seizure of the struck plant to facilitate production of vitally-needed farm machinery during the national food crisis. The union eagerly looked forward to the seizure in hopes that a favorable settlement might be obtained from the government. On the other side, the company equally dreaded the possibility, charging the threat of seizure made sincere collective bargaining virtually impossible. The company accused the Department of Labor of being in"apparent collusion" with the union "to engineer such seizure," a charge Schwellenbach later vehemently denied. On August 12 President Truman announced that the strike did not constitute a national emergency, and the issue died.

In October the company began a back-to-work movement which brought violence and mass picketing. The immediate effect of the violence was a 50-per-cent cut in the number of employees reporting for work. The continued mass picketing made returning to work precarious for several months. October 28 through 31, November 25, and December 4 and 9 there were clashes between the pickets and police. The number of pickets on those days ranged from 700 to 3,000 and the number of police from 30 to 900. Consequently, on December 18 the company filed another complaint with the Wisconsin Employment Relations Board charging Local 248 with illegal picketing and requesting the number of pickets be limited so that the normal police force could control the situation. In its decision dated December 26, 1946, the Board limited the number of pickets to two at each gate.[9]

During this same period a number of other important changes occurred. On October 6 Harold Christoffel returned from the Army to aid in the direction of the strike, and in November R. J. Thomas, now a vice president of the UAW, was designated by the policy committee of the UAW to take charge of the Allis-Chalmers' strike. A number of CIO locals in Milwaukee which had previously been reluctant to support Local 248 because of its Communist leadership began to offer aid. The primary reason for this change was the appeal by anti-Communists for all factions to unite to save the union from what many believed was an attempt by the company to destroy it. For example, at the November 29 meeting of the IUC, administrator Peter Markunas said,

> There is at this time a difference of opinion in the Council, but there is no difference in the needs of the working man and woman. The workers in the Allis-Chalmers plant have the same desires you have in making the same kind of fight that brought about security. Too many take this for granted. Regardless of our political differences, let us unite.

A new challenge came to Local 248. In January, 1947, a group called the Independent Workers of Allis-Chalmers, headed by Walter Peterson, petitioned the Wisconsin Employment Relations Board for a representation election. Although about 4,000 workers were going through the picket lines at the time the election was held, Local 248 received a plurality of the votes cast. Of the 8,259 valid ballots counted, Local 248 received 4,132 votes to 4,010 for the Independent Workers, and 117 votes for no union. Because there were 50 challenged votes, the local failed to receive an absolute majority. The Wisconsin Employment Relations Board prepared to call a run-off election, but before an election could be held, Local 248 called off the strike and returned to work on March 23. According to Robert Buse, president of the local, the decision had been made because of the "wild charges" made by management, the refusal of management to negotiate while there was mass picketing and violence, the two injunctions by the Wisconsin Employment Relations Board, the "smear campaign" launched by Milwaukee newspapers, the organization of a "company union," the "mass arrests" and contempt charges against pickets, the "illegal" representation election held in January, and the testimony of company representatives before the Committee on Education and Labor of the House of Representatives in February, which was designed to institute a "witch-hunt" against the union.

With the workers back in the plant, the company moved to discharge 91 union members and officials, and the union filed unfair-labor-practice charges with the National Labor Relations Board. (Later, the company was upheld in these discharges.) The local set up a "Committee for the Reinstatement of 91 Discharged Allis-Chalmers Workers" to fight the cases and asked the IUC to endorse the program. The IUC voted to give all possible aid to workers unfairly discharged, but the Council set up its own committee to aid the discharged workers because it believed that "part of the money would find its way by direct or indirect means into the treasury of the Communist Party here." This action provoked a flurry of letters charging the IUC with attempting to undermine the position of the discharged workers. The Council was ordered to take no action which would further divide the labor movement.[10]

During this time a number of moves were made to end the deadlock. Walter Reuther had been elected president of the UAW in 1946 over the opposition of a coalition which included the Communists. However, the coalition managed to maintain domination of the executive board of the International union, keeping effective control of the union out of Reuther's hands. Nevertheless, Reuther came to Milwaukee on March 24 to help settle the dispute.

According to the Milwaukee *Journal* of that date, there was a meeting between Reuther, company officials and the anti-Christoffel faction at the home of Reverend Reisner, pastor of the First Methodist Church. However, Reuther's efforts were ineffective because the executive board of the international worked closely with the leaders of Local 248. In May the executive board of the international turned down a petition by two union members who had been defeated in the election of officers for the local in February to call a new officers election. The defeated candidates then began to circulate printed postcards at the plant gates. The cards, addressed to Reuther, asked that Local 248 be placed under an administratorship. Finally on July 23 Walter Peterson, president of the Independent Union, sent a letter to the officers of Local 248 offering to merge the Independent Union with Local 248 if the officers would resign. As might have been expected, the offer was refused.

In June, 1947, the company filed a petition with the National Labor Relations Board asking for a new representation election at the plant. In the election held on July 17, Local 248 won more votes than its opponents, which now included the UAW-AFL as well as the Independent Union, but because there were 247 challenged votes, the local again failed, by 92 votes, to secure an absolute majority. The patternmakers and the electrical testers had requested a separate bargaining unit. This question, plus the counting of the challenged ballots, had to be decided by the National Labor Relations Board. The probability of Local 248 being certified was almost certain, but the Taft-Hartley Act intervened. The new law required the filing of non-Communist affidavits by union officers before the union could be certified. The provision temporarily banned certification of Local 248, and the local dwindled to a handful. Later investigation revealed that the local, which had once numbered over 8,000, dropped to only 184 dues-paying members in November 1947.

The beginning of the end for the Communist leadership of Local 248 came with the November convention of the international UAW. At the convention Reuther's forces gained control of the executive board and voted to sign the non-Communist affidavits. At first Local 248 voted not to sign but shortly afterward reversed its position. Most of the leaders of Local 248 resigned their positions but planned to retain power in the local by electing a slate of dummy officers. This move was thwarted by Reuther who placed the local under an administratorship.[11] (It was important for Reuther to eliminate Communists from the UAW if he was to consolidate his victories in the union.)

The incumbent officers of the local, referring to the March meeting of Reuther, company officials, and anti-Christoffel forces, charged that:

Walter Reuther and his henchmen have for years been trying to destroy our union and we in turn have continuously fought his sell-out activities. He tried to sell the union out to the company during the strike. He failed then and he will fail again. The work of Local 248 will go on. The meeting scheduled for this evening will be held and the work of taking care of the problems of the workers at Allis-Chalmers will not be stymied by any illegal action.[12]

An appeal by Local 248 to the courts to set aside the administratorship failed, and the Communist control of Local 248 ended. With Communist influences removed from the leadership of the Milwaukee County Industrial Union Council, the Wisconsin Industrial Union Council, the United Auto Workers nationally, and now Local 248, the *Wisconsin CIO News* editorialized on January 9, 1948:

> For the first time in many years AC workers face the future secure in the knowledge that the slate has been wiped clean, that a new deal is in the cards, and that they are backed in their demands for a clean, democratic local union by all the strength and power of the entire UAW-CIO . . . and the Wisconsin State and Milwaukee County CIO Industrial Union Councils.
>
> Observing the turbulent experience of Local 248 during its existence one notes a constantly recurring urge on the part of the Allis-Chalmers workers for a union of their own choosing.
>
> In spite of disastrous strikes, prolonged heart-breaking contract negotiations, political factionalism, and all the other ills a union of workers might become heir to, the one predominant factor always rising to overshadow temporary setbacks is the constant and compelling demand for bargaining rights.

At the 1948 convention of the Wisconsin Industrial Union Council, Walter Reuther commented: "We did not lose the Allis-Chalmers strike because we were fighting a tough management, because we have taken on equally tough managements in other situations and have won. We lost there because of a situation in our own house that was wrong—was bad, and which sapped our own strength. I am pointing this out as an object lesson so that never again will we allow this sort of situation to repeat itself within our union."[13]

In October nine of the left-wing leaders of Local 248 were tried and expelled from the local on charges that they had misused $83,000 in union funds. The legal status of Local 248 was finally settled in June, 1948, when it was certified by the National Labor Relations Board. In somewhat of an understatement, Pat Greathouse, the administrator of the local, commented, "Thus ended an 18 month stalemate in labor-management bargaining, unique in the history of labor relations." Two years later Local 248 signed a five-year agreement with the company which included a modified union shop—the first time the company had voluntarily agreed to any form of union security.

In 1948 the Wisconsin Industrial Union Council expelled seven executive board members of the Wisconsin branch of the Political Action Committee using their support of Henry Wallace—the national CIO had endorsed Truman—as an excuse. Most of the seven were fellow travelers. The 1949 convention of the national CIO brought the expulsion of 11 Communist-dominated international unions. As a result some Milwaukee locals, such as the Farm Equipment Workers Local at AMPCO, voted to leave the expelled international and affiliate with another union. (In the AMPCO case, the local affiliated with the UAW.) This eliminated the vestiges of Communist control in the Milwaukee CIO unions and central bodies.

The revulsion against Communism led to some excesses. In an ugly incident at Seaman Body in July 1950, workers in the plant seized a man who had signed the "Stockholm Peace Petition," carried him down four flights of stairs, and threw him into the street. The man was rushed to a hospital where he was reported in fair condition, suffering from a fractured spine and possible internal injuries. The stewards in the local were called into emergency session and, after an hour's discussion, decided to return to the plant and end the disturbance.[14]

Postlude

The period of Communist infiltration and control of CIO unions and central bodies in Milwaukee had been a calamitous episode. In the 1930's the Communists had found opportunities never before opened to them. The deplorable economic conditions of the Great Depression made many amenable to suggestions from any group that "was doing something." The new unions formed under the CIO had few members who knew the struggles with the Communists in the past. Many of the Communists had seemingly-overwhelming energy to carry on the tiring organizational work of the period. For instance, Meyer Adelman, a fellow traveler and long-time secretary-treasurer of the IUC, was arrested in 1938 for failure to obey an injunction to end the Fansteel sit-down strike in Chicago. It was perhaps not in jest that he then said (as quoted in the Milwaukee *Leader* of May 10, 1938), "I have no time to go to jail, I am too busy organizing."

Employers too must bear their responsibility for providing opportunities for Communists. Although writing in a different context, Selig Perlman prophetically wrote in 1922:

... American trade unionism ... seems in a fair way to continue its conservative function—so long as no overpowering open-shop movement or "trustification" will break up the trade unions or render them sterile. The hope of American Bolshevism will, therefore, continue to rest with the will of employers to rule as autocrats.[15]

It should be emphasized that Milwaukee was by no means the only area of Communist infiltration in the Thirties. For reasons similar to those important in Milwaukee, the Communists were able to infiltrate the national headquarters of the CIO—the general counsel, the editor of the *CIO News,* and the director of research and education were either Communists or fellow travelers. The Communists were also able to gain control of CIO affiliates in New York City, California, and Chicago and Illinois. To the 11 Communist-dominated national unions expelled in 1949-50 by the CIO—most notably the United Electrical Workers, the Mine, Mill and Smelter Workers, the International Longshoremen's and Warehousemen's Union, and the Fur and Leather Workers—must be added such unions as the National Maritime and the Transport Workers which followed the Communist line for a time.[16]

The elimination of the conditions that had opened opportunities for the Communists—the return of prosperity, the growth and stabilization of trade unionism, and a gradual, if in many cases reluctant, change in the attitude of employers—brought to a close the possibility of continued Communist influence. The purges of 1946 to 1950 ended it. Probably most important was the growing antagonism on the international front between the Soviet Union and the United States which plainly revealed the primary allegiance of the Communists. The labor movement could not, nor did it want to, continue in power those persons who could not be trusted.

The fruits of some ten years of Communist influence in the Milwaukee labor movement were violence, the suppression of internal union democracy, and the misuse of funds. Further, while it would be a gross exaggeration to say that the Communists caused, or were chiefly responsible for, the split in the Milwaukee labor movement, unquestionably the presence of Communists intensified the conflict. The Socialist leaders of the Federated Trades Council could make no peace with the Communist leaders of the Milwaukee County Industrial Union Council, for the Socialists and Communists of the city were mortal enemies.

The presence of Communists in Local 248 also prolonged the strike needlessly. The charge that the Allis-Chalmers Company sought to destroy the union during the 1946-47 strike seems debatable, but it is quite evident that the company was unwilling to make any settlement as long as Communists remained in control of the local. More generally, the very real problem of Communism in the Milwaukee labor movement gave aid to those who would brand all union leaders as radicals and tattered the reputation of trade unionism in the eyes of the public, forcing an extra task upon the CIO unions, in particular, to regain public prestige.

On balance, the Communists were a net disadvantage to the Milwaukee labor movement. Radicalism is a luxury the American labor movement can seldom afford, particularly when that radicalism is wedded to the interests of another nation.

CHAPTER XVII

Some Recent Developments

UNLIKE its feelings about the First World War, the Milwaukee labor movement had no reservations about American participation in the Second. Although the AFL unions in the state were extremely reluctant to see the United States engaged in any war that could conceivably be avoided, the kinship felt for Germany in the pre-World-War-I days was not repeated in the Thirties and Forties. Germans in the Milwaukee labor movement found no sympathy with a Nazi Germany that had suppressed its free trade-union movement and was antithetical to the principles of "Americanized socialism." The few Nazi sympathizers in Milwaukee were most often German immigrants of the post-World-War-I era or homebred fascists who seldom had any connections with the labor movement. CIO unions in the city tended to follow the attitudes of the general public, with the exception of the Communists who followed the policies of the Soviet Union.

With America actually under attack after Pearl Harbor, citizens of the community (with the exception of the few fascists) were unanimous in their support of the war. Unions were actively involved in the civilian war effort, though organizational activities were not neglected. With the generally-friendly attitude of governmental agencies, such as the War Labor Board, trade-union membership in Milwaukee increased during the war years, even though the time lost due to strikes was but one-third that of the three years immediately preceding the war.

However, the accumulated grievances of the war years, the creeping inflation that offset wage gains, and fears about a postwar depression laid the groundwork for a postwar strike wave. The end of the war in 1945 also brought an end to labor's wartime no-strike pledge, which had been increasingly difficult to implement as the war neared an end. Demands for unions' security, higher wages, and shorter hours, coupled with the unwillingness of employers to concede what they considered unreasonable demands (plus the belief of some employers that this would be a fine time to punish, or even destroy, the "unruly upstart"), brought a tremendous contest of strength in the postwar years. In the city of Milwaukee, the number of man-days lost due to strikes in the years 1945 through 1947 was 18 times that of the war years.

The irritation of the public with the postwar wave of strikes, the few wartime strikes (notably the coal strike of 1943), certain practices of trade unions, and the popular belief that the inflation and shortages of the reconversion period were in some way connected with the actions of the unions, lent urgency to the voices of the opponents of trade unionism. This resulted in the passage of the Taft-Hartley Act in 1947. Wisconsin had anticipated the federal legislation in 1939 with its own Wisconsin Employment Peace Act. Hence, there was no "little Taft-Hartley" act in Wisconsin in the postwar years. However, a short strike against the Milwaukee Gas Company and a national telephone strike brought a law regulating strikes in public utilities in Wisconsin.

Although bitterly opposed by organized labor, the law regulating public utility strikes was passed in 1947. It banned strikes and provided for conciliation of the dispute and, if necessary, compulsory arbitration. Of the 31 cases settled under the law, 9 were ultimately decided by compulsory arbitration. The law did not, however, prevent a short strike of streetcar workers in Milwaukee in 1948 or a strike of gas workers in October, 1949. Both the Amalgamated Association of Streetcar and Busmen's Union and the Gas, Coke, and Chemical Workers Union appealed their cases to the Wisconsin Supreme Court and then to the United States Supreme Court. That court ruled that the Wisconsin law conflicted with the Taft-Hartley Act and was, therefore, invalid.[1]

The political reaction which had produced the Taft-Hartley Act on the national scene and the Public Utility Act in Wisconsin also forced a political re-alignment of labor in the state. The Socialist Party was no longer a factor, the Progressive Party had disbanded, and the Republican Party was dominated by the conservatives, leaving the Democratic Party as the only realistic alternative for the unions.

The drift towards the Democratic Party was not, however, an entirely enthusiastic move on the part of the unions. The majority of Democratic members of Congress had, after all, voted for the Taft-Hartley Act, and the state Democratic Party did not have a notable record as a liberal group in the past. It was also not forgotten that President Truman had asked for a labor-draft bill during the railway strike of 1946 and had failed to make his veto of the Taft-Hartley Act effective. During the low ebb of Truman's popularity in early 1948, the Milwaukee County Industrial Union Council endorsed General Dwight Eisenhower for the presidency. After Truman was nominated by the Democratic Party, the state CIO followed the lead of the national CIO and endorsed Truman, but toyed with the idea of a possible labor party in the future. The president of the state central commented, "We are certain that labor will not allow itself to get in a situation again where its endorsement will be a choice of the lesser of many evils."

However, the unexpected re-election of Truman in 1948, along with a Democratic Congress, helped to dispel the idea of a third party in Wisconsin. The labor unions found a relatively cordial reception from the Democrats and began to cooperate more actively with that party, although in a number of cases the unions continued to endorse Republicans. Mutual interest in fighting the anti-union political trend of the postwar era also brought closer cooperation between the Federated Trades Council and the Milwaukee County Industrial Union Council. Previously, effective political cooperation had been impossible because of jurisdictional conflicts and ideological incompatibility when the Communists were in control of the IUC. While jurisdictional conflicts continued, the desire to present a united and more effective front led to the formation of Labor's Political League in Milwaukee in 1950. The League's executive committee was composed of 15 members from the FTC, 15 from the IUC, and 4 representatives from independent unions.[2]

Although labor-endorsed candidates, particularly in Milwaukee County, have been reasonably successful in elections, the political power of unions has been over-estimated by both friend and foe of the labor movement. Particularly worrisome to the Republicans was the tendency of the unions to endorse primarily members of the Democratic Party in Wisconsin. Consequently, the Republican-controlled legislature passed the Catlin Act in 1955. The law banned direct contributions by labor unions to political parties or individual candidates. The law was bitterly fought by labor unions and by the Democrats. Its provisions, however, were somewhat vague and it is doubtful if labor's political activities were seriously curbed by the measure. Moreover, in 1958 the Democrats were swept into office, and the following year the Catlin Act was repealed.

The forces working toward a merger of labor's political forces in Milwaukee were also important in the organic merger of the AFL and the CIO nationally. Communist influence within the CIO was ended by 1950. The AFL began to attack its own problem of internal corruption by expelling the International Longshoremen's Association in 1953. A promise of a reduction in disputes among national unions came with the signing of a "no-raiding" agreement in 1954. Labor leaders who had been symbolic of the antagonisms of the Thirties had left the scene. These factors, combined with the anti-labor trend of the postwar era, facilitated the merger of the two national federations on December 5, 1955, into the AFL-CIO. As a consequence, all central bodies were ordered to merge.

In Wisconsin and in Milwaukee, the merger did not proceed especially smoothly or rapidly. Disagreement arose over a number of points: apportionment of votes to local unions, representation on the executive boards, financing of union newspapers, and the award of jobs in the central bodies.

Finally, with the aid of the national AFL-CIO, the Wisconsin State Federation of Labor and the Wisconsin Industrial Union Council merged as the Wisconsin State AFL-CIO on July 24, 1958. George A. Haberman, president of the State Federation, was elected president and Charles M. Schultz, president of the state CIO, vice president. More than a year later, September 30, 1959, the FTC and the IUC merged. The new organization, the Milwaukee County Labor Council, represents more than 120,000 workers in the county. J. F. Friedrick, general secretary-treasurer of the FTC, was elected president, Stanley Joers, FTC general organizer, vice president, and Fred Erchul, IUC secretary-treasurer, secretary-treasurer in the new central.[3]

The united city central continues its major functions of providing social services to its members, promoting harmonious community relations, and furthering the political and legislative demands of the trade unions. Whether the Milwaukee labor movement will ever again develop a unique philosophy such as that which characterized the period of the Socialist-labor alliance seems extremely unlikely. With the almost complete assimilation of the Milwaukee labor movement into the American environment and the increased importance of policies established by the national organizations, it has neither the motivation nor the ability to develop an ideology which would set it apart from the main stream of trade-union life. Although there are some in the Milwaukee labor movement who advocate a renaissance of the "spiritual idealism" of the past, any idealism of the future bids fair to be one characteristic of the entire labor movement.

CHAPTER XVIII

An Experiment in Ideology

THE common-law marriage of Socialism and the labor movement in Milwaukee was unique. Here the Socialist Party had its brightest opportunity but then failed. Here the intellectual had his greatest chance to influence the labor movement and succeeded. The history of the labor movement in Milwaukee raises a number of important questions. (1) Why were unions so active in politics? (2) Why did Socialism achieve greater success in Milwaukee than elsewhere? (3) What did the Socialists accomplish, and what heritage did they bequeath to the labor movement? (4) Were relations between employers and unions in the city colored by the ideological preoccupations of labor? (5) Why was there no better cooperation with the Progressives? (6) Why did Socialism ultimately fail? (7) What role does ideology play in the labor movement?

1. Ours is a market-oriented society where all commodities are for sale, and labor, despite the declarations of the Clayton Act, is a commodity. If the economy is competitive, certain goals, such as the efficient allocation of resources, are automatically achieved. Though our society has substantial imperfections in its markets, it frequently appears to produce the competitive result in the long run. However, the narrow goals of economics are not all-important. The ability to determine the social goals of tomorrow or the means we shall use to achieve those goals is equally important—and much more exciting.

For many workers, the union represents the only vehicle for participation in the decision-making process. In an atomistic society freedom and effective participation are protected by the equal distribution of power. But in reality power is unequally distributed. Violence, one element of power, is generally limited to the state; hence, it becomes important to know who controls the state. The ability to persuade people to adopt a certain course of action, another element of power, is not a characteristic shared by all; not every man can be a messiah. Workers share but little in the third element of power, the control of economic resources. They usually control little but their own services.

If the services of workers can be collectively withheld or if workers can find a means to influence government, they enhance their power. Unions provide the mechanism through collective bargaining and political action. Each is almost as old as unionism itself. A crude form of bargaining can be traced back to the journeymen printers in New York City in 1778 and to the masons and bricklayers in Milwaukee in 1847. Political action by workers finds its origin in the Workingmen's Party of Philadelphia in 1828 and in the Milwaukee Labor Reform Association of 1866.

Municipal unionism has long had an advantage in the field of political action. City centrals have usually been involved in local contests—mayors, sheriffs, congressmen, state legislators. In those cases the concentration of union membership in cities was an advantage. To elect a governor or a president is much more difficult. Not until after 1910 did a majority of the nation's population live in urban areas. Even then unions were not strong in all urban areas. To elect local officials, unions did not need to tussle with an electoral college or elect a majority of congressmen from districts scattered over the face of the land. Moreover, in the days before radio and television, communication was infinitely easier if unions could restrict their appeal to members concentrated in a limited geographic area.

Labor's involvement in politics springs from no abstract analysis of power. Had there been no Civil War and no eight-hour movement in the 1860's, there would have been no Milwaukee Labor Reform Assembly. Had there been no long and bitter strike of the cigar makers in 1881-82, the Milwaukee Trades Assembly would probably not have entered the municipal elections of 1882, and Stowell would not have been elected mayor by the labor-Democratic coalition. Had there been no riot in 1886, the People's-Union Labor Party might never have succeeded, perhaps never have been born. Without Dave Rose and municipal corruption, the Socialists would not have been victorious in 1910.

Besides the specific grievances which motivated political action, the role of individuals must not be overlooked. If men such as Lyser and Brucker had not introduced Socialism to Milwaukee in the 1870's, Grottkau could not have caried the banner in the Eighties. Without the raging conflict between Schilling and Grottkau, Berger might never have learned the lessons necessary for the development of an Americanized Socialism. Would the response of the Milwaukee labor movement to Socialism have been the same without a Frank Weber? Probably not. Nor would the alliance have lasted as long without a Seidel and a Hoan in the mayor's office.

Political action is an integral part of the labor movement, not an ephemeral attraction. Unions achieved their earliest political success on the local level. The reasons why unions enter politics are concrete and vary over time. The means which unions use and the success they achieve are heavily influenced by the individuals active on the scene at the time.

2. Early Socialism failed in Milwaukee because it was too sectarian. The squabbles between those Socialists who advocated political action to the exclusion of unionism and those who advocated unions to the exclusion of politics vitiated the efforts of both. The failure of the early Socialists to cooperate with other groups, such as the Greenback Party of the 1870's, undoubtedly meant missed opportunities. Unions led by the Knights of Labor, which advocated producers' cooperatives, were unable to cooperate with Grottkau's Central Labor Union. Grottkau's bolt from the Union Labor Party in 1887 meant the separation of Socialism from the mainstream of union political interest at the time, though probably maintaining the pristine virtue of the Socialists.

The two factors contributing mightily to the ultimate success of Socialism in Milwaukee were the predominance of Germans in the population of the city, and Victor L. Berger.

In 1850, 64 per cent of the city's population was foreign-born, about 60 per cent of them Germans. As late as 1900, 31 per cent were foreign-born with the Germans still accounting for 60 per cent. These figures understate the importance of the German heritage. In some of the elementary schools, subjects were taught in German; English was the foreign language. The children and even the grandchildren of the immigrants were more adept in expressing themeslves in German than in English. The Bennett law of the 1890's was an attempt to accelerate the acculturation process, but it only produced a mighty political reaction.

While the earliest German immigrants, the Forty-Eighters, were swept up in the abolition movement of the Civil-War period and joined the Republican Party, their children and grandchildren could respond to the appeals of Socialist orators speaking in German. The German immigrants of a later period had already been exposed to Socialism in Germany; many had packed it in their trunks and brought it to America with them.

But to Victor L. Berger belongs the ultimate credit. A magnetic personality, he avoided the mistakes of the early Socialists. In their formative stage, the early Socialists refused to work with the Green-backers until it was too late. Grottkau bolted from the Union Labor Party too soon. But Berger was willing to work with the Populists in the 1890's until the time was ripe for a separate party.

Especially important was Berger's recognition of the imperative of a successful alliance with labor. Socialists had had some early political successes in the 1870's but after 1876 their newspaper, *Der Sozialist*, ignored unions. Schilling's political activities reached a pinnacle in 1886-87, but his base in the Knights of Labor eroded, and he was never able to gain support from the AFL unions. Berger, on the other hand, insisted on building a base in the unions and working with the rela-tively-conservative AFL. He did not dogmatically insist that all union-ists must follow his lead. The ranks of labor, he had proclaimed, must be open to all. Even after the Socialists gained control of the FTC in 1899, Berger was more tolerant toward political opposition within the organization than the union leaders themselves.

The Socialists and the unions were further united by common ene-mies. The excessive privileges granted the streetcar company by the city made the Socialists, as well as others, indignant. The vigorous but futile attempts to organize the company in 1896 and 1912 made the company an enemy of the unions. (In one of history's little ironies, Berger was killed in a streetcar accident in 1929.) If Dave Rose could denounce his opposition as a "rabble of pulpit hypocrites, character defilers, red-card Socialists, and a small section of the Mühlenberg Society still worshipping their Kaiser," the FTC could respond that "the late and odoriferous candidate for mayor, whose name disgraces one of our most beautiful and sweet scenting flowers" had uttered "a volume of vitriolic and nauseous political vomit, unbecoming any human being with a grain of intelligence. . . ."[1]

Of course the Socialists and the unions alone could not have achieved political success. Labor unions have always been a minority of the population. Only because the Socialists were willing to accept re-form, rather than emphasizing the long-range goal of a cooperative commonwealth, were they able to enlist the support of the community. The unexcelled political machine built by Berger played up the shocking municipal corruption of the turn of the century. This em-phasis brought political victory early. That was important. Had the Socialists been unable to elect a mayor and a congressman in 1910, one might doubt whether the unions would have long been willing to con-tinue their support.

3. The Socialist Emil Seidel was mayor of Milwaukee from 1910 to

1912 and Daniel Hoan held the office from 1916 to 1940. Several times the Socialists were successful in electing Berger to Congress, but during their period of power in Milwaukee, they socialized nothing. Rather, the Socialists gave the city an efficient and honest government—no mean achievement.

Perhaps more important than their gift to the city was the inheritance Socialists bequeathed to the labor movement. The noted integrity of the Milwaukee labor movement finds its antecedents in the Socialist movement as does the relatively-high degree of democracy, though as Michels' "iron law of oligarchy" suggests, it was not perfect. The local labor movement's receptiveness to industrial unionism, as symbolized by the adoption of the Wisconsin Plan in the 1930's, also finds its origin in the constant agitation of the Socialists for the organization of all workers. Similarly, the Milwaukee labor movement's strong interest in both workers' education and public education is part of that heritage. Without it the Milwaukee Workers College would not have been started in the Twenties. Without it, the University of Wisconsin's School for Workers might never have developed. Labor's interest in public education had its practical as well as its ideological motives. Unions feared that public schools would be used to spread anti-union propaganda. Also, they wanted to make sure that the school board would enforce union wages on school building projects and purchase union-made materials. But equally important was the fact that Socialist ideology placed great importance upon controlling the material fed to the children.

Finally, the interests of the Wisconsin and the Milwaukee labor movement in protective labor legislation was a consequence of Socialist influence. All unions were interested in legislation to restrict the use of the injunction and to outlaw the yellow-dog contract. But these are examples of laws affecting unions themselves. Unemployment compensation, minimum-wage laws, and public old-age pensions were supported by unions in Wisconsin long before they were endorsed by the AFL. The AFL under Gompers recognized that it could not influence government and, therefore, mistrusted it. The FTC was convinced it could influence government and was willing to embrace it as a partner.

4. It would appear that employer-employee relations were little affected by labor's flirtations with ideology. In the early period, E. P. Allis was active in the Greenback Party and perhaps helped bring Schilling to Milwaukee. His paternalistic activities on behalf of his employees were ahead of the times. But none of this kept his factory from being one of the prime targets in the riot of 1886. Val Blatz was a fervent Socialist, but he was an exception, not the rule. The National

Civic Federation, an early experiment in union-employer cooperation, had no noticeable effect in Milwaukee.

Employers in Milwaukee as elsewhere joined the virulent anti-union campaigns that periodically swept the nation. The open-shop movement of 1903-08 found an ardent supporter in Milwaukee's Metal Trades and Founders Bureau. Certainly the Milwaukee Employers Council was no half-hearted exponent of the American Plan in the Twenties, and labor's advance in the early Thirties activated the Citizens Law and Order League and the Milwaukee branch of the National Metal Trades Association.

Were relations any worse? Undoubtedly some employers were alarmed by the alliance with Socialism. Undoubtedly this influenced their decisions, just as Allis-Chalmers was opposed to settlement of the 1946-47 strike as long as the Communists remained in control. Yet, John R. Commons of the University of Wisconsin was proud of the cooperation which employers in the state gave on questions of labor law. The Milwaukee Merchants and Manufacturers Association, which became the Milwaukee Chamber of Commerce in 1917, played an important part in the preparation of workmens'-compensation legislation and helped improve the state-employment office in Milwaukee. Though often opposing new labor laws, the Wisconsin Manufacturers Association, founded in 1911, and the State Chamber of Commerce, formed in 1929, have helped to improve existing laws. This cooperation not only improved the laws but helped to make the progressive labor laws of the state permanent.

5. If the Socialists and the Progressive Republicans had worked closely together, their success might have been even more notable. But this was not possible. Personality conflicts, such as existed between Berger and LaFollette, were compounded by a rural-urban split and ideological differences over the appropriate attitude toward capitalism. They appealed to different ethnic groups, and their attitudes about the world at large differed. Berger and La Follette were united in the First World War by a common opposition to the war. La Follette left a heritage of isolationism that held sway in Wisconsin for years. Berger's opposition to the war had a different base: the belief in the essential unity of labor throughout the world.

The Socialists and the Progressives were rivals for votes in Milwaukee. The Progressive Republicans joined the coalition that ousted Seidel from office in 1912. In 1914 Seidel ran for the United States Senate. The vote he gained in Milwaukee probably cost Francis McGovern, a Progressive Republican, the election.[2] The two attempts at coalition—
La Follette's presidential bid in 1924 and the Farmer-Labor Progres-

sive Federation of the Thirties—sapped the strength of the Socialists and produced few notable results.

6. Why did the Socialist Party in Milwaukee ultimately fail? In many respects the factors responsible for the success of Socialism were ultimately its undoing. The Socialists had emphasized reform, and the reforms of Wilson's New Freedom and Roosevelt's New Deal wooed away the conservative "sewer Socialists." Berger had vigorously opposed the radical IWW, and the Bolshevik revolution won the allegiance of the restive left. The Socialist Party was built on the foundation of unionism, and labor declined in the Twenties. Socialism had scant appeal to the new unionism of the Thirties. The conservatives came to support FDR, and the Communists locked the door to Socialism wherever they held control.

The Socialists had built a fort in Milwaukee but were unable to duplicate their success on the state or national level. The development of national labor agreements, improvements in communication and transportation, and the impact of the New Deal tended to centralize the important decision-making centers. Local groups were robbed of significant content. Unions found that they must negotiate with political parties able to command attention among a larger group of people if they were to achieve their constantly-changing goals.

In Milwaukee Socialism spoke with a German accent. This had been an asset, but it became a liability. While almost 20 per cent of Milwaukee's population in 1900 had been born in German lands, this had shrunk to 5 per cent in 1940. Under the strain of the First World War, elementary schools abandoned instruction in German; it was now relegated to the status of a foreign language. With the advent of the Second World War, elementary schools no longer taught German even as a foreign language.

The overwhelmingly-German membership of the Socialist Party in Milwaukee was known throughout the nation. David Shannon relates the story, probably apocryphal, of the Milwaukee Socialist who was explaining the political defeat of a Socialist candidate with a Polish name. "If we had had someone with a good American name like Schimmelpfennig," said the Milwaukeean, "we would have won."[3]

Other immigrant groups found little appeal in Socialism. The Irish, who came to Milwaukee about the same time as the Germans, the large number of Poles, who started to become important after 1870, and other, smaller groups, like the Italians and Yugoslavians, had had little exposure to Socialism in their home country. Many from these groups stayed outside the labor movement until the days of the CIO.

Quite probably the attitude of the Roman Catholic Church played a role. In 1904 the Socialists' newspaper charged that the Catholic Church was aiding the open-shop crusade of the employers and commented: "So you see, Mr. Workingman, you are not only oppressed by the greed of the capitalist class, but the Church is also being used against your efforts to improve the conditions of your class." In the mayoralty campaign of the same year, the clergy of the Church uncompromisingly denounced the Socialists. Polish priests even invited Dave Rose to speak to their congregations the Sunday before the election, staggering their meetings to make it possible for Rose to visit every church. The Church's adamant opposition to Socialism also undoubtedly affected the Polish Catholics' attitude towards FTC-affiliated unions which were known to be closely allied with the Socialists. While the Socialists and the unions did gain Catholic members, as did the Communists in the Thirties, their real strength lay elsewhere.[4]

Even though Frank Zeidler, a Socialist, was mayor of Milwaukee from 1948 to 1960, his victories could hardly be attributed to the work of the Socialist Party. In Zeidler's 1956 race the issue of Socialism was again raised by the Milwaukee *Sentinel.* The voting pattern bore little resemblance to the patterns in the heyday of the Milwaukee Socialist Party. Zeidler carried all the wards in the city except his opponent's home ward and the "Republican Eighteenth." This more closely suggests a split between Democrats and Republicans than between Socialists and anti-Socialists.

The strains of the First World War, the decline of unions in the Twenties, the assimilation of the immigrants, and the traumatic developments of the Thirties sealed the fate of the Socialist Party in Milwaukee. An exciting experiment had ended. But while the party died, ideology continues. No person is without an ideology, though he may be unable to verbalize it. The labor movement is also affected by ideology. What role does it play?

7. Unquestionably the major gift of unionism to American society has been the development of collective bargaining and the grievance procedure. These constantly-evolving institutions have established a form of industrial government. It is also true that the working rules of unions are a very real and basic part of those organizations. But so is participation in the political process. Labor parties as such have been few and far between in American history, and the obstacles to the development of a successful one today are formidable. To be politically successful, therefore, unions must of necessity enter into alliances with other groups. Certainly exclusive emphasis on collective bargaining and union work rules would provide too narrow a base for an alliance. We see evidence today of the attempt to adopt a wider appeal. Labor's

support of social security, its advocacy of civil-rights legislation, and its preference for public over private power are a part of it. True, in each case unions have practical reasons for their position, but labor's public posture can hardly be attributed to a desire to control jobs, unless words are defined so broadly that they lose all meaning.

Can a wide appeal be successfully united with the labor movement's more parochial interests? Yes. The Milwaukee labor movement, despite its reverses in the past and despite the death of the Socialist Party, bears testimony to that. And so does the evolving alliance between labor and the Democratic Party.

The planks in the appeal are part of an ideology. The ideology cannot be implanted by outsiders who expect it to be swallowed whole by the labor movement without any protest or reshaping. Rather a pragmatic ideology—a virtual contradiction in terms—must evolve. Organizations have no inner logic which makes it possible to predict precisely the ideology of the future. We must wait to see what ideas men develop, not what history dictates.

The development of any ideology brings a class of true believers—fanatics; they, however, are the men who fashion the reality of tomorrow. At times, the labor movement may appear bereft of any ideology. This is but a phase of an almost exclusive emphasis on the parochial interests of unions. Those interests can never be forgotten, but the total repudiation of ideology may trap unions into the sin of Esau.

Notes
Bibliography
Index

Notes

Works listed in the Bibliography are cited in shortened form in the Notes.

CHAPTER ONE

1 Still, *Milwaukee*, pp. 570–77.

2 Berthrong, "Social Legislation," pp. 125–29, 144–61, 175–90.

3 Milwaukee *Daily Sentinel,* May 10, 1881; Wisconsin Bureau Labor Statistics, *First Biennial Report,* pp. 138–39.

4 Milwaukee *Daily Sentinel,* Feb. 11, 1845. There is no evidence that the "Trades Union" referred to was a real union.

5 Milwaukee *Sentinel,* Aug. 24, 1847; Mueller, "Milwaukee Workers," p. 205; Still, *Milwaukee,* p. 65; Buck, *Pioneer History,* II, 50. Reports on many of the early strikes are fragmentary.

6 Mueller, "Milwaukee Workers," pp. 205–6; Milwaukee *Sentinel,* Aug. 1, 1848.

7 Milwaukee *Sentinel,* Aug. 30, Sep. 1, 1851.

8 Mueller, "Milwaukee Workers," p. 206; Osten, "The Annekes," *Milwaukee Turner,* III, 5.

9 Merk, *Economic History,* pp. 162–63.

10 Buck, *Milwaukee Under the Charter,* III, 439–41; Milwaukee *Sentinel,* Jul. 12, 13, 1853.

11 Milwaukee *Sentinel,* Aug. 18, 31, Sep. 7, 8, 10, 12, 1853.

12 *Ibid.,* Jan. 18, 22, 1855.

13 Mueller, "Milwaukee Workers," p. 206; Merk, *Economic History,* pp. 162–63.

14 Milwaukee Writers Project, "History of Milwaukee County," p. 310.

15 Merk, *Economic History,* pp. 160–61; Mueller, "Milwaukee Workers," pp. 207–8.

16 Milwaukee *Sentinel,* Jan. 13, Jul. 27, 30, 1860, Oct. 28, 1862, Jan. 15, 16, 17, 19, 21, 24, 1863, Apr. 12, 1864; Wisconsin Bureau Labor Statistics, *Second Biennial Report,* pp. 204–5.

17 Wisconsin Bureau Labor Statistics, *Second Biennial Report,* pp. 206–7; Mueller, "Milwaukee Workers," p. 208; Merk, *Economic History,* pp. 175–76.

18 Merk, *Economic History,* p. 166; Milwaukee *Sentinel,* Oct. 2, Dec. 7, 8, 1866.

19 Milwaukee *Sentinel,* Feb. 11, Mar. 13, 1861, Aug. 4, 1870.

CHAPTER TWO

1 Milwaukee *Sentinel*, Nov. 7, 1848; Berthrong, "Social Legislation," p. 169; Merk, *Economic History*, pp. 163, 182; Mueller, "Milwaukee Workers," p. 208.

2 Mueller, "Milwaukee Workers," p. 212; Commons, *Documentary History*, IX, 177, 131; Merk, *Economic History*, pp. 179–80; Milwaukee *Sentinel*, Nov. 7, 10, 11, 1865.

3 Milwaukee *Sentinel*, Dec. 1, 1865, Jan. 17, 23, 27, Feb. 9, 10, 21, Mar. 17, 30, 31, 1866; Merk, *Economic History*, pp. 180–81.

4 Berthrong, "Social Legislation," pp. 170–72; Milwaukee *Sentinel*, Jan. 21, 1867.

5 Berthrong, "Social Legislation," pp. 172–75; Milwaukee *Sentinel*, Feb. 11, Mar. 4, 9, 11, 14, Apr. 6, 1867.

6 Milwaukee *Sentinel*, Mar. 19, 1866; Wisconsin Bureau Labor Statistics, *Second Biennial Report*, pp. 314–15.

7 Milwaukee *Sentinel*, Apr. 24, 29, Jul. 6, 9, 25, 1867; Merk, *Economic History*, pp. 178, 181–82.

8 Milwaukee *Sentinel*, Jul. 8, Aug. 26, Sep. 22, 27, Oct. 20, Nov. 1, 3, 1869; Merk, *Economic History*, pp. 183–85; Mueller, "Milwaukee Workers," p. 212.

9 Merk, *Economic History*, pp. 167, 175; Mueller, "Milwaukee Workers," p. 210; Milwaukee *Sentinel*, Dec. 20, 1861.

10 Mueller, "Milwaukee Workers," pp. 210–11; Merk, *Economic History*, pp. 174–78.

11 Merk, *Economic History*, p. 170 n.

12 Mueller, "Milwaukee Workers," pp. 209–10; Merk, *Economic History*, pp. 176–77; Lescohier, *Knights of St. Crispin*, pp. 5–6; McNeill, *The Labor Movement*, p. 199; Milwaukee *Sentinel*, Jan. 4, Apr. 4, 1874; *KOSC Monthly Journal*, L, 117–18.

13 *Workingman's Advocate*, Jun. 11, 1870, cited in Merk, *Economic History*, pp. 182–83n.

14 Merk, *Economic History*, pp. 173–74; Milwaukee *Sentinel*, Oct. 7, 8, 14, 1868, Mar. 20, 27, Apr. 6, Aug. 5, 1872, Feb. 25, 1876, Nov. 1, 7, Dec. 27, 1877, Oct. 10, 1878, Jul. 19, 1879.

15 Milwaukee *Sentinel* Jul. 1, 1872.

16 *Ibid.*, Jul. 2, 3, 6, 13, 1872.

17 *Ibid.*, May 3, Jul. 26, 27, 30, Sept. 2, 8, 9, 20, Nov. 12, 1873, Jan. 10, Mar. 26, 28, Apr. 4, 23, Nov. 11, 1874, Feb. 4, 1875, Jan. 13, 15, Feb. 25, May 3, 9, 10, 13, 25, 1876.

18 Merk, *Economic History*, pp. 185–86.

CHAPTER THREE

1 Still, *Milwaukee*, p. 574; Holzman, "The German Forty-Eighters," pp. 55–56.

2 Holzman, "The German Forty-Eighters," pp. 57–58; Mueller, "The Socialist Movement," p. 57; Milwaukee Writers Project, "History of Milwaukee County," pp. 310–11.

3 Wachman, *History of the Social-Democratic Party,* p. 10; Olson, "The Milwaukee Socialists," p. 10.

4 Commons, *History of Labor,* II, 232–33, 281.

5 Milwaukee *Sentinel,* Mar. 27, May 18, Jun. 2, 1876; *Der Sozialist,* Feb. 17, Jun. 29, Jul. 8, 1876; Olson, "The Milwaukee Socialists," pp. 10–11.

6 Milwaukee *Sentinel,* Jul. 8, 1876.

7 Commons, *History of Labor,* II, 270–71; Milwaukee *Sentinel,* Jul. 13, Sep. 14, 16, 1876, Mar. 12, 13, 27, 1877; *Der Sozialist,* Sep. 14, 23, 28, 29, 30, Oct. 15, 1876; Milwaukee Writers Project, "History of Milwaukee County," p. 213.

8 *Milwaukeer Sozialist,* Nov. 7, 1877; Witte, "Labor in Wisconsin History," p. 86. Witte's account errs in stating that Allis was endorsed by the Socialists in 1877.

9 Milwaukee Writers Project, "History of Milwaukee County," pp. 310–12; Commons, *History of Labor,* II, 273–81; Olson, "The Milwaukee Socialists," pp. 8–12; Milwaukee *Sentinel,* Jul. 25, 28, 30, 1877, Aug. 8, Oct. 25, Nov. 17, 1879; *Der Sozialist,* Aug. 1, 11, 1877; *Milwaukeer Sozialist,* Apr. 2, 3, 1878.

CHAPTER FOUR

1 Milwaukee *Sentinel,* Jul. 2, 4, 18, Aug. 8, 1878; Jun. 12, Jul. 19, 21, 1879.

2 *Ibid.,* Jan. 7, 8, 19, 1880; Dec. 19, 1881, Jun. 2, July 8, 1882; Wisconsin Bureau Labor Statistics, *First Biennial Report,* p. 123.

3 Milwaukee *Sentinel,* Jan. 2, Apr. 21, Aug. 31, 1880, Apr. 23, May 6, Aug. 30, 1881.

4 Wisconsin Bureau Labor Statistics, *First Biennial Report,* p. 132; *Printers Daily Bulletin,* May 5, 1881.

5 Milwaukee *Sentinel,* Jul. 27, Aug. 26, 27, 28, 30, 31, Sep. 1, 3, 4, 9, 10, 1880.

6 *Ibid.,* Apr. 29, May 2, 5, 6, 7, 10, 11, 16, 1881; *Printers Daily Bulletin,* May 5, 7, 1881.

7 Typographical Union Local 23, "Milwaukee Constitution, June 1881."

8 *Printers Daily Bulletin,* Apr. 29, 30, May 2, 7, Aug. 2, 6, 20, Sep. 3, 1881, Feb. 28, Mar. 6, 13, 1884; Milwaukee *Sentinel,* Apr. 26, 1881, May 24, Jun. 9, 1882; Wisconsin Bureau Labor Statistics, *First Biennial Report,* pp. 149–51, and *Second Biennial Report,* pp. 267–68, 372–74; Milwaukee *Labor Review,* Apr. 24, 1886.

9 Quoted in Wisconsin Bureau Labor Statistics, *First Biennial Report,* pp. 121–22.

10 Milwaukee *Daily Journal,* Jan. 4, 1883; *Printers Bulletin,* Sep. 3, 1881; Milwaukee *Sentinel,* Sep. 3, 5, 1881; Commons, *History of Labor,* II, 321.

11 Milwaukee *Sentinel,* Mar. 12, 16, 20, Apr. 3, 8, 1880.

12 *Trades Assembly Bulletin,* Apr. 1, 1882; Milwaukee *Sentinel,* Feb. 13, Mar. 6, 21, 25, Jun. 9, 1882; *Printers Bulletin,* Nov. 5, 1881.

13 Milwaukee *Sentinel,* Jan. 14, Mar. 2, 6, 7, 21, 23, 25, 26, 28, 31, Apr. 5, 1882; Still, *Milwaukee,* p. 282.

14 Milwaukee *Sentinel,* Aug. 31, Sep. 21, Nov. 8, 1882; Witte, "Labor in Wisconsin History," p. 86.

15 Milwaukee *Sentinel,* Jun. 12, Sep. 25, 1882; Milwaukee *Daily Journal,* Jan. 4, 1883, Jun. 16, 1884, Jan. 8, Jul. 14, 1885; Wisconsin Bureau Labor Statistics, *First Biennial Report,* pp. 121–23.

16 Wisconsin Bureau Labor Statistics, *First Biennial Report,* pp. 127–32, and *Second Biennial Report,* pp. 446–52.

17 Commons, *History of Labor,* II, 76, 161–68, 241–44; McNeill, *The Labor Movement,* p. 201; Milwaukee *Sentinel,* Dec. 3, 1881; postcard from Lewis Ranch to Schilling, Feb. 14, 1881, and partial biography of Schilling (n.a., n.d.), in Schilling papers; Usher, *The Greenback Movement,* p. 60; Still, *Milwaukee,* p. 592.

18 Wisconsin Bureau Labor Statistics, *Second Biennial Report,* p. 317, and *First Biennial Report,* pp. 145–59; Milwaukee *Sentinel,* Apr. 15, 1882; Milwaukee *Daily Journal,* May 15, 1886.

CHAPTER FIVE

1 Wisconsin Bureau Labor Statistics, *First Biennial Report,* pp. 140–44; Milwaukee *Sentinel,* Oct. 31, 1877, Nov. 1, 3, 4, 12, 1881.

2 Milwaukee *Sentinel,* Nov. 26, 1881.

3 *Ibid.,* Dec. 5, 12, 13, 19, 1881; Jan. 5, 1882.

4 *Ibid.,* Nov. 28, 1881, Feb. 6, 1882.

5 Wisconsin Bureau Labor Statistics, *First Biennial Report,* p. 126, and *Second Biennial Report,* pp. 212–13, 256; Milwaukee *Daily Journal,* Nov. 17, 24, 1882, May 2, 1883.

6 Milwaukee *Daily Journal,* May 12, 1886; Wisconsin Bureau Labor Statistics, *Second Biennial Report,* pp. 213–16, 254–56, 274–82, 374.

7 Wisconsin Bureau Labor Statistics, *Second Biennial Report,* pp. 256–267, 385; Milwaukee *Daily Journal,* May 20, 1886.

8 Milwaukee *Daily Journal,* May 27, 1884, May 8, 10, 1886; Milwaukee *Labor Review,* Apr. 5, May 6, 1886.

9 *Social Democratic Herald,* Jul. 16, 1898; *Arbeiter-Zeitung,* May 4, 1886; Commons, *History of Labor,* II, 281, 287, 296, 387, 516; Wisconsin Bureau Labor Statistics, *Second Biennial Report,* p. 326.

10 Milwaukee *Labor Review,* Apr. 3, 1886; Wisconsin Bureau Labor Statistics, *Second Biennial Report,* pp. 217–18.

11 Wisconsin Bureau Labor Statistics, *Second Biennial Report,* p. 319.

12 *Ibid.,* pp. 335–36.

13 *Ibid.,* pp. 325–41; King, "Memories of a Busy Life," pp. 374–77; Milwau-

kee *Daily Journal*, Apr. 30, May 1, 3, 4, 5, 7, 12, 1886; Milwaukee *Labor Review*, May 8, Oct. 16, 1886; *Arbeiter-Zeitung*, May 4, 1886; Wisconsin Adjutant General, *Biennial Report*, pp. 13–26, 40; Milwaukee *Daily News and Daily Review*, Mar. 26, 1890.

14 Wisconsin Bureau Labor Statistics, *Second Biennial Report*, pp. 362–72.

15 King, "Memories of a Busy Life," p. 377; Witte, "Labor in Wisconsin History," p. 137.

16 Wisconsin Bureau Labor Statistics, *Second Biennial Report*, pp. 335–38, 376; Milwaukee *Labor Review*, May 15, Jun. 12, 1886; Berthrong, "Social Legislation," p. 315; Usher, *The Greenback Movement*, correction inserted after p. 92.

17 Wisconsin Bureau Labor Statistics, *Second Biennial Report*, pp. 266, 366; Milwaukee *Labor Review*, May 29, Jul. 3, 10, 17, 1886.

18 Milwaukee *Daily Journal*, May 6, 7, 8, 12, 20, Jun. 14, 15, 16, 17, 18, 19, 20, 21, Jul. 1, 19, 1886.

19 Milwaukee *Labor Review*, Jun. 5, 1886; Remey and Bruce, "A Half Century in Business Effort," part I, ch. III, 22.

20 Wisconsin Bureau Labor Statistics, *Second Biennial Report*, pp. 338–39; Milwaukee *Labor Review*, May 29, Jun. 19, Jul. 10, 17, Sep. 4, 11, 18, 25, Oct. 2, 1886; Heath, *Social Democracy Red Book*, p. 39.

21 Milwaukee *Daily Journal*, Nov. 1, 1886.

22 *Ibid.*, Nov. 6, 24, 1886; Witte, "Labor in Wisconsin History," p. 137; Wisconsin Bureau Labor Statistics, *Second Biennial Report*, pp. 341–44; Milwaukee *Daily Journal*, May 7, Jun. 8, Jul. 19, Nov. 15, 29, Dec. 31, 1886; Milwaukee *Labor Review*, Jun. 5, 12, Jul. 3, Aug. 21, Nov. 6, 13, 1886, Apr. 23, 30, May 7, 17, 1887; Milwaukee *Daily Review*, May 22, 1888; *Arbeiter-Zeitung*, Jan. 28, 1887.

CHAPTER SIX

1 Witte, "Labor in Wisconsin History," pp. 137–38; Holzman, "The German Forty-Eighters," p. 60; Milwaukee *Labor Review*, Apr. 9, 1887; Milwaukee *Daily Review*, Apr. 6, 1887.

2 Commons, *History of Labor*, II, 465-68; Still, *Milwaukee*, pp. 284-85; Milwaukee *Labor Review*, Sep. 10, 1887, Mar. 24, 1888.

3 Milwaukee *Daily Review*, Mar. 28, 29, 30, 1888.

4 *Ibid.*, Apr. 4, 1888.

5 *Ibid.*, Apr. 5, May 6, 1888; Milwaukee *Labor Review*, Mar. 24, 31, 1888; Still, *Milwaukee*, pp. 284–86.

6 Still, *Milwaukee*, p. 592; Milwaukee *Labor Review*, Jun. 16, 23, 1888; Milwaukee *Daily Review*, Apr. 4, Nov. 7, 1888; Milwaukee *Daily News and the Daily Review*, Jun. 30, Aug. 10, Sep. 9, Oct. 8, 1889, Mar. 25, Apr. 2, Jun. 16, 18, Aug. 2, Sep. 6, Oct. 13, Nov. 5, Dec. 18, 1890, May 16, 20, 1891; Milwaukee *Daily News*, Nov. 30, 1891; Commons, *History of Labor*, II, 469.

7 Milwaukee *Labor Review*, Jan. 29, Feb. 19, Dec. 17, 1887; Milwaukee *Daily News and the Daily Review*, Nov. 15, 1890; Milwaukee *Leader*, Mar. 15, 1930; FTC Constitution, reprinted in *Wisconsin Labor* (1939), 41.

8 Milwaukee *Labor Review*, Jun. 4, 1887. All emphasis in the original.

9 *Ibid.*, Sep. 10, 24, 1887; Milwaukee *Daily Review*, Mar. 2, 1889; Milwaukee *Daily News and the Daily Review*, Nov. 25, 1889, Jun. 19, 1890, Apr. 28, 30, May 7, Jul. 11, 1891; *Milwaukee Directory*, 1880 through 1895 editions.

10 Wisconsin Bureau Labor Statistics, *Third Biennial Report*, p. xxvii.

11 Milwaukee *Daily News and the Daily Review*, Jun. 20, 29, Dec. 6, 1889, Jan. 3, 17, Feb. 7, 24, Apr. 18, 22, May 2, 8, 12, 1890; Milwaukee *Daily Review*, Feb. 7, 16, 1889; Commons, *History of Labor*, II, 475.

12 Quoted in Foner, *History of the Labor Movement*, II, 171–72.

13 Milwaukee *Labor Review*, Apr. 16, May 7, 14, Jun. 4, 1887; Milwaukee *Daily News and the Daily Review*, Sep. 25, 1889, Apr. 17, 1890; Milwaukee *Daily News*, Dec. 1, 14, 1891; Milwaukee *Labor Press*, Feb. 11, 1943; Commons, *History of Labor*, II, 488; "An Appeal to Organized Labor," flyer in papers of Milwaukee Brewers Union, Local 9.

14 Milwaukee *Daily News and the Daily Review*, Jan. 16, Feb. 2, 16, Mar. 10, 11, 18, Apr. 1, 2, 8, 10, 14, 20, May 1, 6, 7, 8, 12, 18, Jun. 4, 29, 1891; Commons, *History of Labor*, IV, 336.

15 Milwaukee *Daily News and the Daily Review*, Oct. 9, 10, 11, 14, 15, 16, 1889; Milwaukee *Journal*, Feb. 4, 7, 1895; Milwaukee *Labor Press*, Feb. 25, 1943; Milwaukee *Sentinel*, Feb. 14, 1895.

16 Wisconsin Legislator, *Assembly Journal*, Apr. 22, 1919, pp. 864-65; Still, *Milwaukee*, pp. 370–71; Wisconsin Board Arbitration and Conciliation, *First Biennial Report*, pp. 11–23.

17 Quoted in Campbell, *Wisconsin in Three Centuries*, IV, 99.

18 Wisconsin Board Arbitration and Conciliation, *First Biennial Report*, p. 12; Mueller, "Milwaukee Workers," p. 222.

19 Milwaukee *Daily Review*, Sep. 19, 20, 1888; Milwaukee *Labor Press*, Feb. 11, 1943; Wisconsin *Vorwärts*, Jan. 6, 1893; Berthrong, "Social Legislation," pp. 360–61.

20 Schmidt, "History of Labor Legislation," p. 28; Wisconsin Labor Relations Board, *Report*, p. 1; summary of proceedings of first WSFL convention in *Wisconsin Labor* (1924), n.p.

CHAPTER SEVEN

1 Milwaukee *Daily News and the Daily Review*, Dec. 8, 1890.

2 *Ibid.*, Apr. 18, 1890.

3 Wisconsin *Vorwärts*, Jan. 3, 6, May 5, 1893, Jul. 2, 1894; Milwaukee Writers Project, "History of Milwaukee County," p. 312; Olson, "The Milwaukee Socialists," pp. 12, 17–20.

4 Olson, "The Milwaukee Socialists," pp. 24–25; see also Wachman, *History of the Social-Democratic Party*, p. 24; Commons, *History of Labor*, II, 515-16.

5 Wachman, *History of the Social-Democratic Party*, pp. 10–14, 34; Klotsche, "The 'United Front' Populists," pp. 382–84; Perlman, "History of Socialism," pp. 24–31; Still, *Milwaukee*, p. 301; Olson, "The Milwaukee Socialists," p. 109; Milwaukee *Leader*, Mar. 15, 1930; Milwaukee *Daily News and the Daily Review*, May 16, Nov. 21, 1890; Wisconsin *Vorwärts*, Jan. 3, 1893, Nov. 2, 1894.

6 FTC *Constitution* (1893), pp. 5–6; summary of WSFL proceedings, 1894, in *Wisconsin Labor* (1924), n.p.

7 Perlman, "History of Socialism," pp. 32–36.

8 *Ibid.*, p. 33; Commons, *History of Labor*, IV, 227; Wachman, *History of the Social-Democratic Party*, pp. 17–24; *Social Democratic Herald*, Sep. 10, 17, 1898.

9 Dec. 24, 1899, quoted in Wachman, *History of the Social-Democratic Party*, p. 35.

10 *Ibid.*, pp. 35–36; Perlman, "History of Socialism," pp. 35–37.

11 *Social Democratic Herald*, Apr. 26, 1902, Jul. 18, 1903; summary of WSFL proceedings, 1904, in *Wisconsin Labor* (1924), n.p.

12 FTC *Constitution* (1893).

13 FTC *Minutes* (hereafter *FTCM*), Jun. 17, 1908.

14 *Ibid.*, Oct. 3, 17, 1900, Mar. 19, 1902, Nov. 15, 1905, Jun. 6, 20, 1906, Feb. 6, 1907.

15 *Ibid.*, Apr. 3, Jun. 5, Aug. 20, Dec. 18, 1901, Oct. 1, 15, Dec. 17, 1902, Aug. 15, Dec. 16, 1908, Nov. 3, 1909, Jan. 5, Apr. 20, 1910; *Social Democratic Herald*, Nov. 30, 1901, Jan. 13, 20, 27, Oct. 6, 1902, Jun. 6, 1903, Jul. 13, 1907.

16 *FTCM*, Apr. 7, Jun. 16, 1909.

17 Wachman, *History of the Social-Democratic Party*, p. 40; Olson, "The Milwaukee Socialists," pp. 92 n., 231–33; Drosen, "The History of Socialism," p. 15.

18 *FTCM*, Oct. 3, 1900, Apr. 17, May 15, Nov. 20, Dec. 14, 1901.

19 *Ibid.*, Oct. 16, 1901.

20 *Ibid.*, Jun. 18, 1902, Apr. 15, Oct. 7, 1908.

21 *Social Democratic Herald*, May 31, 1902.

22 *FTCM*, Jul. 26, 1902.

23 Commons, *History of Labor*, IV, 151.

24 *Social Democratic Herald*, Jan. 16, 1907; *FTCM*, Jan. 16, 1907.

25 *Social Democratic Herald*, Aug. 13, 1907; *FTCM*, Dec. 4, 1907.

26 *FTCM*, Aug. 20, Oct. 15, Dec. 3, 17, 1902, Mar. 4, 1903, Jan. 4, 1905, Aug. 1, Sep. 5, Oct. 3, 1906, Jul. 17, 1907; *Social Democratic Herald*, Jul. 26, Dec. 6, 1902, Jan. 2, Aug. 13, 1904; Commons, *History of Labor*, IV, 151; *Voice of the People*, Nov. 5, 1910.

27 *Social Democratic Herald*, Jan. 21, 1905.

28 Berger and Thomas, *Voice and Pen of Victor L. Berger*, p. 699.
29 *Social Democratic Herald*, Mar. 24, 1905; cited in Perlman, "History of Socialism," p. 41.

CHAPTER EIGHT

1 Haferbecker, *Wisconsin Labor Laws*, pp. 6–10; Hofstadter, *The Age of Reform*, pp. 238–39.
2 Ameringer, *If You Don't Weaken*, p. 298.
3 Maxwell, *La Follette*, pp. 3–9.
4 Schmidt, "History of Labor Legislation," pp. 37–96; Haferbecker, *Wisconsin Labor Laws*, pp. 34–61.
5 Schmidt, "History of Labor Legislation," pp. 375–79.
6 *Ibid.*, pp. 181–96.
7 *Ibid.*, pp. 154–65.
8 *Ibid.*, pp. 226–38; *FTCM*, Nov. 4, 1914, Dec. 15, 1915.
9 Schmidt, "History of Labor Legislation," pp. 323–26; Wisconsin Labor Relations Board, *Report*, p. 1.
10 Wachman, *History of the Social-Democratic Party*, pp. 24–74; Still, *Milwaukee*, pp. 303–20; Shannon, *The Socialist Party*, p. 23; Drosen, "The History of Socialism," pp. 15–16; Olson, "The Milwaukee Socialists," pp. 225–26.
11 Remey and Bruce, "A Half Century in Business Effort," part II, ch. V, 7.
12 *FTCM*, Oct. 19, 1910, Mar. 15, Oct. 4, 18, 1911, Jan. 17, May 3, 1912, May 7, Dec. 17, 1913, Sep. 2, Oct. 21, 1914, May 19, Sep. 15, 1915; Schmidt, "History of Labor Legislation," pp. 374-75; Lescohier and Peterson, *The Alleviation of Unemployment*, p. 123.

CHAPTER NINE

1 Wisconsin *Vorwärts*, Dec. 24, 1899; *Social Democratic Herald*, Dec. 26, 1903, Jun. 18, 1904; *FTCM*, Mar. 20, Oct. 2, Nov. 6, 1901, Dec. 3, 1902, Apr. 1, 1903, Jan. 9, 1904, Nov. 19, 1913.
2 *Social Democratic Herald*, Apr. 23, May 14, Jun. 11, 1904, Oct. 5, 1907; *FTCM*, Jan. 4, Oct. 4, Nov. 15, 1905, Mar. 17, 1909.
3 *FTCM*, Mar. 7, 1906, Feb. 6, May 1, 15, Oct. 2, 1907, Mar. 4, Nov. 4, 1908, May 5, 1909; *Social Democratic Herald*, Feb. 18, 1905, Feb. 17, 1906, Feb. 2, Sep. 14, 1907, Feb. 29, 1905.
4 *FTCM*, Nov. 7, 21, 1900, Jul. 17, Sep. 18, 1901, Jan. 15, Feb. 5, Mar. 5, 19, Apr. 2, 16, 1902, Apr. 1, 1903; Mueller, "Milwaukee Workers," p. 225.
5 Letter from Gird Korman to author, Nov. 11, 1957; Milwaukee Foundrymen's Association, *Constitution*, p. 11.
6 Wisconsin Board Arbitration and Conciliation, [*Third*] *Biennial Report*, pp. 26–38, and *Fourth Biennial Report*, pp. 27–28; Commons, *History of Labor*, IV, 110–14; *Social Democratic Herald*, Apr. 12, 1902.

7   *FTCM*, Mar. 18, 1903.

8   *Social Democratic Herald*, Mar. 28, 1903, Jan. 2, Jul. 9, 1904, Jan. 23, Jun. 4, Sep. 17, 1907, Sep. 11, 1909; Commons, *History of Labor*, IV, 133 ff.

9   *Social Democratic Herald*, Jul. 9, 1909.

10 Remey and Bruce, "A Half Century in Business Effort," part I, ch. I, 1, Ch. II, 6–7; Schmidt, "History of Labor Legislation," pp. 35–36, 166–171; Perry, "The Milwaukee School of Trades," pp. 78–79; *Social Democratic Herald*, Oct. 5, 1907. The School of Trades became Boys' Technical High School.

11 Commons, *History of Labor*, IV, 116; *Social Democratic Herald*, Jan. 27, May 5, 12, Jun. 2, 9, 16, 23, Aug. 11, Oct. 20, Nov. 17, 1906.

12 Quoted in Schmidt, "History of Labor Legislation," pp. 273–74; see also Wisconsin Board Arbitration and Conciliation, *Fourth Biennial Report*, pp. 10–15.

13 *Social Democratic Herald*, Mar. 16, Jul. 20, Aug. 3, 1907, Jan. 11, May 16, Oct. 17, 24, 31, 1908; *FTCM*, Jul. 3, 1906, Apr. 3, 1907, May 6, 1908; Milwaukee *Sentinel*, Jan. 4, 1907.

14 Wisconsin Legislature, *Assembly Journal*, Apr. 22, 1919, p. 876, Apr. 24, 1919, pp. 908–9, and transcript of hearings in Milwaukee by the General Legislative Committee (1919), pp. 2–91, 735–895, 1,369–73, 1,154, 1,789–1,901.

CHAPTER TEN

1   *FTCM*, Aug. 5, 1914.

2   Summary of proceedings of 1915 WSFL convention in *Wisconsin Labor* (1924), n.p.; *FTCM*, Dec. 15, 1920.

3   Letter from Frank Weber and others to Wisconsin Branch, National Security, League, Jun. 9, 1916, in FTC *Papers*, Jun. 21, 1916.

4   *FTCM*, Dec. 20, 1916.

5   *Ibid.*, Feb. 7, 1917.

6   *Ibid.*, May 2, 1917; Commons, *History of Labor*, IV, 421–22.

7   *FTCM*, May 2, Jun. 20, Aug. 1, 15, Sep. 19, Dec. 5, 19, 1917; Olson, "The Milwaukee Socialists," pp. 364–65; Milwaukee County Council of Defense, *Report*, pp. 4–9.

8   *FTCM*, Aug. 7, Oct. 2, 1918.

9   Quoted in Olson, "The Milwaukee Socialists," p. 107.

10 Drosen, "The History of Socialism," pp. 37–44.

11 Milwaukee *Journal*, Jul. 22, 1918; Shannon, *The Socialist Party*, pp. 85, 100.

12 *FTCM*, Aug. 15, Oct. 3, 17, Nov. 7, 1917, Jan. 2, Dec. 4, 1918, Apr. 21, May 19, 1920.

13 *Voice of the People*, Mar. 10, 1918.

14 Wisconsin Trades Union Liberty League, *Proceedings* (1915), p. 7 and

(1920), pp. 3, 28.

15 *FTCM*, Feb. 20, Mar. 6, Dec. 18, 1918, Jan. 15, Feb. 19, Mar. 19, Apr. 2, May 7, Jun. 4, 18, Jul. 2, 16, Aug. 6, Nov. 19, Dec. 17, 1919, Jan. 7, Feb. 4, Dec. 15, 1920.

16 *Ibid.*, Jan. 16, 1920; Drosen, "The History of Socialism," p. 80.

17 *FTCM*, Jun. 6, 1917, Feb. 6, Mar. 6, Nov. 6, Dec. 18, 1918, Mar. 19, Sep. 17, Nov. 5, 19, Dec. 3, 17, 1919, Apr. 21, 1920; circular letter from Labor Foreward Movement, signed by Green (*ca.* Oct. 1918) in Theatrical Stage Employees, *Papers*; FTC *Papers*, "First Report of the Strikers' Aid Committee," and "Treasurer's Final Report, Strike Co-op Aid Committee"; Schmidt, "History of Labor Legislation," pp. 280–85; *Builders Bulletin*, Apr.–May 1920, p. 11.

18 Schmidt, "History of Labor Legislation," pp. 313–15; *FTCM*, Sep. 17, 1919; see also FTC *Papers*, notarized statement of Nathaniel Wescott, Nov. 5, 1919.

CHAPTER ELEVEN

1 *FTCM*, Jan. 7, Jun. 16, Sep. 15, 1920, Jan. 5, Jun. 1, Aug. 3, Oct. 5, Nov. 2, 1921, Apr. 19, May 3, Aug. 2, Oct. 4, Dec. 6, 1922, Mar. 7, 21, Apr. 18, May 2, 1923, Jan. 2, Apr. 2, 1924, Jan. 7, 21, May 20, Jun. 3, Jul. 1, Nov. 18, Dec. 2, 1925, Jan. 6, 1932; Cady, *Free America!*

2 FTC *Papers*, letter from Weber to members of Milwaukee Unions, Dec. 21, 1927, and letter from Weber to William Coleman, May 8, 1929.

3 *Builders Bulletin*, Apr.–May 1920, p. 6, Jul. 1, 1921, p. 5, Jan.–Feb. 1922, p. 26; Schmidt, "History of Labor Legislation," pp. 35–39; Lorwin, *The American Federation*, p. 202.

4 Letter from Milwaukee Employers Council reprinted in *Master Builder*, Sep. 1923, p. 19.

5 *Master Builder*, Jun. 1931, p. 5; *FTCM*, Mar. 19, Aug. 6, 1919, Jul. 7, Sep. 1, Oct. 6, 20, Dec. 1, 15, 1920, Feb. 16, Jul. 20, Aug. 3, 1921, Mar. 19, 1924.

6 Schmidt, "History of Labor Legislation," pp. 37–42, 285–329, 370–78.

7 *FTCM*, Apr. 18, 1928; Josephson, *Sidney Hillman*, p. 250; Olson, "The Milwaukee Socialists," p. 502.

8 Schmidt, "History of Labor Legislation," pp. 301–3, 326–29; *FTCM*, May 7, 1924.

9 Schmidt, "History of Labor Legislation," pp. 315, 322.

10 *FTCM*, Aug. 15, 1923, Oct. 6, 1926, Aug. 15, 1928, May 7, 1930; see also Hoan, *City Government*, pp. 302–3.

11 *FTCM*, Aug. 18, Dec. 1, 1920, Jan. 19, May 18, Jul. 6, 20, Oct. 5, Dec. 7, 21, 1921, Apr. 19, 1922, Nov. 4, 1925, Jan. 19, 1927, Feb. 18, 1931, and letter from Board of Trustees, Milwaukee Workers College to affiliated unions, Jan. 1, 1922; Still, *Milwaukee*, p. 528; *Emancipator*, Aug. 1940; Milwaukee *Labor Review*, Oct. 1, 1887, Jun. 16, 1888; Wisconsin Bureau

Labor Statistics, *Third Biennial Report*, p. xxvii; Milwaukee *Daily News and the Daily Review*, Oct. 17, 1890.

12 Schwartztrauber, "Workers' Education," pp. 27–55, and *The University of Wisconsin School*, pp. 11–15; FTC *Papers*, "Report of Board of Trustees, Milwaukee Workers College" (*ca.* 1922).

13 *FTCM*, Apr. 2, 1919, Jun. 16, 1920, May 18, Oct. 5, Nov. 2, 16, 1921, Dec. 6, 1922, Nov. 6, 1929, Feb. 5, May 21, Aug. 6, Nov. 19, 1930; Hoan, *City Government*, pp. 212–13; Milwaukee Writers Project, "History of Milwaukee County," pp. 325–26; Olson, "The Milwaukee Socialists," p. 467.

14 *FTCM*, Nov. 16, 1927.

15 *Ibid.*, Mar. 16, 1921, May 15, 1929.

16 Olson, "The Milwaukee Socialists," pp. 397, 403–4, 475; Roberts, "Farm Organizations and Labor," pp. 22–23; summary of WSFL 1921 and 1922 conventions in *Wisconsin Labor* (1924), n.p.; Drosen, "The History of Socialism," 77–83.

17 Letter from J. J. Handley to Ed. Murray, May 21, 1931 in WSFL *Papers*.

18 Copies of speeches by Frank Weber, Sep. 4, 1922, *ca.* 1923 in FTC *Papers*.

19 *FTCM*, Feb. 2, 1916, Jan. 21, 1920, Nov. 16, Dec. 7, 1921, Mar. 3, Nov. 3, 1926, Aug. 7, 1929.

CHAPTER TWELVE

1 *FTCM*, Mar. 19, Nov. 19, Dec. 17, 1930, Mar. 4, 1931, Jan. 21, Apr. 30, Jul. 15, Sep. 2, Dec. 2, 1932; letter from FTC to Robert F. Wagner, Apr. 29, 1930, in FTC *Papers;* Still, *Milwaukee,* p. 479.

2 Still, *Milwaukee*, p. 528; Olson, "The Milwaukee Socialists," p. 493–94; Wisconsin Emergency Relief Administration, *Review*, pp. 10–23.

3 Schmidt, "History of Labor Legislation," pp. 331–69; *FTCM*, Apr. 3, Jul. 17, 1935, Jan. 6, 20, Feb. 3, Apr. 7, 1937, Mar. 2, 16, Apr. 6, 1938; Haferbecker, *Wisconsin Labor Laws*, pp. 122–30.

4 Haferbecker, *Wisconsin Labor Laws,* p. 161; Schmidt, "History of Labor Legislation," pp. 304–7.

5 Still, *Milwaukee*, pp. 498–99; U.S. Senate, Committee on Education and Labor, *Violations of Free Speech*, p. 80.

6 Hoan, *City Government*, pp. 216–19.

7 Milwaukee *Labor Press*, Feb. 25, 1943; "Store Unions," *Business Week*, Dec. 8, 1934, pp. 12–13; *FTCM*, Jan. 2, 15, Mar. 20, 1935, May 19, 1937; statement by J. F. Friedrick, tape recording of discussion by FTC representatives, May 23, 1951, in Wis. Hist. Soc.; for more information on Seide, see the *Emancipator*, Sep. 1940; Milwaukee *Labor Press*, May 27, 1943.

8 Still, *Milwaukee*, pp. 499–500, 530; Hoan, *City Government*, pp. 220–21, 352–56; *Guild Striker*, May 13, 20, Jul. 1, 16, 30, 1936; *FTCM*, Nov. 20, 1935, Feb. 5, 19, Mar. 18, Apr. 15, May 6, 20, Jul. 3, Sep. 2, 1936.

9 U.S. Senate, Committee on Education and Labor, *Violations of Free*

Speech, pp. 858–60, 989, 1,002, 1,788; letter from A. J. Lindemann and Hoverson Co. to their employees, Jan. 15, 1936, in FTC *Papers*; Krakowski, "Press Treatment of Wisconsin Labor Issues," p. 83; Wisconsin Labor Relations Board, *Report*, pp. 3–6; Haferbecker, "Wisconsin Labor Legislation," pp. 162–65.

CHAPTER THIRTEEN

1 *FTCM*, Aug. 19, Oct. 2, 21, Nov. 4, Dec. 2, 1936.
2 WSFL, *Proceedings* (1936), p. 76; Krakowski, "Press Treatment of Wisconsin Labor Issues," pp. 15–19.
3 Krakowski, "Press Treatment of Wisconsin Labor Issues," p. 182; *FTCM*, Sep. 16, 1936.
4 *FTCM*, Sep. 16, 1936; Still, *Milwaukee*, p. 500.
5 *FTCM*, Mar. 17, 1937.
6 *Ibid.*, Mar. 17, Apr. 7, May 5, 1937.
7 Milwaukee *Leader*, Jul. 8, 30, 1937; Milwaukee *Wisconsin News*, Aug. 12, 1937; Milwaukee *Journal*, Mar. 7, 8, Sep. 7, 1937; Krakowski, "Press Treatment of Wisconsin Labor Issues," pp. 25–29; *FTCM*, Jan. 6, 1932; *Emancipator*, Nov. 1, 1936; *Allis-Chalmers Workers Union News*, Aug. 2, Sep. 30, 1937; Stoughton *Courier-Hub*, Aug. 23, 1937.
8 Krakowski, "Press Treatment of Wisconsin Labor Issues," pp. 23–24; Milwaukee *Leader*, May 24, 26, Jun. 2, Jul. 9, 1937; Milwaukee *Journal*, May 25, 1937; Milwaukee *Wisconsin News*, Jun. 1, 1937; Madison *Wisconsin State Journal*, May 28, 1937; *FTCM*, Nov. 16, Dec. 7, 1938; Gordon, "The Listing Provision," p. 24.
9 Wisconsin Labor Relations Board, *Report*, pp. 9–10.
10 Haferbecker, *Wisconsin Labor Laws*, p. 165–74; Roberts, "Farm Organizations and Labor," pp. 27, 39.
11 Two letters from Meyer Adelman to Herman Seide, both dated Jan. 23, 1939, and letter from Seide to Adelman, Feb. 2, 1939 in IUC *Papers*.

CHAPTER FOURTEEN

1 *FTCM*, Oct. 5, 1932, Mar. 20, Sept. 18, Dec. 18, 1935, Sep. 2, 16, Oct. 7, 1936, Nov. 3, 1937; letter from Frank Weber to AFL Committee on Labor Press and Publications, Jul. 12, 1932, in FTC *Papers*; Olson, "The Milwaukee Socialists," p. 524; *Chicago Tribune*, Dec. 9, 1937; Raney, *Wisconsin*, p. 366–67.
2 *Emancipator*, Nov. 1, 1936.
3 *FTCM*, Jul. 1, Nov. 18, 1936, Apr. 21, May 5, 1937, Jul. 6, 1938; Olson, "The Milwaukee Socialists," pp. 547–59; Milwaukee *Sentinel*, Aug. 8, 1938; Shannon, *The Socialist Party*, p. 246; *Wisconsin CIO News*, Jun. 4, 1938; *Emancipator*, Dec. 1937.
4 *FTCM*, Oct. 21, 1942; Olson, "The Milwaukee Socialists," pp. 570–71;

for additional information on Friedrick, see *Emancipator*, Oct. 1940; Milwaukee *Labor Press*, Feb. 15, 1943, Mar. 31, 1960.

CHAPTER FIFTEEN

1 Letter from J. J. Handley to Michael E. Sherman, Mar. 14, 1930, in WSFL *Papers*.

2 Letter from Frank Weber to Matthew Woll, Mar. 2, 1932, and letter from Herman Seide to Roy Burt, Feb. 28, 1935, in FTC *Papers*; *Wisconsin Voice of Labor*, Sep. 1, Dec. 15, 1934, Feb. 28, Mar. 1, May 1, 1935; Shannon, *The Decline of American Communism*, p. 12; Derber and Young, *Labor and the New Deal*, pp. 79–90.

3 Olson, "The Milwaukee Socialists," pp. 519–20; Ozanne, "The Effects of Communist Leadership," pp. 190–92, 274–75; U.S. Congress, House of Representatives, Committee on Education and Labor, *Amendments to the NLRA*, pp. 1,349–50; *Allis-Chalmers Workers Union News*, Aug. 2, Nov. 26, Dec. 10, 1937, Jan. 7, 1938.

4 Krakowski, "Press Treatment of Wisconsin Labor Issues," pp. 32–36; letter from Emil Costello and Gunnar Mickelson to CIO locals, Jan. 15, 1939, and telegram from Harold Christoffel and others to John L. Lewis, Jul. 20, 1938, in IUC *Papers*; Milwaukee *Journal*, Aug. 16, 1937, Jun. 10, 1938; Milwaukee *Sentinel*, Jun. 12, Aug. 8, Oct. 6, 1938; Milwaukee *Leader*, Jun. 18, Jul. 11, 1938; Appleton *Post-Crescent*, Jul. 16, 1938; Wausau *Record-Herald*, Jul. 18, 1938; Oshkosh *Northwestern*, Jul. 20, 1938; Kenosha *Labor*, Aug. 5, 1938; Milwaukee *Wisconsin News*, Aug. 9, 1938; *Chicago Tribune*, Aug. 10, 1938; Ashland *Press*, Oct. 27, 1938; Kenosha *News*, Oct. 26, 1938; *Wisconsin CIO News*, May 7, 1938, Mar. 13, 1939; Milwaukee *Labor Press*, Apr. 29, 1943; U.S. Congress, House of Representatives, Committee on Education and Labor, *Amendments to the NLRA*, pp. 78–79, 1,346–49, 1,443; Ozanne, "The Effects of Communist Leadership," pp. 204–8, 291. In 1943 Kiebler was elected to the FTC executive board as a representative of the UAW-AFL, the remnants of the Martin faction in the UAW-CIO.

5 Report of trial committee to the IUC, Nov. 23, 1938, in IUC *Papers*.

6 U.S. Congress, House of Representatives, Committee on Education and Labor, *Amendments to the NLRA*, pp. 1,351, 1,432–34, 3,610–16; Ozanne, "The Effects of Communist Leadership," pp. 210–15; Wisconsin Employment Relations Board, *Third Annual Report*, p. 10.

7 Quoted in Seidman, *American Labor*, p. 44.

8 Ozanne, "The Effects of Communist Leadership, pp. 290–94; U.S. Congress, House of Representatives, Committee on Education and Labor, *Amendments to the NLRA*, pp. 1,346, 2,134.

CHAPTER SIXTEEN

1 U.S. Congress, House of Representatives, Committee on Education and

Labor, *Amendments to the NLRA*, p. 1,354; Ozanne, "The Effects of Communist Leadership," p. 274; Kruger, "A Study of Collective Bargaining," pp. 83–84.

2 Resolution of USWA Local 1,114 enclosed in letter from Krause to Linus Lindberg, Sep. 25, 1946, and letter from IUC to Henry Wallace, *ca.* Sep. 1946, in IUC *Papers*.

3 *Wisconsin CIO News: Local 248 Ed.*, Mar. 8, Aug. 16, Oct. 4, 18, 1946; *FTCM*, Jul. 17, 1946.

4 Interview of author with Fred Erchul, IUC sec.-treas., Mar. 7, 1957; Milwaukee *Labor Press*, Sep. 5, 1946; *Wisconsin CIO News: Local 248 Ed.*, Nov. 9, 30, 1945, Sep. 20, 1946; IUC *Minutes*, Oct. 13, 16, 1946.

5 Signed statement of the election commissioners, Nov. 7, 1946, in IUC *Papers*. Momblow had been elected IUC president on Oct. 17, 1945, to replace Buse who was later elected president of the state CIO council. Buse had previously become president of the IUC and Local 248 to replace Christoffel who had been drafted into the army.

6 Report of election results, Oct. 17, 1946, in IUC *Papers*.

7 Haywood-Brophy Reports in *Wisconsin CIO News: Local 248 Ed.*, Nov. 8, 1946.

8 *Ibid.*, Oct. 25, Nov. 29, Dec. 13, 1946; see also *Wisconsin CIO News*, Dec. 5, 12, 19, 1947; telegram from John Brophy to Glenn Clarke, Sep. 20, 1947, in IUC *Papers*.

9 Ozanne, "The Effects of Communist Leadership," pp. 233–38; U.S. Congress, House of Representatives, Committee on Education and Labor, *Amendments to the NLRA*, pp. 1,354–65, 1,408, 2,025–30, 2,994–97, insert #5 after p. 1,442; *Wisconsin CIO News*, Jan. 4, Feb. 15, Mar. 8, 15, Apr. 26, 1946; *Wisconsin CIO News: Local 248 Ed.*, May 3, 31, Jun. 7, 14, 1946.

10 IUC *Minutes*, Nov. 29, 1946; *Wisconsin CIO News: Local 248 Ed.*, Oct. 11, Nov. 29, Dec. 13, 1946, Jan. 3, 10, Feb. 14, Mar. 14, 28, Apr. 18, 1947; U.S. Congress, House of Representatives, Committee on Education and Labor, *Amendments to the NLRA*, pp. 1,395, 2,049; Ozanne, "The Effects of Communist Leadership," pp. 238–39; Kruger, "A Study of Collective Bargaining," p. 87; letters from Glenn M. Clarke to John Brophy and from Brophy to Clarke, May 12, 20, Jul. 9, 14, 1947, and letter from R. J. Thomas to Philip Murray, Jul. 3, 1947, in IUC *Papers*.

11 *Union Daily*, Jul. 24, Oct. 23, Nov. 12, 20, 25, 26, Dec. 2, 4, 5, 1947; *Wisconsin CIO News: Local 248 Ed.*, May 9, Jul. 25, 1947; *Wisconsin CIO News*, Nov. 28, 1947; Ozanne, "The Effects of Communist Leadership," pp. 196, 240; Kruger, "A Study of Collective Bargaining," pp. 87–88.

12 *Union Daily*, Dec. 3, 1947.

13 Quoted in Ozanne, "The Effects of Communist Leadership," p. 241.

14 *Ibid.*, p. 244; *Wisconsin CIO News*, Jun. 4, Aug. 6, Oct. 8, 1948, Nov. 11, 1949, Jul. 7, 28, 1950.

15 Perlman, *A History of Trade Unionism*, pp. 305–6.

16 Saposs, *Communism in American Unions*, pp. 130–35.

CHAPTER SEVENTEEN

1 *FTCM*, Jan. 2, 15, Mar. 6, 20, Jul. 3, Nov. 6, 1935, Aug. 4, 1937, Jan. 7, 1942; *Wisconsin Labor* (1935), p. 29; Still, *Milwaukee*, pp. 463–64; "Wisconsin State Federation of Labor's Position on the Conscription Measures," *ca.* 1940, "Lend Lease Bill," *ca.* 1940, and "Statement in support of the La Follette Resolution . . . for a referendum . . . on the declaration of war," *ca.* Oct. 1941, in WSFL *Papers*; Haferbecker, *Wisconsin Labor Laws*, pp. 174–75; Milwaukee *Labor Press*, Mar. 1, 1945; *Wisconsin CIO News*, Oct. 7, 14, 1949.

2 Haferbecker, *Wisconsin Labor Laws*, p. 178; Milwaukee *Journal*, Mar. 31, 1956; Milwaukee *Labor Press*, Jul. 25, 1959; *Wisconsin CIO News*, Apr. 7, Sep. 3, 1948, and Nov. 26, 1948 for information on the County Non-partisan Citizens' Conference for Political Education used by CIO unions in 1948; see also Milwaukee *Labor Press*, Oct. 23, 1947, for information on the Political Education Committee used by AFL unions.

3 Milwaukee *Journal*, May 2, 1957; *Wisconsin CIO News*, Sep. 7, Oct. 5, 1951; Milwaukee *Labor Press*, May 29, Jun. 13, Jul. 18, Aug. 22, 1947, Jul. 10, 31, 1958, Sep. 3, Oct. 8, 1959.

CHAPTER EIGHTEEN

1 *FTCM*, Apr. 2, 1924; Still, *Milwaukee*, p. 327.
2 Maxwell, *La Follette*, pp. 200–1.
3 Shannon, *The Socialist Party*, p. 23.
4 *Social Democratic Herald*, Jun. 11, 1904; Wachman, *History of the Social-Democratic Party*, pp. 52–53; *FTCM*, Nov. 15, 1905; Roy, *Communism and the Churches*, p. 132.

Bibliography

The standard general history of the labor movement is the four volumes by John R. Commons and Associates, *History of Labor in the United States.* Valuable one-volume histories are Foster R. Dulles, *Labor in America,* and Joseph G. Rayback, *A History of American Labor.* A series of essays in Milton Derber and Edwin Young, eds., *Labor and the New Deal,* give insight into the developments of the Thirties. Joel Seidman, *American Labor from Defense to Reconversion,* is an excellent study of the period around the Second World War.

Bayrd Still, *Milwaukee,* is an invaluable history of the city. Also useful is H. Russell Austin, *The Milwaukee Story.* Daniel W. Hoan, *City Government,* gives a passionate view by the long-time Socialist mayor.

There are very few sources of information on the Milwaukee labor movement prior to 1880. Especially helpful was an index to the Milwaukee *Sentinel* prepared by the WPA in the Thirties. The index, covering the years 1837 to 1879, has subject and name cards for all local items; it is in the possession of the Milwaukee Public Library. Frederick Merk's *Economic History of Wisconsin During the Civil War Decade* and Don D. Lescohier's monograph, *The Knights of St. Crispin, 1867–1874,* were useful.

Frank A. Flower, Commissioner of the Bureau of Labor Statistics in the 1880's, gives a diffuse but comprehensive account of developments in the *First* and *Second Biennial Report* of the Bureau. The labor collections of the State Historical Society of Wisconsin were invaluable. In addition to union newspapers and miscellaneous documents, I found the papers of the FTC and the IUC a particular treasure. The Society also houses papers from a number of local unions in Milwaukee and the Wisconsin State Federation of Labor.

Two brief accounts of the development of labor in the state are Edwin E. Witte, "Labor in Wisconsin History," and the unpublished manuscript by Theodore Mueller, "Milwaukee Workers." A typed copy of that manuscript, as well as a few other pertinent documents, can be found in the records of the Milwaukee County Historical Society.

David A. Shannon, *The Socialist Party of America,* is the best account of the national party's history. Marvin Wachman's excellent monograph, *History of the Social-Democratic Party of Milwaukee: 1897–1910,* is competently supplemented by Frederick I. Olson, "The Milwaukee Socialists, 1897–1941." Interesting accounts can also be found in Hanni M. Holzman, "The

German Forty-Eighters and the Socialists in Milwaukee," Selig Perlman, "History of Socialism in Milwaukee," and Rosalind M. Drosen, "The History of Socialism in Milwaukee: 1910–1930."

Victor L. Berger's views are reflected in the editorials and speeches reprinted in Meta Berger and Elizabeth H. Thomas, eds., *Voice and Pen of Victor L. Berger.* The socialist newspapers can be found in the files of the Wisconsin and the Milwaukee County Historical Societies.

Richard Hofstadter, *The Age of Reform,* is a very interesting interpretation of the progressive movement. A good account of the movement in Wisconsin can be found in Robert S. Maxwell, *La Follette and the Rise of the Progressives in Wisconsin.* By far the best biography of La Follette is the two volumes by Belle Case La Follette and Fola La Follette, *Robert M. La Follette.*

Two illuminating studies of the role of the Communists in the American labor movement are Max M. Kampelman, *The Communist Party vs. the CIO,* and David J. Saposs, *Communism in American Unions.* Robert W. Ozanne, "The Effects of Communist Leadership on American Trade Unions," contains a more extensive discussion of the situation in Local 248 at Allis-Chalmers.

The labor education movement is described in Ernest E. Schwarztrauber, *The University of Wisconsin School for Workers.* Labor legislation in the state is covered in Donald J. Berthrong, "Social Legislation in Wisconsin: 1836–1900" and Gertrude Schmidt, "History of Labor Legislation in Wisconsin." The development of labor legislation is summarized and brought up to date in Gordon M. Haferbecker, *Wisconsin Labor Laws.*

There are very few histories of municipal unionism. Special mention should be made of Grace H. Stimson, *The Rise of the Labor Movement in Los Angeles,* and Barbara W. Newell, *Chicago and the Labor Movement.* An indispensable source of statistical information is Bureau of the Census, *Historical Statistics of the United States.*

MANUSCRIPT COLLECTIONS

Barbers International Union of America, Local 50, Journeymen. 1915–1919. 1 vol. U. S. MSS 89A in the State Historical Society of Wisconsin, Madison.

Carpenters District Council, Milwaukee. 1887–1926. 11 vols. U. S. MSS 96A in the State Historical Society of Wisconsin, Madison.

Emergency Employment Situation in Wisconsin. Letters urging retainment of the U. S. Employment Service. 1918–1919. 1 box. Wis. MSS. 11DZ in the State Historical Society of Wisconsin, Madison.

Federated Trades Council of Milwaukee. 1900–1946. 18 vols., 2 boxes, 1 pkg. U. S. MSS 26A, HG/5MIF in the State Historical Society of Wisconsin, Madison.

Federated Trades Council of Milwaukee. Tape recording of round table discussion by representatives of the Federated Trades Council, May 23, 1951. 3 reels. Tape Recording 29A in the State Historical Society of

Wisconsin, Madison.

Industrial Commission of Wisconsin. 1937–1942. 2 boxes. U. S. MSS 30A in the State Historical Society of Wisconsin, Madiosn.

Laundry and Dry Cleaning Drivers, Local 360. 1936-1947. 10 boxes, 13 vols. U. S. MSS 54A in the State Historical Society of Wisconsin, Madison.

Longshoremen's Association, Local 815, International. 1935–1949. 1 box, 11 vols. U. S. MSS 100A in the State Historical Society of Wisconsin, Madison.

McCullough, Harold R. M. (comp.). Scrapbook of newsclippings concerning Frank Weber. 1 vol. U. S. MSS 87A in the State Historical Society of Wisconsin, Madison.

Milwaukee County Industrial Union Council. 1938–1948. 17 boxes. U. S. MSS 65A in the State Historical Society of Wisconsin, Madison.

Milwaukee Labor College. Hearings by the Special Educational Committee of the Federated Trades Council concerning the abandonment of the Milwaukee Labor College because of alleged infiltration of Communist or radical influences. 1939. 1 folder. U. S. MSS 35A in the State Historical Society of Wisconsin, Madison.

Operating Engineers International Union, Local 311. 1906-1950. 6 boxes, 11 vols. U. S. MSS 108A in the State Historical Society of Wisconsin, Madison.

Rauch, H. Herman Papers. 1937–1948. 9 boxes. U. S. MSS 29A in the State Historical Society of Wisconsin, Madison.

Schilling, Robert Papers. 1852–1922. 1 box. U. S. MSS 109A in the State Historical Society of Wisconsin, Madison.

Theatrical Stage Employees, International Alliance, Local 18. 1894–1944. 6 boxes, 8 vols. U. S. MSS 25A in the State Historical Society of Wisconisn, Madison.

Typographical Union, Local 23. 1859–1948. 1 box, 1 folder. U. S. MSS 113A in the State Historical Society of Wisconsin, Madison.

University of Wisconsin, Extension Division, School for Workers. 3 boxes. Series 18/12/11 in the State Historical Society of Wisconsin, Madison.

Wisconsin Labor Relations Board. 1937–1939. 40 boxes. Series 12/0/1, 12/0/3 in the State Historical Society of Wisconsin, Madison.

Wisconsin State Federation of Labor. 1911–1953. 5 boxes. U. S. MSS 27A in the State Historical Society of Wisconsin, Madison.

Workers Alliance of America. 1935–1936. 1 pkg. U. S. MSS 31A in the State Historical Society of Wisconsin, Madison.

LABOR AND EMPLOYER PAMPHLETS, LEAFLETS, AND PROCEEDINNGS.

"An Appeal to Organized Labor and Its Friends in the States and Canadas." Milwaukee Brewers Union, Local 9, *ca.* 1888. In the State Historical Society of Wisconsin, Madison.

Artisan Day Souvenir. Milwaukee: Federated Trades Council, 1894.

Artisan Day Souvenir. Milwaukee: Federated Trades Council, 1895.

Artisan Day Souvenir: Milwaukee Trades Union Label Bulletin. Milwaukee: Trades Union Label League, 1899.

"Both Sides: The History of the Pending Printers' Strike." Milwaukee: Typographical Union, Local 23, April 27, 1881.

Cady, Samuel H. *Free America! (A Plain Statement of How the Federated Shop Craftsmen Conducted Their Strike on the Chicago and North Western Railway In Wisconsin In 1922.).* ca. November 1922.

Directory of Organized Labor in Milwaukee. Milwaukee: Fred. W. Stearns, 1891.

End of the Century Labor Day Souvenir. Milwaukee: Milwaukee Trades Union Label League, 1900.

50th Annual Convention Wisconsin State Federation of Labor. Souvenir Program. Milwaukee: August, 1942.

Milwaukee Federated Trades Council. *Constitution and By-Laws of the Federated Trades Council of Milwaukee, Wis.* Milwaukee: Edw. Keogh, 1893; 2d. ed., 1900.

――――. *Constitution and Parliamentary Rules of the Federated Trades Council of Milwaukee and Vicinity.* Milwaukee, August 1, 1940.

――――. *The Federated Trades Council Directory of Milwaukee, Wis.: Containing a Complete List of All Labor Organizations in Milwaukee, With the Time and Place of Meeting, Corresponding Secretaries and Their Addresses, History of Trade Unionism, Its Objects and Purposes, Factory Laws, Lien Laws and Laws of Preferred Claims and Articles From Brilliant Labor Leaders and Writers.* Milwaukee: Trade and Labor Assoc., 1892.

――――. *Quarterly Bulletin of the Federated Trades Council of Milwaukee and Vicinity.* October-November-December, 1901.

Milwaukee Iron Molders Union No. 121. *By-Laws of the Iron Molders Union No. 121 of Milwaukee.* Milwaukee: Edw. Keogh, 1900.

Milwaukee County Industrial Union Council. *Constitution of the Milwaukee County Industrial Union Council.* Milwaukee, 1951.

Milwaukee Foundrymen's Association. *Constitution and By-Laws of the Milwaukee Foundrymen's Association.* Milwaukee, March, 1904.

Milwaukee Printers Protective Fraternity No. 16. *Constitution, By-Laws, and Rules of Order of the Milwaukee Printers Protective Fraternity No. 16.* Milwaukee, 1900.

Trades Assembly Bulletin. Milwaukee, April 1, 1882.

Trades Union Liberty League of Wisconsin. *Proceedings of the First Annual Convention and By-Laws of the Trades Union Liberty League of Wisconsin.* ca.1915.

――――. *Convention Proceedings,* 1918.

――――. ――――, 1920.

"To Organized Labor and Friends." Federated Trades Council, April 2, 1902. HG 5MIF in the State Historical Society of Wisconsin, Madison.

Typothetae of Milwaukee. *Constitution and By-Laws.* Milwaukee: Evening Wisconsin Company, 1897.

Wisconsin Labor. Official year book of the Wisconsin State Federation of Labor. 26 vols. 1924–1950.

Wisconsin State Industrial Union Council CIO. *Proceedings Fourth Annual Convention.* 1941.

————. *Proceedings Third Annual Convention.* 1940.

NEWSPAPERS AND PERIODICALS.

A. F. of L. Milwaukee *Labor Press,* February, 1943 – December, 1959.

Allis-Chalmers Workers Union News, August, 1937 – March, 1938.

Appleton *Post-Crescent,* July, 1938.

Ashland *Press,* October, 1938.

AUA Reporter, June, 1945 – January, 1952 (variously titled, scattered). Publications of the Associated Unions of America.

Badger Workmen, June, 1901. Publication of the Ancient Order of United Workmen.

Chicago Tribune, December, 1937; August, 1938.

Daily Picket, May, 1946 – December, 1947 (titled *Union Daily* after March, 1947). Publication of the United Auto Workers, Local 248.

Emancipator, 1936–1948. Publication of the International Ladies Garment Workers Union, Local 188.

Freedom in Employment, September, 1926 – January, 1932. Publication of the Milwaukee Employers Council.

Guild Striker, May, 1936 – July, 1936 (scattered). Publication of the Milwaukee Newspaper Guild.

Kenosha *News,* October, 1938.

Kenosha *Labor,* August, 1938.

Labor Views, February, 1944 – January, 1946. Publication opposing the Communists, Socialists, Democrats, and the CIO-PAC.

Master Builder, January, 1916 – March, 1933 (titled the *Builders Bulletin,* 1917–1922, scattered). Publication of the Master Builders Association of Wisconsin.

Milwaukee *Advertiser,* 1836–1941.

Milwaukee *Daily News and the Daily Review,* 1889–1891.

Milwaukee *Labor Review,* April, 1886 – June, 1888 (scattered).

Milwaukee *Leader,* 1911–1942 (variously titled).

Milwaukee *Journal,* January, 1842 – February, 1842.

Milwaukee Journal, 1882–1957.

Milwaukee *Sentinel,* 1845–1956 (variously titled).

Milwaukee *Volksblatt,* April, 1883 – November, 1888. (scattered). Published by Robert Schilling.

Milwaukee *Arbeiter-Zeitung,* May, 1886 – January, 1887 (scattered). Publication of the Central Labor Union.

Oshkosh *Northwestern,* July, 1938.

Political Action, September – October, 1912. Publication of the Socialists.

Printers Bulletin, April, 1881 – May, 1882; February, 1884 – March, 1884 (scattered, variously titled).

Social Democratic Herald, July, 1898 – September, 1913.

Socialist Campaigner, August, 1931 – October, 1932 (scattered).

Der Sozialist, November, 1875 – May, 1878 (variously titled).

Stoughton *Courier-Hub,* August, 1937.

311 Log Sheet, January, 1954 – December, 1955. Publication of the International Union of Operating Engineers, Locals 311 and 311A.

Voice of the People, October, 1910 – November, 1910; March, 1918. Campaign publication of the Socialists.

Wausau *Record-Herald,* July, 1938.

Wisconsin CIO News, March, 1938 – December, 1956.

Wisconsin CIO News: Local 248 Ed., March, 1943 – August, 1947.

Wisconsin Federationist, March, 1946 – June, 1952.

Wisconsin News (Milwaukee), 1937–1938.

Wisconsin State Journal (Madison), May, 1937.

Wisconsin Union Teacher, March, 1938 – March, 1946.

Wisconsin Voice of Labor, September, 1934 – May, 1935 (scattered). Publication of the Communist Party, Wisconsin District.

Wisconsin Vorwärts, 1893–1910. Publication of the Socialists.

Union Signal, 1894–1902. Populist-labor publication.

Union Teacher, November, 1935 – November, 1937.

PUBLIC DOCUMENTS.

Channing, Alice. *Employed Boys and Girls in Milwaukee.* Children's Bureau, United States Department of Labor. Publication No. 213. Washington: Government Printing Office, 1932.

In the Matter of the Investigation of the Milwaukee Electric Railway & Light Company and Kindred Associations by the General Legislative Committee of the Legislature of Wisconsin Pursuant to Joint Resolution No. 5–A. Hearings held in Milwaukee, Wisconsin, January 24 to February 28, 1919. 5 vols. Typewritten. In the office of the Secretary of State of Wisconsin.

Jamieson, Stuart. *Labor Unionism in American Agriculture.* Bureau of Labor Statistics, United States Department of Labor. Bulletin No. 836. Washington: Government Printing Office, 1945.

Milwaukee Citizens Committee on Unemployment. *Annual Report.* 25 annual reports covering the years from October, 1912 to June, 1938.

Milwaukee County Council of Defense *Report on Twenty Months of War-Time Service in Milwaukee: May 1st, 1917, to January 1, 1919.* Milwaukee, 1919.

United States. Bureau of the Census. *Historical Statistics of the United States.* Washington: Government Printing Office, 1960.

United States. Congress. House of Representatives. Committee on Education and Labor. *Amendments to the National Labor Relations Act.* Hearings, 80th Congress, 1st Session, on Bills to Amend and Repeal the National Labor Relations Act, and for Other Purposes, February 5–March 15, 1947. Washington: Government Printing Office, 1947.

———. ———. Committee on Un-American Activities. *Hearings Regarding Communism in Labor Unions in the United States.* 80th Congress, 1st Session, February 27, July 23–25, 1947. Washington: Government Printing Office, 1947.

———. Senate. Committee on Education and Labor. *Violations of Free Speech and Righs of Labor.* Hearings, 74th Congress, 2nd Session, on S. Res. 266, 1936–1937. Washington: Government Printing Office.

Wisconsin Adjutant General. *Biennial Report . . . for the Two Fiscal Years Ending September 30, 1886.* Madison: Democrat Company, 1887.

———. State Board of Arbitration and Conciliation. *[First] Biennial Report . . . , 1895 & 1896.* Madison: Democrat Printing Company, 1897.

———. *[Second] Biennial Report . . . , 1897 & 1898.* Madison: Democrat Printing Company, 1899.

———. *[Third] Biennial Report . . . , 1899 & 1900.* Madison: Democrat Printing Company, 1901.

———. *Fourth Biennial Report . . . , September 31, 1900 to September 30, 1902.* Madison: Democrat Printing Company, 1903.

———. *Fifth Biennial Report . . . , June 30, 1902 to June 30, 1904.* Madison: Democrat Printing Company, 1905.

———. *7th Biennial Report . . . Dated Dec. 1, 1908.* Typewritten.

———. *Eighth Biennial Report of the Secretary . . . , Dec. 1, 1908 to Dec. 1, 1910.* Madison: Democrat Printing Company, 1910.

———. Bureau of Labor and Industrial Statistics. *Second Biennial Report . . . , 1885–1886.* Frank A. Flower, Commissioner. Madison: Democrat Printing Company, 1886.

———. *Third Biennial Report . . . , 1886–1887.* Frank A. Flower, Commissioner. Madison: Democrat Printing Company, 1888.

———. *Tenth Biennial Report . . . , 1900–1901.* Halford Erickson, Commissioner. Madison: Democrat Printing Company, 1902.

———. Bureau of Labor Statistics. *First Biennial Report . . . , 1883–1884.* Frank A. Flower, Commissioner. Madison: Democrat Printing Company, 1884.

———. Commissioner of Labor and Industrial Statistics. *Fourth Biennial Report . . . , 1888–1889.* H. M. Stark, Commissioner. Madison: Democrat Printing Company, 1890.

Wisconsin Emergency Relief Administration. *A Review of Work Relief Activities: April, 1934 to August, 1935.* Madison, 1935.

———. Wisconsin Employment Relations Board. *Third Annual Report . . . , for the Fiscal Year Ended June 30, 1941.* Madison: Democrat Printing Company, 1942.

Wisconsin Free Employment Offices. "Annual Report of Milwaukee Committee on Unemployment," *Bulletin of the Industrial Commission of Wisconsin,* Vol. 2, No. 9, pp. 220–32. May 20, 1913.

Wisconsin Labor Relations Board. "Report Covering the Period from April 28, 1937 to November 30, 1938." Madison, December 22, 1938. Mimeographed.

——. Legislature, 1931. Interim Committee on Unemployment. *Report....* Madison: Industrial Commission, 1931.

Wisconsin Legislature, Assembly, Special Committee Reports. "In the Matter of the Legislative Investigation of Cessation of Street Car Service in the City of Milwaukee on Janauary 1, 1919, Pursuant to Join Resolution No. 5, A., of the Legislature of 1919." 54th Regular Session—18th Biennial Session, April 22, 1919. *Assembly Journal,* pp. 862–886.

——. "Supplementary Report of Milwaukee Street Railway Investigating Committee." 54th Regular Session—18th Biennial Session, April 24, 1919. *Assembly Journal,* pp. 908–909.

——. Senate. "Partial Report of the Special Joint Committee Created Pursuant to Joint Resolution No. 42, A. (1941)." *Senate Journals,* pp. 2189–2201.

MAGAZINE ARTICLES.

King, General Charles. "Memories of a Busy Life," *Wisconsin Magazine of History,* V (1921–1922), 360–381.

Klotsche, J. Martin. "The 'United Front' Populists," *Wisconsin Magazine of History,* XX (June, 1937), 375–389.

KOSC Monthly Journal, L (January, 1873).

Osten, Walter [Theodore Mueller]. "The Annekes," *The Milwaukee Turner,* III (June, 1942), 5, 7.

Perry, Charles F. "The Milwaukee School of Trades," *The Annals of the American Academy of Political and Social Science,"* XXXIII (1907), 78–84.

"Store Unions," *Business Week,* December 8, 1934, 12–13.

Witte, Edwin E. "Labor in Wisconsin History," *Wisconsin Magazine of History,* XXV (1951–1952), 83–86, 137–142.

BOOKS AND UNPUBLISHED MANUSCRIPTS.

Austin, H. Russell. *The Milwaukee Story: The Making of An American City.* Milwaukee: The Journal Company, 1946.

Altmeyer, A. J. *The Industrial Commission of Wisconsin: A Case Study in Labor Law Administration.* University of Wisocnsin Studies in the Social Sciences and History, No. 17. Madison: University of Wisconsin, 1932.

Ameringer, Oscar. *If You Don't Weaken: An Autobiography.* New York: H. Holt and Co., 1940.

Berger, Meta, and Elizabeth H. Thomas, (eds.). *Voice and Pen of Victor L. Berger.* Milwaukee: Milwaukee Leader, 1929.

Berthrong, Donald John. "Social Legislation in Wisconsin: 1836–1900." Unpublished Ph.D. dissertation, University of Wisconsin, 1951.

Brown, Ray Andrews. *The Administration of Workmen's Compensation.* University of Wisconsin Studies in the Social Sciences and History, No. 19. Madison: University of Wisconsin, 1933.

Buck, James S. *Milwaukee Under the Charter.* 2 vols. Milwaukee: Vol 1, Symes, Swain & Company, 1884; Vol. 2, Swain & Tate, 1886.

———. *Pioneer History of Milwaukee.* 2 vols. Milwaukee: Vol 1, Milwaukee News Company, 1876; Vol. 2, Symes, Swain & Company, 1881.

Campbell, Henry Colin. *Wisconsin in Three Centuries: 1634–1905.* 4 vols. New York: Century, 1906.

Commons, John R., and others. *Documentary History of American Industrial Society.* 10 vols. Cleveland: Arthur H. Clark, 1910.

———. *History of Labor in the United States.* 4 vols. New York: Macmillan Company, 1918–1935.

Derber, Milton, and Edwin Young. *Labor and the New Deal.* Madison: University of Wisconsin Press, 1957.

Drosen, Rosalind Margaret. "The History of Socialism in Milwaukee: 1910-1930." Unpublished Bachelor's thesis, University of Wisconsin, 1931.

Dulles, Foster R. *Labor in America.* New York: T. Y. Crowell Company, 1949.

Feinsinger, Nathan P., and William Gorham Rice, Jr. *The Wisconsin Labor Relations Act.* Bulletin of the University of Wisconsin, Serial No. 2254, General Series No. 2038. Madison: University of Wisconsin, 1937.

Foner, Philip S. *History of the Labor Movement in the United States.* Vol. II. New York: International Publishers, 1955.

Ginger, Ray. *The Bending Cross: A Biography of Eugene Victor Debs.* New Brunswick: Rutgers University Press, 1949.

Givens, Richard Ayres. "The Milwaukee Brewery Strike of 1953." Unpublished Master's thesis, University of Wisconsin, Madison, 1954.

Glasier, Gilson G. (ed). *Autobiography of Roujet D. Marshall.* Vol. II. Madison, 1931.

Glassberg, Benjamin. *Across the Desk of a Relief Administrator.* Chicago: American Public Welfare Association, 1938.

Gordon, Myron Lee. "The Listing Provision of the Wisconsin Labor Relations Act and Its Relationship to Company Unionism in Wisconsin." Unpublished Master's thesis, University of Wisconsin, 1939.

Haferbecker, Gordon Milton. "Wisconsin Labor Legislation." Unpublished Ph.D. dissertation, University of Wisconsin, Madison, 1952.

———. *Wisconsin Labor Laws.* Madison: University of Wisconsin Press, 1958.

Heath, Frederic (ed.). *Social Democracy Red Book.* Terre Haute: Debs Publishing Company, 1900.

Hoan, Daniel W. *City Government: The Record of the Milwaukee Experiment,* New York; Harcourt, Brace, 1936.

Hofstadter, Richard. *The Age of Reform.* New York: Knopf, 1955.

Holzman, Hanni M. "The German Forty-Eighters and the Socialist in Milwaukee: A Social Psychological Study of Assimilation." Unpublished Master's thesis, University of Wisconsin, 1948.

Josephson, Matthew. *Sidney Hillman: Statesman of American Labor.* Garden City, New York: Doubleday & Company, 1952.

Kampelman, Max M. *The Communist Party vs. the CIO.* New York: F. A. Praeger, 1957.

Krakowski, Paul. "Press Treatment of Wisconsin Labor Issues, 1936–38." Unpublished Master's thesis, University of Wisconsin, 1947.

Kruger, Daniel Herschel. "A Study of Collective Bargaining in Wisconsin." Unpublished Ph.D. dissertation, University of Wisconsin, 1954.

La Follette, Belle Case, and Fola La Follette. *Robert M. La Follette.* New York: Macmillan, 1953.

Lescohier, Don D. *The Knights of St. Crispin, 1867–1874: A Study in the Industrial Causes of Trade Unionism.* Bulletin of the University of Wisconsin, No. 355. Economic and Political Science Series, Vol. 7, No. 1. Madison: University of Wisconsin, 1910.

————, and Florence Peterson. *The Alleviation of Unemployment in Wisconsin.* Madison: Industrial Commission of Wisconsin, 1931.

Lorwin, Lewis L. *The American Federation of Labor.* Washington: The Brookings Institution, 1923.

McNeill, George E. (ed.). *The Labor Movement: The Problem of To-Day.* Boston: A. M. Bridgman & Company, 1887.

Maxwell, Robert S. *La Follette and the Rise of the Progressives in Wisconsin.* Madison: State Historical Society of Wisconsin, 1956.

Merk, Frederick. *Economic History of Wisconsin During the Civil War Decade.* Madison: Wisconsin State Historical Society, 1916.

Millis, Harry A., and Royal E. Montgomery. *Organized Labor.* Vol. III of *The Economics of Labor.* 3 vols. New York: McGraw-Hill, 1945.

Milwaukee Directory. Milwaukee: Alfred G. Wright, 1882–1930.

Milwaukee Writers Project. "History of Milwaukee County." Milwaukee, typewritten copy in Milwaukee Public Library, 1947.

Mueller, Theodore. "Milwaukee Workers," in "History of Milwaukee County." Typewritten copy in Milwaukee County Historical Society records. 1940.

————, "The Socialist Movement in Milwaukee." Unpublished MS in Milwaukee County Historical Society.

Newell, Barbara W. *Chicago and the Labor Movement.* Urbana: University of Illinois Press, 1961.

Olson, Frederick I. "The Milwaukee Socialists, 1897–1941." Unpublished Ph.D. dissertation, Harvard University, 1952.

Ozanne, Robert Willard. "The Effects of Communits Leadership on American Trade Unions." Unpublished Ph.D. dissertation, University of Wisconsin, 1954.

Perlman, Selig. "History of Socialism in Milwaukee." Unpublished Bachelor's thesis, University of Wisconsin, 1910.

––––––. *A History of Trade Unionism in the United States.* New York: Augustus M. Kelley, 1922.

Raney, William Francis. *Wisconsin: A Story of Progress.* New York: Prentice-Hall, 1940.

Rayback, Joseph G. *A History of American Labor.* New York: Macmillan, 1959.

Remey, Oliver E. and Wm. George Bruce. "A Half Century in Business Effort: History of the Merchants and Manufacturers Association Covering the Period from March 9–1861 to December 31–1911." Milwaukee: Board of Directors of the Merchants and Manufacturers Association, *ca.* 1911. Typewritten.

Roberts, Julia Adelai. "Farm Organizations and Labor in Wisconsin." Unpublished Master's thesis, University of Wisconsin, 1946.

Roy, Ralph Lord. *Communism and the Churches.* New York: Harcout, Brace, 1960.

Saposs, David J. *Communism in American Unions.* New York: McGraw-Hill, 1959.

Schmidt, Gertrude. "History of Labor Legislation in Wisconsin." Unpublished Ph.D. dissertation, University of Wisconsin, 1933.

Schwarztrauber, Ernest E. *The University of Wisconsin School for Workers: Its First Twenty-Five Years.* Madison: School for Workers, 1949.

––––––. "Workers' Education: A Wisconsin Experiment." Unpublished Ph.D. dissertation, University of Wisconsin, 1941.

Seidman, Joel. *American Labor from Defense to Reconversion.* Chicago: University of Chicago Press, 1953.

Shannon, David A. *The Socialist Party of America.* New York: Macmillan, 1955.

––––––. *The Decline of American Communism.* New York: Harcourt, Brace, 1959.

Still, Bayrd. *Milwaukee: The History of a City.* Madison: State Historical Society of Wisconsin, 1948.

Stimson, Grace H. *The Rise of the Labor Movement in Los Angeles.* Berkley: University of California Press, 1955.

Usher, Ellis B. *The Greenback Movement of 1874–1884 and Wisconsin's Part In It.* Milwaukee: Ellis B. Usher, 1911.

Wachman, Marvin. *History of the Social-Democratic Party of Milwaukee: 1897–1910.* Illinois Studies in the Social Sciences, Vol. 28, No. 1. Urbana: University of Illinois Press, 1945.

Writers' Program of the Work Projects Administration. *Wisconsin: A Guide to the Badger State.* New York: Duel, Sloan and Pearce, 1941.

Index